Out On Your Feet

Out On Your Feet

The Hallucinatory World of Hundred-Mile Walking

JULIE WELCH

First published in Great Britain
2009 by Aurum Press Ltd
7 Greenland Street
London NW1 0ND
www.aurumpress.co.uk

A catalogue record for this book is available from the British Library.

ISBN 978 1 84513 427 3

10 9 8 7 6 5 4 3 2 1
2013 2012 2011 2010 2009

Typeset in Garamond and Meta with Amasis.
Printed in Great Britain by Clays Ltd, St Ives plc

CONTENTS

The most fulfilling human projects appeared inseparable from a degree of torment, the sources of our greatest joys lying awkwardly close to those of our greatest pains

ALAIN DE BOTTON

Exercise should be savage and rude

MAO ZEDONG

If only the whole world was like the LDWA

JUNE COLE

ACKNOWLEDGEMENTS

I HAVE RECEIVED A GREAT DEAL OF HELP from LDWA members, many of whom appear in these pages. I am grateful to them all, as I am to Lesley Sparshatt and Lucy Morrill for their hospitality and to Peter Wood, of West Yorkshire LDWA and The Irregulars, who wrote such an excellent route description for the Yoredale Hundred. Essential background information was provided by Geoff Saunders and Paul Lawrence, and Sue Newman provided invaluable documents in the form of LDWA Newsletters, numbers 1 to 8.

This book would not have come about had it not been for the late Pat Kavanagh, who first had the idea that all those mad walks I told her about deserved chronicling, and I should also like to thank Graham Coster, who believed her. Without Avril Stapleton's help and encouragement, I would never have done the Hundred. Most of all, though, I would like to salute all the Hundred-ers past, present and future. They really are a special breed, and it was a great moment when I became one of their number.

ONE
I Will Follow You into the Dark

THIS IS THE MADDEST THING YOU CAN DO to yourself, ever. Except maybe throwing yourself off the Clifton Suspension Bridge, and even that would be over quickly. This goes on practically for eternity, and you're not even halfway. It turns your feet into bleeding stumps, your muscles into concrete and your brain into oatmeal. In the last five minutes, you've pictured yourself in a taxi, just to torture yourself; in your mind's eye, you're having a hot shower and someone is waiting to hand you a fluffy towel and a pair of cashmere socks.

You have been on the hills for eleven hours, clutching your route description, nineteen pages of dampening A4, heading for places with *League of Gentlemen* names like Fang and Drool; whether you get to find them is another matter, because the instructions are written in a language analogous to English. Here's an example: *Go thru to X field by fence on Lt to field corner and enter overgrown sunken Trk (B070) to keep AH for 600m thru several Gts (Trk becomes well used after 1st rusty Gt).*

You were able to understand this at ten in the morning, when you were fresh. But as time wears on, now you've been climbing all day and you're suffering from the incremental fuckwittedness caused by the drip-drip-drip of fatigue and cold, it's all too easy to go wrong. And then you have to double back, trying to remember which way you came from, worryingly aware that time's getting short. So when you're back on track you force yourself to run with increasingly stiff and painful strides to make sure you reach the next checkpoint before it closes.

Run. What a nostalgic memory that evokes, like 'comfortable' and 'really enjoying this'. You ran the first eleven miles and after that, as the climbs got steeper and you had to start walking, you were still *walking bloody quickly*. You're still walking now, but with 35 miles under your feet you're down to a plod. And there's another 65 to go.

The batteries of your iPod have just died, so you can no longer listen to its motivating cargo of *Eine Kleine Nachtmusik* for the long distance walker: Death Cab for Cutie's 'I Will Follow You into the Dark'; The Proclaimers' '500 Miles'; 'Dancing in the Dark' (*dancing.* Ha. Ha. Ha). You're dawdling along, self-pityingly prodding the controls to see if you can wring any more life out if it, when there's a flash of colour, and a woman of about twenty-five in a bright red fleece goes belting by, followed by two lads in hiking gear. None of them see you because to them you're completely static, in a boring way like a bin or a pile of builder's old rubble.

Old. That's how you feel. With grating joints and bent shoulders, and a sharp pain in one instep, and big blue veins standing out on your hands.

Oh, get a grip. It's not as though you're past it. For a long distance walker, you've yet to reach your prime. Boyd Millen was 59 when he started his international racewalking career. He walked a hundred miles over the Pennines to mark his sixtieth birthday. In snow. Wearing trainers without any socks. Henry Bridge of Soham – still at it past eighty. Some of these people don't take up the sport till they've qualified for the winter fuel allowance.

And here come a horde of rusty old gits, whizzing past like Coe and Ovett in their heyday. One of them slows down long enough to hand you a strip of ibuprofen as you wince at the pain suddenly afflicting your left knee. 'Take a couple of these,' he advises. 'Drugs are widespread!'

Why does he have to sound so cheerful? Bastard.

But you plod on, thinking of where you'd be if you weren't out here.

In a line of stationary traffic waiting to go through the Blackwall Tunnel.

Or staring at a computer screen, trying to renew your Norton Internet Security software without signing up by mistake to a different package at nearly three times the price.

Or riding on a Network Southeast train full of drunks eating KFCs.

It's no contest, is it?

CHECKPOINT 7. Bedlam. Only 38 miles into the route, and outside it people are already grabbing the door handles of the death cab, trying to get in. More than fifty of the five hundred starters have already dropped out. With 9,000ft of ascent on the first day alone, it's the toughest Hundred anyone can remember.

But then, they say that every year. Anyway, you're not giving up now. You can't. For months, the Hundred and you have been trapped in a love-hate relationship. You've gone on training walks together. Thirties, forties, fifties: you've fought your way through them all. It's beaten you up and reduced you to tears, yet you still keep coming back. A couple of days is all it takes, and you'll forget the bad bits, the sore feet and bramble gouges and liquid cowshit flooding your trainers, and think only of the good things: banter, mates, the feeling of shared suffering and endeavour, the way grass turns pale green by the light of the moon.

Tuna bap. Fistful of raisins from a Tupperware container. Then it's head torch on, and out into the twilight. Now your luck's in. You get picked up by Sally, an accountant from Worcester, and her partner Rob. They've done a Hundred every year for the last ten, they know the ropes. It's lovely having friends to chat to in the dark; makes you start to feel quite larky. And now here's another bunch of people. Jim is wearing a Newcastle shirt. You're a Spurs fan, so you bond over a discussion about what it is to support delusion-inducing football clubs. Benita, possibly released into the community but somehow fascinating, is kitted out in dangly earrings, Doc Martens and what appear to be baby doll pyjamas. David, a first-timer, is a genial puffed-out ultra runner in Madras check beach shorts worn with a Berghaus fleece, and Stanley is a magnificent bearded *homme d'un certain age* in pleated trousers, army boots and schoolteacher jacket. You're in puckered tracksters, smelly thermals and red hat. You're all the people you'd move away from if they sat next to you on the tube.

CHECKPOINT 8. Another nine miles done. In two and three-quarter hours! God, you're rather good at this. You'll be storming into the finish by tea time tomorrow. You might even run the final hundred yards, just to show your complete mastery of the genre. Inside Drool Village Hall, it's warm and welcoming. The food is just what you need, and you never thought you'd say that about tinned rice pudding. Jim stuffs himself with cheese straws and peanut butter sandwiches while telling you this is his third attempt at a Hundred. Both other times he had to drop out at 70 miles.

He's mad. If you've dropped out twice already, you just have to accept you can't do it. Why punish yourself again?

Oh well. Let's do it. Out into the gripping night. Everyone switches on their head torches again and streams away like a line of miners, heading up into the forest.

Another mile of climbing. Your heart is thudding like the bass in 'Walk the Line'. Way ahead, a string of pearls is rising slowly into the sky, or so it appears at first gaze. After that you begin

OUT ON YOUR FEET

faintly to make out a grey-green hump against the backdrop. The tiny pearls are the lights of other competitors' head torches, and the hump is . . .

. . . Another climb. A 1,800ft climb. Blithering, blithering God.

Never mind. Here are some more new friends. Andy is on his seventh Hundred. You have incredible hallucinations on the second day, he says, productions in exquisite HD like it's really happening. In the 2004 Exmoor he saw a Shakespeare play enacted by a roadside on a brightly lit stage, with people in doublets and codpieces and plumey hats. Margarita, his partner, who's only on her third Hundred, chips in with the time on the 2003 White Rose when the stones on the path in front of her started moving. Rob mentions the last two miles of the 1997 Downsman, walking through his second sunrise followed by marching trees. 'And behind the trees there was a herd of elephants moving. I couldn't see them but they were there. I heard them trumpeting.'

This is a long, long haul. It just . . . keeps on . . . going up. And up. Your quad muscles hurt. The only way to keep climbing is to pile-drive your thighs into the path with the palms of your hands for leverage.

Right. Take it one mile at a time. At least the tracks are fairly obvious. It's not like the open moorland you get in the Fellsman. I won't have to find my way over pathless heather in the dark. Twenty more hours, increasing agony, no sleep, but then it'll be over. I'll have done it! I'll feel great!

No I won't. I'll feel crap. Actually, I might quit at the next checkpoint. I just don't want to do this any more.

CHECKPOINT 9. It's a tent, appearing suddenly out of dense darkness. A frozen hand, its owner partially clad in a sleeping bag, appears out of the vent to clip tallies.

Bugger him, I can't give up here. Not when he's sacrificed his Saturday night for us, huddling under canvas on a cold mountain in the dead of night, just to keep us all going.

Anyway, I don't feel that bad. I can't quit when I'm not even shuffling.

The Hand mumbles your numbers to another sleeping bag inside. The zip closes with a cheery 'Good luck'. Fumblingly you stuff your tally back into your rucksack and follow the others into the dark. You and Jim have agreed to finish this Hundred together. Celebrate by getting together afterwards next time Newcastle play Spurs. In fact you're practically on the brink of civil partnership when there's a distant zigzag of lightning, a drum roll of thunder and rain in torrents.

Everyone stops to clamber into waterproofs except for Benita, who puts on a raincoat and shower cap. It takes so long to get your stuff out of the rucksack you're drenched already. The harder the storm lashes, the more silvery-black everything turns. Each individual raindrop seems to glint and flash, like a sack of needles being emptied through the air. Whatever is ahead, path, pool, sheep, foothills, is behind a curtain of plummeting water. The backdrop of the mountains is indistinguishable from moor and sky. As soon as you do up the last zip, the rain stops.

Drip, drip, drip. Moan, moan, moan. You're already lagging behind the others when a bramble as taut as a tripwire catches your foot.

You go flying.

Sit there for a bit, regrouping.

I must be conscious because I can feel rain running down the back of my neck. And because I can feel my shoulder hurting. And because I can't feel my hand, which is numb.

And I've landed on my rucksack. Which is wet outside *and* inside, thanks to a burst pouch of sports drink.

Now what do I do?

'YOU ALL RIGHT THERE?' asks Jim. Everyone is standing round, holding out their hands to pull you to your feet.

'Yeah, fine,' you mumble. 'Just got to sort myself out. I'll catch you up.'

You start hunting in your rucksack for the drinks pouch. Then you stop.

Yes, this is it. I've had enough of this for one lifetime.

You throw sticky wet stuff out. Outdoor Leisure maps the size of loaves. Loo paper for on-route exigencies. Strips of ProPlus. Quadruple-strength painkillers. Energy bars made of budgie seed and minced cardboard. Your phone's covered in bits of fluff and dust, it's the world's first flock mobile.

I won't need any of this. I'm quitting.

Thing is, it takes ages to clear out a rucksack. For five minutes you sit there, chilling like a Sancerre, strangely fuddled, full of vague indecision: whether you could stay here and wait to be helped, or whether people would just scud past you, heads down, and you'd die. Months later they'd find a skeleton, in trainers and red hat.

You shine a torch on your hand. Your left palm is turning the colour of Paul McCartney's hair.

But dammit, what kind of wimp am I? It's not as if I'm going to be walking on my hands.

Minutes later you're moving again.

It's a harrowing few minutes, having decided it would be a brilliant idea to catch up the others by *running* after them. This time you stumble to a halt after five hundred yards. Pause button jammed. You pretend you're only stopping to check the route description, but it's no good. You have gone beyond non-enjoyment now. Beyond indifference, beyond dislike.

I hate this sport. *Hate* it. The most pointless activity known to man. No money in it. No glory. Nobody writes about it in the papers. You aren't given a goody bag full of freebies like in big-city marathons. It's not like fell running, all romantic dash and glamour. Even curling isn't as silly as this. At least it's an Olympic event.

You stagger along, considering finding your way in secret to a road. You could say you were just going to 'pop into the bushes', then you'd hit tarmac. With judicious use of the OS map you could probably get away with that for quite a few miles. It'd be exciting, like a clandestine tryst.

Only the trouble is, you can't find where you are on the map. You're carrying a compass but you're useless with it. You might as well try and find your way with a can opener.

So it's back to the route description. Here goes.

FORTIFIED BY THE BUDGIE SEED and the last of the ibuprofen you lumber onwards with Jim, Benita, David and Stanley. This section has walls. Walls, fields and walls. Lots of fields and walls. They help you navigate but it's becoming harder and harder to keep track of where you are. Count the walls. And the fields. A left, a right and through the little gate. Read the map. Across and down the field – along a wall, through a gate, across another field . . . it's like a drunk session on Google Earth. With added rain.

What's going on now?

Somewhere along the way everyone seems to have missed a crucial kink through a caravan park.

You huddle in a sheep field while David and Stanley pore over the map. Time passes at the rate of the Northern Ireland peace talks.

'I think we ought to turn left here,' says David, flapping the map like a toreador.

'No,' barks Stanley. 'It's much further on.'

'Trust me, I've recce'd this bit,' says David.

They march off. You, Jim and Benita trail after them, keeping tabs on them at first by the little bobbing beams of their head torches, then when the lights disappear just trundling morosely forward till you hear raised voices.

Stanley and David are standing at the corner of a field.

'You're an absolute bastard,' Stanley is roaring. 'You led me astray completely. You don't know the difference between the left of a hedge and the right of a hedge. Follow hedge on right. You followed hedge on left.'

'I won't be spoken to like this,' says David in the tone of a man who requires a door to slam, and storms off.

You, Stanley, Jim and Benita go back to the caravan park and wander about in it for another twenty minutes, looking for the way out. You head down the only track you haven't tried and find David sitting on a stile.

'You again,' says Stanley. 'You bloody bugger.'

'I've lost my compass,' bleats David.

You can't stand them any longer. You tramp along in the darkness, ten yards in front of them, buffeted by wind, lashed by rain. Up ahead, the trees on the hillcrest appear to be belly-dancing. The horizontal hold in your brain is going already, while the blisters on your left foot are so sore you can't put your heel down. You're walking like Larry Grayson.

Night blankets the valley as you descend into the village of Fang.

CHECKPOINT 10. Inside the community centre is a smell of damp tuna sandwiches, embrocation and wet clothes, and a flash of brightness at a corner table where a young woman, flame hair limp and darkened with sweat, tends her feet next to a man in a thermal hat. He looks like Van Gogh in his self-portrait, with that bandaged head and those enormous eyes haunted by defeat and despair. Two bodies are stretched out on the floor.

It's two in the morning. You claim your limp tuna sandwich then start to change your socks, but blood has superglued them to your raw, skinned feet, so you leave them and sit there trying to psych yourself up for the next stretch. You've never gone further than 54 miles before. This will be new territory. Exciting. An adventure. And the whole of this stretch is along a national trail, so there'll be waymarks to help with navigation. And then, at mile 60, the breakfast stop.

You squint at the route description. It hurts to read now. *This leg should give you a comfortable ramble on pleasant turf-carpeted paths with short stretches along roads . . .*

Roads! My friend tarmac! I can do this!

Leaving the warmth and light seems one of the hardest things you've ever done. And the road stretches are agonising to your sore, skinned feet. Plodding, stumbling, limping along, you can't bring yourself to talk. You just want to shuffle along, you and your pain. Your wrist is the size of a Ginster's pasty. It hurts to swing your arm as you walk. You can't think of anything except this terrible, throbbing pain. Oh yes you can. You can also think of the way your eyes feel as though someone's laid gravel in the sockets. Your left leg won't bend any more and someone is trying to sever your right leg below the knee.

You must be near the next checkpoint now, surely. How many more miles?

'Two,' David mutters through parched lips.

Two miles. That's, like, on the moon.

CHECKPOINT 11. Through another godforsaken village you've staggered, past windows where people are drawing back curtains and doors with Sunday papers sticking out of letterboxes. Outside the Scragg Temperance Hall, bodies are propped, heads lolling, spreadeagled against walls, oblivious to brambles and weeds. Someone is sobbing, inconsolable at having had to give up. It's like the aftermath of a shootout in a Wild West saloon. Survivors stagger away, heading for the next checkpoint. Inside, among baggage piled up like burst sacs and empty chrysalises, are people with towels over their heads, people in trances, people who look at death's door, people tending red, macerated feet, tugging off boots and trainers, soaking their feet in grey washing-up bowls.

Very slowly and carefully, you weave your way through the bodies and flop into an empty chair. You've come 60.9 miles. There's another 39.1 to go. You can't even face the 0.1.

'Sorry, Jim, I'm quitting.'

Blood red of eye, Jim nods at you uncomprehendingly and hobbles off into the dark.

He's mad. Look at him. He won't get another mile.

You are not mad, you think to yourself as you wait for the body bus to pick you up and take you back to the finish. You're being sensible, giving up before you do yourself serious damage. There's always next year.

Yeah, I did pretty well. Sixty-point-nine miles. Practically two and a quarter marathons. There's not many who could do that. Three cheers for me!

And half an hour later, you're slumped in disappointment and self-hate. Sensible? Who are you kidding? Your self-respect is in tatters.

I'm a complete and utter wimp. Everyone must despise me. Go on – you know they do. What a ninny.

THE EVENT HQ is a sixth form college. Behind a door with a sign pinned on it that says 'Morgue' you stretch out your throbbing body as best you can on the floor of the gymnasium next to all the other snoring wimps and groaning wrecks. You wake just as a young woman finishes. Everyone is cheering. She smiles, takes a bow, then falls to the floor. People rush forward, pick her up and lay her tenderly on a trestle table.

You while away the rest of Sunday by hanging around the control desk, listening to the reports coming in from checkpoints. David and Stanley are still going.

Benita the madwoman has gone walkabout and Search & Rescue have just radioed in to say they've found her.

Jim, now at the speed of growing asparagus, is still out there, among the mountains.

Sunday turns into Monday. You envy the people who've finished, sleeping with their heads on the table. And the people holding their backs, with lopsided shoulders, and the ones who daren't take their trainers off because of what they might see, and the ones smiling vacantly and talking crap.

It's after dawn when the news comes in that David and Stanley are on the final approach. They're best mates by now.

David tries to give him a man-hug. Stanley intercepts quickly by shaking his hand, clapping him on the shoulder and calling him Dave.

'Any idea where Jim's got to?'

David looks at you, narrow-eyed. 'He's down by the water,' he says in a low, conspiratorial voice. 'With the snails.'

Down by the water. That's the second from last checkpoint. He has ten more miles to do.

The sun is high in the sky by the time the shout goes up that someone else is on the final approach. You step gingerly outside to look. There's a dead man walking. It's Jim, tilted to one side, painfully slow, every step a massive effort of will and determination. In the time it's taken him to get here from the 60-mile checkpoint he's aged from a man in his mid-forties to someone who looks as though he qualifies for a telegram from the Queen.

He has tears in his eyes. Is in that faraway state of weary rapture, experiencing a moment as intense as that felt on the brink of any long-dreamt bigtime sporting triumph: think Goran Ivanisevic's lonely ecstasy as he served to win Wimbledon at last, at last. It's been so long coming.

He props himself up in the doorway, pulls himself up with a grimace and drops his tally on the desk. Then he collapses in the nearest chair.

Even though each small movement is agony, you squat down and unlace his trainers with your good hand. It's the least you can do. What a hero.

You're terribly envious. You want it. You want to complete a Hundred so badly. That feeling of *I've done it*. Dues paid. You didn't give in. You climbed over the wall of physical and mental torment and slithered down the other side.

There's only one thing for it. I'll have to come back next year and try again. The Hundred, you big, beautiful bastard. As long as it takes. I'll tame you yet.

TWO
This Walking Life: 2007

Sat May 26–28 2007
Cant Canolbarth Cymru (The Mid Wales 100)
Taith drwy Galon Cymru. *A journey through the heart of Wales. 100ml and 14,000ft of ascent in 48hr starting from the Pavilion, Llandrindod Wells, Powys. A circuit of the County of Radnorshire crossing Aberedw Hill, Glascwm Hill, Radnor Forest, visiting the Elan valley and the historic Abbey Cwm Hir. The route varies from little used tracks and bridleways to parts of Glyndwr's Way and the Wye Valley Way. The only 100 with a 7ml entirely downhill section. All entrants must be over 18 and have completed a 50ml event in the previous 12 months. Entry £38 to inc full route description, food and drink at 15 Cps, meal, showers and sleeping area at end, cert, badge and results sheet . . .*
Strider,
The Journal of the Long Distance Walkers Association

MOST OF BRITAIN WAS EMBARKING IDLY ON a Bank Holiday weekend Saturday as 460 long distance walkers and runners set out on the Mid Wales Hundred, the Long Distance Walkers Association's flagship event of 2007. Also known as the more lyrical-sounding Cant Canolbarth Cymru, this non-stop 48-hour challenge took place in and around Llandrindod Wells on a route carefully devised and tested over three years by two of the LDWA's affiliated local groups, Mid Wales and Marches. The 14,000ft of climb included a diversion up the 2,100ft Black Mixen after the hill originally intended for the path turned out to feature unexploded munitions. Slower entrants endured two nights of bitter cold as rain pelted over Radnor Forest and the Cambrian Mountains. The last section, touted as an easy three miles over the fields from Newbridge back to Llandrindod via Disserth, was actually one of the hardest because there were more stiles to be climbed in that stretch than all the rest put together. Try lifting a leg over a stile after 97 miles and you'll see the difficulty.

First to finish, in just over 22 hours, was Jez Bragg, the UK Trail Running champion. The fastest woman finisher, in 27 hours 42 minutes, was the runner Marie Doke, a computer programmer from London. Little more than half an hour later came one of the earliest walkers back – Ken Falconer, maths professor at St Andrews and editor of *Strider*. As always, though, the biggest applause was for entrants who came struggling into Llandrindod Wells as the hands of the clock ticked inexorably towards ten o'clock, and everybody in the finishing hall waited, holding their breath and willing on people who had been out there since Saturday morning and walked through two sunrises in a row.

But almost as stamina-packed that weekend was the performance of the weather. The rain began at midday on the first day and continued throughout the event. On the second day the temperature never rose above 7° C. Conditions were so bad at one checkpoint that marshals filled all the kettles and containers they could find with boiling water and gave them to people to hug. One woman came out of the second last checkpoint, a tent by the dam at the end of Graig Goch Reservoir, and turned left instead of right. Someone managed to grab her before she fell in.

'We had eight or nine hypothermics at the seventy-eight-mile point, three irrecoverable,' said Neil Fullwood, an organiser. 'They didn't die on us but we had to send them to hospital with exposure.'

'There was one guy found raving around on the road just after the penultimate checkpoint,' added another organiser, Chris Dawes. 'Oh, and a girl with a leg infection packed up at ninety-eight miles.'

They also had a mystery helper, who arrived in a big Land Rover on the first night and took off with some retirees. 'Quite clearly he was listening in on radio transmissions,' said a third organiser, Janet Pitt Lewis. 'I sent out an urgent message: no walker to get into *any* unidentified Land Rover.' The retirees were delivered safely back to base and he disappeared after the first night, never to be seen again, leaving the organisers to speculate whether he was someone's husband, a Hundred groupie or a local undertaker trying to drum up custom.

Just another Hundred, then. In *Strider*, the LDWA's magazine, reports by finishers combined enthusiasm and gratitude with that mustn't-grumble undertone that is peculiarly English: 'The walk truly was wonderful, good views, weather – well, could have been worse'; 'Apart from the pain I think I will probably look back on the weekend and say I enjoyed it'; 'Weather was challenging to say the least, but got there in the end.'

There were tales from other finishers, too. A 54-year-old local GP, Mike Warrick, who came home second, 45 minutes behind Jez Bragg, said he'd had the run of his life but that on the Sunday morning, on the trail alongside the Elan reservoirs, his brain shut down and he kept falling asleep: 'Each time I was jolted awake by walking off the path.'

Pam Girdwood, a 24-year-old walker from Northumberland, had less than a mile to go when she lost her way. 'I spent half an hour trying to find the road while hallucinating rats and traffic cones.'

Martin Burnell, a brawny, hairy plumber from Hertfordshire, raved about it. 'I loved it. When we walked down to the reservoir, a really wild and lonely bit of moorland, all the elements were against you, everything was trying to knock you down. It was the best bit of the whole walk.'

Martin finished in just over 35 hours. Another Hundreder, Merv Nutburn, a former primary school teacher from Kent, would normally have run the event. This time he walked it with 22-year-old Kerry Scrivener, who had been slowed down by an injury incurred two weeks previously on a fun run. 'That was fine,' said Merv. 'I've always wanted to see what it was like to go through two nights.'

Well, what was it like?

'Great. At the breakfast stop this Australian said, "Mind if I tag along with you?" So we turned it into a party and went along singing "Always Look on the Bright Side".' They arrived back after sunrise, shortly before Avril Stapleton, a retired human resources manager. She was shepherding round Ian McLeod, a very strong but partially sighted walker of seventy-one. 'We got to seventy miles,' Avril said, 'and we were wet and cold and Ian was ready to give up, but I said, "We've come this far, it would be a shame to stop now".'

But if you find it beyond comprehension that two bedraggled pensioners would carry on walking thirty miles in a downpour on top of the seventy they've already done, then hear this. Betty Lewis, a wispy 74-year-old grandmother from Wiltshire with snow-white hair, became the oldest ever female finisher when she came back in 45 hours 45 minutes.

'I've got a theory,' said John Walker, the chemical engineer who went round with her, completing his seventh Hundred in the process. 'The later you are in life when you start, the longer you're OK. Start in your twenties and your skeleton's worn out by middle age. Someone like Betty could go on well into her eighties because her bones aren't worn out.'

John first met Betty when she went out walking with his local group, Wiltshire LDWA. Already over seventy, she had never walked further than ten miles before and John thought she looked rather weak. Eighteen months later, he said with wonder, she was completing a Hundred.

Betty's daughter Sahrah was walking it with them. At one of the later checkpoints Betty gave her a painkiller which she washed down with a cup of tea before climbing a hill and falling asleep on her feet. John, who was talking to her at the time, watched Sahrah's eyes close. She slid down him – 'like in a Popeye cartoon' – and ended up in a crumpled heap on his boots. By then, Betty had started falling over too. When John gave her a hand up, he was amazed at how little she weighed. She was as fragile and beautiful as a dandelion clock. 'We were nearly the last to finish,' he said. 'It took almost forty-six hours of hard slogging. But I can't describe it, the elation you feel. It's unique. It blows your mind.'

THE HUNDRED was the only event that weekend in the LDWA calendar, but a trawl through the August issue of *Strider* revealed a world in itself, with its own social structure, rituals and codes of behaviour, of people doing back-to-back events at weekends, devising routes, uncovering new footpaths, collecting Wainwrights, designing badges and certificates and – sometimes in the middle of the week as well as at weekends – walking prodigious amounts of miles.

'Past Events' contained a report by Neil Fullwood on February's South Shropshire Circular. Andrew Clabon reported on April's 100km Dorset Giant. Jill Green, the veteran international racewalker, wrote up the 40-mile Ridgeway Walk.

Within a month of the Hundred, Pam Girdwood completed the 52-mile Durham Dales Challenge. Marie Doke was first woman finisher on the Three Rings of Shap, a tough 62-miler in Cumbria, for the third successive year.

The event featured in the 'Good Badge Guide' was Capability's

Overview, a 21-miler organised jointly by East Yorkshire LDWA and Sledmere. The newly designed embroidered badge was thought up by John Davis, a 78-year-old journalist and walker who specialises in creating off-footpath routes in the farming country, and depicted 'the mythical sea god Triton who adorns the gate pillars at Sledmere House'.

The National Committee was continuing to give thought to linking the 2012 Hundred to Olympic year with a route visiting a number of the London area venues.

Roy Davies, a member of East Lancashire LDWA, described his experience of designing the Wycoller Hoof, a new 30-mile challenge event.

Keith Warman, a quantity surveyor from Kent, had taken over George Foot's role as keeper of the Hundreds database.

There were reports of 'Social Walks' laid on by local affiliated groups that had taken place in the previous few months. Albert Bowes, a builder from Stockton-on-Tees, led a group from Cleveland LDWA around the Bilsdale Circuit, 30 miles with almost 5,000ft of ascent. In April, Kent LDWA's Graham Smith, a local newspaper editor from Deal, led a 38-mile Four Pits Walk, linking Tilmanstone, Snowdown and Betteshanger, the three Kent coal mines that closed in the eighties, with Chislet, shut down in 1969. 'Group Social Walks' to come included Calderdale's 39-mile Bowland Fells, led by Anton Criritis, Cleveland's 33-mile Three Circles With Ron, led by Ron Caygell, and 'Brill (well, reasonably good) Walk', John Esslemont's 20-miler to Brill windmill for Thames Valley group.

The Events Diary for August and September featured a choice of fifties – the distance it was necessary to complete in order to qualify for next year's Hundred, the Yoredale. Some had already made the grade by finishing the Mid Wales. Others, like me, would be heading for Sheringham, on the coast of north-east Norfolk, for the Poppyline Fifty. In the following ten months we would do the marathons, thirties, fifties and 100kms that would get us in shape, deliberating over choice of trainers, poring over maps, going home with our certificates carefully shielded from the sweaty contents of our kitbags.

You might catch sight of some of us setting out on a 30-miler in a long, exuberant line from a village hall or a car park, heads down, seemingly oblivious to the surrounding scenery. Ramblers and tourists we'll meet on the way will ask the questions they always ask: 'Are you on some kind of event? How long is it? Are you doing it for charity?' Their parting shot is usually, 'You must be mad.'

Frankly, if walking thirty miles for fun strikes anyone as idiotic it's just as well they haven't heard of the Hundred – and I've met some long distance walkers who think even a non-stop hundred miles once a year isn't adequate. The weird thing is that while clambering out of a mud gully in the dead of night, or being bored out of my mind as I hobble in mid-afternoon along a bone-hard field path, or come close to tears of frustration if I realise I've strayed off route and will have to spend the next hour retracing my steps, I've often contemplated never doing it again but have never questioned the normality of the activity.

From the day I first met the long distance walkers nothing about them seemed crazy to me. I quite understood why finishing was what really mattered. That if the route description tells you to walk three sides of a rectangle around a field it's very bad form to save thirty yards by cutting a corner, even if nobody is looking. That Vaseline helps. That falling down in a faint is an occupational hazard, the same as hallucinations and blisters and lost toenails. That the fortitude and bloodymindedess required to get to the finish is a perfect example of the British character. And that more than anything else if you write off long distance walking as mad you just don't get the point. Which is that this is one of the most challenging, addictive, aesthetically pleasing, physically draining and emotionally satisfying sports ever created.

THREE
The Novice

THE HUNDRED AND I GO BACK A LONG WAY. All these years on, I still get flashbacks to that weekend in November 1996: the bleary-eyed pre-dawn drive through the dismal outer fringes of east London, in the kind of weather that makes you want to turn round and go home; the venue at Gilwell Park on the edge of Epping Forest, a cavernously decrepit scout hut with an insanitary-looking kitchen and bare floorboards creaking under the weight of some 250 people.

What an assortment of people it was. At road races everybody, from podgy fun runner to grizzled veteran, looked recognisably part of the same sport. We were all members of the running community, vested and shorted. Here was the most bizarre mix I'd ever seen gathered for a sporting event.

There were a few couples, a few lads and girls and some women who, like me, were on their own. But the scout hut appeared mainly to be filled by middle-aged white men. Some were identifiably athletic – rangy ectomorphs as tall as Douglas firs, wiry little ultra-runners in prehistoric tracksters. Others looked as though they'd kitted themselves out from a consignment of secondhand clothes meant for overseas refugees. There were hairy cavemen, chubby pie-eaters, squares with glinty glasses and Boy Scout shorts. Some were beyond middle age, even – stout elderly blokes in corduroys and thick socks, one or two with magnificent manes of grey hair, like distinguished knights of the theatre, plus a really weird stone-deaf one with a floaty white beard.

I wasn't taking it very seriously. It sounded a bit of a laugh – a sort of comic-book version of the London Marathon, times two and a half. It was just another in the line of challenges that I was reporting on for my newspaper. Two months before, I'd cycled from London to Paris in three and a half days. I was training for my first London Marathon. I'd discovered that endurance sport was something I enjoyed – some of the time, anyway. The crucial attribute I possessed, probably as a result of spending several years at a boarding school on the UK's wind-lashed, fogbound eastern seaboard, was stoicism.

Anyway, so. The newspaper wanted a feature about walking. Steven Seaton, editor of *Runner's World*, came up with a name I'd never heard of: the Long Distance Walkers Association. A lot of distance runners, he explained, used the association's events for winter training. One phone call later, I found myself signing up to something else I'd never heard of: a challenge walk.

I was attracted by its sheer extravagant loopy obscurity. The Three Forests Way wasn't a Hundred, but at 100km it still seemed fabulously mad. Sixty-two miles. In 26 hours. The furthest I'd ever gone on foot was a ten-mile run. But I only had to walk this. And with more than a day to do it in. How hard could it be?

I was hopelessly ill-informed. What? They didn't use roads? No mile-markers? How did we know which way to go? I was issued with a route description on several sheets of A4 paper, a compass I didn't know how to use and a map I didn't know how to fold up, let alone interpret. And then we set off into the morning.

I remember the exhilaration of the first couple of hours, queuing for each stile in a line of people jostling to get to it like footballers at a corner kick; hastening along bridleways carpeted with fallen leaves; skimming over blades of grass frosted to the sharpness of fishbones; feeling triumphant when I was in the earliest group to reach Checkpoint 1. This turned out to be a picnic table on a common. Here, in the watery November sunlight, two helpers offered jugs of weak pink and yellow cordial, a Tupperware box filled with sultanas and a plate of hard-wearing biscuits.

I belted along on my own. Blimey, I was good at this. It was easy. There was no need to look at the route description. I just had to plunge through the forest behind the bunch of tall, stringy men who sailed along at the front with no apparent effort. Though my legs seemed to be moving twice as fast as theirs, I was still clinging to their backs as we reached the 13-mile checkpoint, a barn in which all the bales and farming implements had been pushed to the sides to make room for a random selection of folding chairs.

It was like a child's birthday party in there. A huge table groaned with home-made cakes, jelly, cheese straws, date balls, bowls of crisps and platters of sandwiches. A tea urn sighed and puffed. Marshals rushed around asking what they could do for you and plying you with a choice of drinks. I remember noticing, as I sat on a stripey beach chair enjoying tea and flapjack and putting off going back out into the cold, that (a) the people I'd been pursuing had already swallowed a drink and left, and (b) my leg muscles had seized so I had difficulty getting up.

A gnarled *ancien* in tracksters gave me a couple of Anadin and I got going again, stamping out the stiffness. The people I'd been pursuing were long gone but I kept walking, albeit more slowly. Some time later – it seemed like days – I realised I'd done 21 miles, further than I'd ever gone on foot before. Far from feeling exultant, I went dramatically into a low. Twenty-one miles. Another 41 to go. I wasn't even halfway. How was I going to do this? All of a sudden my calf muscles felt as though they'd been hollowed out then filled with plaster. And soon after that, as if it had all been coordinated, the tips of my toes thumped once too often against the toebox of my trainers and all the blisters exploded at once.

The low mood passed. Walking into the November sunset sent shivers down my spine. I'd never seen the flat, arable land of my childhood look so seductively lovely. Huge tracts of soil and stubble turned gold and pink in the setting sun. We passed through ancient Essex villages, neat and picturesque with their clapboard cottages. On the skyline were little country churches with dumpy spires. We clumped along footbridges over ditches of glinting water lit up like Tiffany lamps by the fading sun.

It was still light, just, when we emerged into a village high street where the last of the Saturday shoppers were going about their lives. As I thought of these people listening to the football results and queuing at checkouts I had a sense of having been doing something extraordinary, of having moved through a parallel universe. The checkpoint was in the local pub. On one side were the civilians, boozing, and on the other side was the LDWA table, loaded with another slap-up tea. It was quaintly magical.

And yet, really, I'd had enough. It had been a great experience, but I quite wanted to go home now and put my feet up. As if she sensed my hesitation, a tall, vigorous, booted woman in her fifties marched me towards the door. 'Come on,' she said. 'Now you've slowed down a bit, you're welcome to walk with me.'

As we left the pub and turned down a footpath the last light was ebbing from the sky. The creeper-plaited hedges, the distant brown clumps of woodland and the sprawling beige fields abruptly took on the mystery of night. Part of me marvelled at the way everything looked different and mysterious. All the senses were heightened. Head torches appeared as little points of light, threading through the dark.

The other part of me thought, Yeah, but I could get the same effect sitting in the pub garden. And I could have vodka and orange with it. And bloody hell, it was hard clambering over stiles now. I gritted my teeth and concentrated on matching my new friend's long, raking strides. At least I didn't have to talk. She did enough for both of us.

'Hundreds, they're the best thing of all . . . fell into a river on the last one . . . had to do ninety-seven miles on a sprained ankle . . . saw fairies all dancing with their little wands . . . If you finish this you'll have your qualifier for next year's Hundred . . .'

I dropped further and further behind. She carried on talking for a few minutes till she glanced sideways. Noticing I wasn't there, she glided into the distance, head held high.

The next hour panned out, basically, the way all doomed long distance walks do. The heaviness in the legs, the head-dropping dispiriting feeling of being left on your own, the realisation that you're probably doing less than one mile an hour, the chattering teeth, the latest crop of blisters.

I had no idea just how long it would take to cover a relatively short distance at night across country. It wasn't like staggering home after a party because the last train had gone. A mile, normally a ten-minute jog, was a titanic undertaking. I couldn't even have sped up if I'd been able to. It was too dark to see where I was going. I skated over the wet beech leaves, helplessly trying to angle the beam of my head torch on the route description. It bore no relation to anything I could see, so I hung on grimly, following the beam of another head torch that bobbed in the distance. Only two things kept me going, rather than sitting down and sobbing, head in hands: first, if I lost sight of the torch beam in front I was completely finished because I had no idea where I was; and second, when I reached the next checkpoint I could give up.

The next checkpoint – at last I was there. It was a refreshments hut by a lake in Hatfield Forest and the warmth and light hit me like a shock. When I took off my jacket I started shaking uncontrollably. People fussed round me, putting it back on. I was given hot chocolate and a Mars bar. Gradually I came back to life. Thirty-nine miles. Hadn't I done well?

Relief that I'd decided to give up turned to astonishment, then consternation, as I watched a portly middle-aged man on the floor with his boots off. Inspecting socks that were red with blood, he shrugged ruefully, put his boots back on, swigged the last of his tea and set out into the dark.

He must be some kind of super-hero, I decided. He was in much worse shape than me. And a lot less fit, by the look of him.

Then I got a second jolt. Bobbie, a Norfolk girl with a sweet, round face who I'd talked to at an early stage of the walk, looked at me aghast.

'You can't give up,' she said. There was genuine passion in her voice. 'You'll hate yourself. An hour from now you'll be crying your eyes out in the loo. You'll go home to your family and hang your head in shame.'

I thought, on the contrary, that I'd go back to my family and be ridiculed for getting myself in such a state. Then again, another 23 miles – surely I could manage that. It was only walking.

I tacked on to the group who were just leaving – a bunch of runners too exhausted to run any more. And then . . . don't get me started. I could go on longer than the Ancient Mariner about how the next five miles passed. We spent half an hour trudging back and forth over a common trying to identify which of seven trees in front of which of two white houses had to be aimed for. We slogged along the side of arable fields, over rutted tracks mined with rabbit holes and snagged with brambles that wrenched the ankles and bruised the feet. We seemed to be going along the same field, like a tape loop, with the same cow propping its bum against the same stile.

We were a shambling bunch, limping, grunting, groaning. Just to intensify my boredom and misery, it started to rain. My eyes joined in, streaming tears of irritation caused by the accumulation of sixteen hours' worth of dust and grit behind my contact lenses. It was marginally less uncomfortable if I closed the right eye. Pain was shooting through my foot, not the sharp pain of blisters but the deep-seated, tender agony of swollen tendons and ligaments. Every step I took felt as if someone had hit my instep with a gavel. As we left the field path and filed through a dark, warmly pungent farmyard I stumbled and bashed my good foot against a hot black mound which got up and galloped away.

Another bloody cow.

I was half-blind. I could only walk on tiptoe. My left foot had stopped doing what a foot was for and was merely a hub of throbbing pain. But it wasn't just my foot and my eye. Every part of my body was sending out messages.

I CAN'T TAKE MUCH MORE OF THIS.

I DON'T WANT TO DO THIS ANY MORE.

I DON'T CARE ABOUT FINISHING. I JUST WANT THIS TO STOP.

Sawbridgeworth. Even now I only have to see that name on a road sign to be back in a world of exquisite agony as the last half-mile of tarmac met my feet. Wincing, I hobbled finally into another dilapidated scout hut, picked my way around the prone forms of two walkers flat out on the bare floorboards and flopped into an old armchair.

I wolfed down another meal – this one consisted of soggy potatoes and tasteless stew. It tasted wonderful. Anything would have – sheep's eyeballs vinaigrette, tian of worms. It was just so good not to be walking any more. And hadn't I been brave to get this far? Carrying on from the last checkpoint – blimey, that showed guts. Forty-three miles! Nearly one and three-quarter marathons!

I dozed off for an hour between the other people I'd come in with. Even now I remember the fatuity of my triumph as, waking up, I looked for them and found they'd all gone except one.

'Where are the others?' I asked.

'They decided to carry on. Nutters, aren't they?'

'Ye-ees.' I nodded thoughtfully. 'Nutters.'

Of course they were. Completely barking.

Three hours later, after a lift back to the finish in the body bus, I sat down to a full English breakfast in the scout hut. Someone found an empty film canister from their rucksack so I could store the contact lens I'd taken out to relieve my sore, scratched eye. As I tucked in next to all the people who had finished, a strange feeling came over me. I felt unworthy to share their table. And as the sky grew light and I limped out to the car park to drive home, I paused to watch the sweepers bring back a sort of gallant ruin, a solemn old chap plodding ponderously but determinedly towards the end.

'Who's that?' I asked one of the sweepers.

'Gerald. He always finishes last.'

But at least he finished, I thought.

And I hadn't. I was completely gutted. I didn't do it. I didn't finish. Forty-three miles. It was just *lame*.

AS TIME WENT BY, I learnt that this feeling of shame was familiar to any true long distance walker. Dogged insistence on carrying on seemed to be part of the sport's defining ideology. In the words of Reg Kingston, the retired general surgeon who acts as medic-in-residence for the LDWA's magazine, *Strider*: 'On Hundreds it's part of the camaraderie for organisers and other walkers to try and push them through to the finish. From a medical point of view, you'd want to be pushing them off to the casualty unit.'

But the sport's demand for cavalier disregard of potentially crippling injury appeared an essential quality, along with the playing down of what they'd achieved, the lack of crowing and the quixotic insistence on calling the sport long distance walking even if some or all of it was conducted at a run. Not to mention that camaraderie, the Blitz-spirit cheerfulness in extremis and the abandonment of genteel niceties once you'd been on the trail for a few hours. 'My sister-in-law asked me, "Where do you go to the toilet?"' said Shropshire walker Margaret Smith. 'I told her, "Well . . . you know . . . behind a bush." "Ooh, I couldn't do that," my sister-in-law said. People look at you as though you're alien.'

I could have listened all day to the tales of the Hundreds.

'My first was the 1983 Snowdonia,' said George Foot, a gangly and engaging retired lecturer from Devon. 'My friend Arthur Vince persuaded me to go with him and I hadn't a clue what was involved. I was wearing thick felt cut-offs – Bermudas. That was the sort of thing people went walking in then, but I looked an absolute prat. When I set off it was very wet and the trousers soaked up a lot of water. We got hopelessly lost at night and by the time we got to the breakfast stop at Porthmadog, via three or four miles of road, the skin on the balls of my feet was completely removed. When I got to the seventy-mile checkpoint, they asked, "Do you want to retire?" I thought to myself, I've done seventy miles, I don't want to retire now.'

George carried on, walking on the sides of his feet, with people overtaking him. By the time he reached the 82-mile checkpoint he was almost catatonic with depression, and was given a sleeping bag into which he crawled. After half an hour's unconsciousness and a plate of jam sandwiches he went on his way transmogrified, exuberantly shaking his fist at the heavens where his father now resided, the father who had told an eleven-year-old George that he was a bad walker. At the finish, he edged stiffly into a tent and passed out again. By the time his friend Arthur turned up, gaunt and hollow-eyed, he had set like cement. 'We got into the car. Arthur hadn't had any sleep and I couldn't move, so I drove and he got out to fill up when we needed petrol. I was due to catch a train home from Bristol Temple Meads but I couldn't get up and down the steps to the platforms so Arthur took me home with him. When I got out of the car I could only stagger across to the front door. I couldn't walk normally for three weeks, the whole thing was absolute agony and I was hooked.'

'My first Hundred was the 1994 Dartmoor,' said Merv Nutburn. 'I ran it with a guy called Mick Hyde. We were still novices – we got lost between the start and the first checkpoint. Got in there with twelve seconds to spare, which put pressure on us to get to the next checkpoint in time, so then you start using up mental as well as physical energy. Anyway, I got to the last checkpoint and mentally I was dead. I'd reached that moment when you think, I can go no further. I just sat down. That was it. I'd had it. Someone grabbed me by the scruff of the neck, pushed me out. "Off you go, I'll lead you," they said.'

Merv hadn't a clue where he was. All that registered on his consciousness were the lights as they went down into the finish at Tavistock. He got in, removed his shoes and just sat, a staring sac of bones and organs. 'I was absolutely numb. I had no feeling whatsoever. Even though I'd completed it, I felt it had beaten me. So I had to do it again. That's how I got hooked.'

But what was it in this hideous-sounding experience that was so compelling? Were there any prizes? None. What did the winner get, then? There were no winners. It wasn't a race. Anyone who finished got a round of applause, that was all. Plus a badge and certificate. Oh, and a special badge when they finished their tenth Hundred.

To me, that lent this prodigious feat nothing less than profundity. No one, though, seemed to see any splendour in what they were doing. 'We were on the 1991 Lancastrian, my first Hundred,' said Annie Foot, George's wife. 'At ninety-seven miles some idiot started talking about the stars. The galaxy. We lost *him* before the end.'

So, none of that airy-fairy nonsense, thank you. The default attitude was dismissiveness. 'It's like being in labour,' said a friend, Jan, veteran of sixteen Hundreds. 'It's fantastic when it's all over.'

'You've won your battle against yourself,' said my friend Avril. And that was something that did come over, time and again – a kind of uncowed quality peculiar to long distance walkers. 'It's nothing much, but *you* did it,' said Bobbie Sauerzapf, a veterinary surgeon from Norfolk and the one who exhorted me not to give up on the Three Forests Way. 'You kept going when your whole body was pleading with you to stop. You proved that you aren't a quitter. You have something that the others in the office haven't.'

This impression of being determined to see something through was reinforced time and time again as I sat working on my newspaper piece. Who were the legends? Obscure names were given to me: Roger Cole, owner of a water treatment company in Leicester, who had done every Hundred since the first, when he finished severely dehydrated and with his trainers covered in blood, and who had completed the 2005 Chiltern Landmarks Hundred three months after surgery for a brain tumour; Henry Bridge, who dragged his frail old body to the finish of his tenth Hundred aged 81; Boyd Millen, who as soon as he finished chemotherapy for terminal bone cancer went up Low Man in the Lake District on crutches. And that's when I began to find some defining quality of long distance walkers. They *carried on*.

'It was towards the end of the second Cleveland, in 1978, and I was going at one mile per hour,' said Keith Chesterton, the LDWA historian. 'I'd had problems with my shoes and I'd got blisters from early on. Then I got a lot more blisters. Blisters on blisters. I ignored them. I was grimly determined. By the end they were down to the bone but I was so determined I would have carried on even if I'd got two broken legs.'

'On one Hundred, at eighteen miles, I fell running downhill,' said Annie Foot. 'All I could think of was, Ooh, my legs are all right. Then at the sixty-mile checkpoint Jean, one of our friends, said my jaw was dislocated. I thought it had been hurting a bit.'

'On the 2002 Lakeland I was with a lady called Alison,' said Jill Green. 'She was injured. She was a GP and she knew what she'd got. I said, "You're only worried because you're a doctor and you know about it. We just say, 'I've got a bad leg'."

'"Well, if I go on, I won't be able to walk for a week."

'"Will you be able to walk after a week?"

'"Yes."

'"Well, what's the problem? You've come all this way. You keep with me and you'll be all right."'

Not content with finishing 100 miles non-stop, some went

on to do 25, even 40 more. In 1991 George Foot walked 200 miles, from top to bottom of Wales. At the start he picked up a pebble on Llanfairfechan beach and carried it on a continuous journey that took him over a few 3,000-footers ('it was a lot quicker than lots of little ups and downs going round the sides') and through three nights, on the last of which the ground turned into a beautiful coloured mosaic of blues and yellows. Every hill he saw was pitched with tents that weren't there. He weaved down a road, amazed at how fast he was going. His son Barney, deputed to mind him, kept up by going slowly. 'I finished at Dunravin Bay where I threw the pebble into the sea. It was a total high.'

It was the hallucinations and the visual effects of the longer walks that intrigued me. The fifties, 100kms and Hundreds could test you to near-destruction but the payoff was the stuff you saw. Some of it wasn't there, but it was all brilliant. 'The senses are heightened,' said my friend Fabrice, who ran his first Hundred, the Mid Wales, in 27 hours. 'You're on your own. The mind empties itself. No worries any more. Your eyes are looking in front of you, so you're feeling comfortable – you're not looking down, your head hasn't dropped. I love going through fields at night with animals. Running alongside a river when the sun rises and hundreds and hundreds of rabbits come out over the banks. It's a beautiful experience which you have to go through a lot of hard work to get to.'

Here was a sport, too, I speculated, that replicated life – pain, beauty, pratfalls, absurdities, imperfections, moral relativism and all. For instance, there seemed to be an interesting tension between the official ideal – 'it's not a race, it's a personal challenge' – and the private, sometimes zestfully attritional, contests that actually went on.

'One year I finished the Surrey Summits 100km really fast,' said George. 'A whole lot set off at speed. I finally started catching them up in the two o'clock to six o'clock stretch and caught up with the leading group at the food stop. They went off without me. I set off behind them with my friend Tim Carter. First checkpoint at dusk, they were just leaving as we came in. Tim and I tallied and set off again. We came up behind them on Puttenham Common and passed them downhill.

'Tim and I went flat out, headlamps on. I knew the way like the back of my hand. The other group were following us, not looking at the route description. Tim and I switched our headlamps off. They couldn't see us. They had to stop and work out where they were going. We got round in under sixteen hours, really fast. The group who I had been nasty to were well behind us – but they'd left me behind earlier, so that was all right.'

'There are a lot of people who are competitive in the sense of "Oh, I'm not being beaten by him",' said John Sparshatt, a former Scene of Crime Officer with Leeds constabulary and the organiser of three Hundreds. 'I've been on events when I've thought, Oh, I must keep ahead of him because he's older than me. There were a couple of old guys on a famous walk in Lancashire who vied desperately every year to be the oldest finisher.'

'It was the Two Crosses Walk, and it had an award, the Old Man of the Crosses, for the oldest completer,' said John Westcott, a long-term LDWA member from Surrey. 'Henry Bridge was born in 1912 but Bill Stirling, another of these incredibly elderly people, was born in 1910. Henry was a better walker but Bill kept going for it and completing it. So Henry never got it.'

Private competition between peers, though, was acceptable. What was really bad form, apparently, was short-cutting – deviating from the route description to save a few miles.

'On the 1996 Yorkshire Dales, over thirty people were going along a lane to avoid a meandering river bank,' said Keith Warman, the LDWA's Hundreds database holder. 'There's even a school of thought that frowns upon, say, going diagonally across a field when you're asked to go left or right along the side.'

'A problem we've had in the past is that if one sees another short-cutting, they'll follow, particularly if they're treating it as a race,' said John Sparshatt. 'It's mainly runners, because they're competitive. I think it's disappointment you feel really. You put in such a lot of hard work and people take advantage. Unless you have checkpoints at every corner it's difficult to stop. I'm sure it's only a small minority. Most don't, as a matter of honour.'

If short-cutting was the deadly sin, it seemed to be the enduring of prolonged, possibly hilarious, discomfort in order to finish that earned the medals. The greater the physical travails, the more harrowing the progress, the more florid the mental disintegration and the more ridiculous a state someone finished in, the louder the applause.

'On the 2002 Lakeland my buttocks actually fused together,' said Martin Burnell. 'I suppose the top layer of skin mixed with sweat and formed a glue. Sticky bum syndrome. Got all horrible and sore and sticky up there. At one of the checkpoints Norman, the guy I was with, got a load of toilet tissue and shoved it up his bum, then pulled his pants back up and carried on walking. His hand kept gravitating down to his bottom where he was obviously trying to rearrange things. It must have been awful because toilet tissue disintegrates, he must have been in a right state at the end of it.'

'On the Exmoor in 2004, I acted as sweeper to a walker from Kent, Roger Munn, who was in a particularly bad way,' said Shirlie Gill, Keith Warman's partner. 'There was thick fog all around us, and it was just beginning to get light after the second night. The walker Roger had been with had gone on, so it was just the two of us. I said, "If we step it out, Roger, we can get in by quarter to ten." We went along this straight bit on a ridge and I'm saying, "Open your eyes, Roger. Longer steps. This is where you're going to step it out." His knee was murder. He was crying with pain all the way down the hill. "Ten steps, Roger, then you've got to bend a bit." We got to the bottom. He was walking into parked cars. "Open your eyes, Roger." And this lady wound her window down and called, "Have a nice walk!" "Yes I am, thank you," said Roger.'

'Sandra was American,' said John Sparshatt. 'She had these walking poles so she was known as the Lady with the Sticks. She wanted to do the 1998 White Peak. She couldn't map read for love nor money, so the only way to get her to complete was if there were people leading her. I helped her through the second night with my friend Stevie and on the penultimate section, leading up to the Cat and Fiddle, which was our last checkpoint, she was struggling. It was dark, coming light and she'd been walking more than forty hours. She could see all these animals beside her in the road. Honestly. Zoo animals! Really weird stuff. She kept telling us, "There's a zebra!" We were approaching the Cat and Fiddle, and they were all clapping her in. So she thought that was the finish! Which was terrible because then I had to make her understand that we still had the finish to get to.'

So what happened?

'Off we went down a track. She kept saying, "You're taking me off down here to murder me. I'm going to tell your wife about you."

'I kept saying, "No, no, I'm not. I'm taking you to the finish," but she wouldn't have it. "You are not. You're going to murder me. I'm going to tell your wife about you." Every time somebody came towards us she started again. Stevie and I were looking at one another. I mean, I was a police officer, I knew what it looked like. We're with a woman in a psychotic state and if anybody had come up and asked us, "What are you doing with this woman?", we couldn't have justified ourselves. It was only us that wanted it by then, not her. Because she was absolutely gone. We eventually got back at ten to ten on Sunday morning. Forty-seven hours fifty. We stopped outside to let her enter the finish hall on her own. She *loved* it. She seemed quite normal.'

ALL THAT, OF COURSE, lay in the future. For the present, I was flaked out on a sofa back in London, wincing and hobbling in the aftermath of my first attempt at a long distance walk. In the days that followed I seemed strangely unable to get it together in normal life. My view of the world seemed different, like if you've just returned home after spending the last twenty-five years on a remote island. Maybe it was the connection to something primitive and feral. Maybe nightwalking had managed to make the daytime world seem dreary and colourless. Whatever it was, for a few weeks afterwards part of me was still back in the forest, crashing around in the bushes just yards away from people getting on with their normal lives.

But that wasn't really what hooked me.

What hooked me was that I was younger and fitter than a lot of these people. How come they were able to keep going and I wasn't?

I tried reasoning with myself. I couldn't have finished. My foot was the size of a snowshoe.

And a voice in my head murmured, *Could still have done it. Could have hopped.*

Instead of putting the whole ridiculous, painful experience behind me, the uncomfortable feeling of shame persisted. I hadn't finished.

Looking back, I'm taking a leap in the dark here, but it seems to me that the defining moment was when I opted to walk on after Hatfield Forest. If I'd done the rational thing and retired there, I would have limped home, written the feature and forgotten about it. Instead I went on. Doing so flipped me into a different level of the sport. It became more than merely walking a long way. Those last few miles seemed to grip me. It was then that this sport grasped my soul in some kind of half-nelson. *You won't give up till you do it.*

Of course, my thoughts at the time were nowhere near so grandiose and profound. All I did was wait till I could walk again without howling with pain, drive back to Sawbridgeworth and complete the miles I hadn't done. Then I sent in my entry for the Hundred.

YOREDALE HUNDRED 2008

Saturday, Sunday & Monday 24, 25 & 26 May

Route Description

This is the route description for the Event.
The following should be noted:
1. As always the description should be used in conjunction with the
appropriate maps.
2. There are no route abbreviations. If you need to 'X st on rt to X fb
to go thru kg and trn lt' you will be told to 'cross stile on right to cross
footbridge to go through kissing gate & turn left'.
3. Please try to avoid doing anything that would compromise the good
relationships that have been developed with the landowners. Whilst
none of the route is on private land it does belong to someone.
Please feel free to publicise the event as you enjoy walking
along the route.

1: Aireville School, Skipton (SD 977 519) to Gargrave (SD 934 546) *Distance: 5.02 miles; Ascent: 184 feet; Descent: 244 feet*

Here we go, then: 101.8 miles of Yorkshire's best scenery. One serious climb, one night yomp up the Pennine Way to Kidhow Gate, and fifty miles more than I've ever walked before.

I queue for breakfast in the school assembly hall, only to realise I've discovered a powerful new appetite suppressant. It's a simple combination of adrenalin, disorientation and naked fear. Every gram of motivation, all the confidence I've developed from the marathons, thirties and fifties of the last year, all the fitness I've gained through running forty miles a week, has disappeared.

Instead I think I might die. All I can focus on is a small stretch of path – no, not a path, but a series of descending slabs the size of pixels – that curves round a boulder as you come off the top of Ingleborough.

The dictionary definition of vertigo is 'a sensation of whirling and loss of balance, caused by looking down from a great height'. But that's not quite it. What's getting me is sheer funk – what if I fail, what if I don't deliver the goods? – combined with excess of imagination; in real time and space I'm queuing at the tea urn, giving little jaunty waves of recognition to everyone I know, but in my mind's eye I'm trying to ease myself round the edge of that terrifying crag. On that path six feet long and the width of a hair ribbon. There's a thousand-foot drop on the left. One mis-step and I'll be involuntarily tombstoning into Black Shiver. And then I'll have to retire, but I won't lose face because I'll be dead. It's a win-win situation. Kind of.

By way of displacement activity, I fiddle with my tally, which I've hung around my neck. In the end I tie it on the back of my rucksack, trying not to gag at the smell of bacon butties.

Then I consider the rucksack itself. It's stuffed to bursting and will feel as if I'm carrying a dead crow around on my back. Deciding on what's to go in it has caused me the kind of angst people normally reserve for choosing a flatmate. Well, I could be living with these things for the next 48 hours.

First, there's the compulsory kit. Two waterproofed maps: Explorer 002 Yorkshire Dales (Southern & Western) and 030 Yorkshire Dales (Central & Northern). You have to carry them even though you're never going to look at them. They're long distance walking's equivalent of the Gideon Bible in hotel rooms.

What I will be looking at is the route description, a hefty wodge of A4. I've also brought a supplementary route description, much

OUT ON YOUR FEET

simplified and in large, bold, unmistakable print for the later hours of the event when I lose my wits; put together, the entire package is almost as big as *Vogue*. I'm carrying a compass and map case, a whistle and survival bag. Emergency rations, mug and fleece. I have the waterproofs: a new, very expensive Goretex lightweight top plus the elderly, bulky green pair from Millets that I bought for my first ever long distance walk, the Three Forests Way, where all this madness started. And a head torch, including spare bulb and batteries. And change for a public phone, because you can't rely on a mobile in case it's out of range. I have to say, it's not often you'll find a red telephone box on a sheep moor, so good luck with that one.

I'm also carrying the usual extras: emergency toilet paper, eye drops and container for my contact lenses, painkillers, NUUN tabs for electrolite replacement, tube of Eumovate for bumular chafing problems, hat, gloves, and monster packet of ProPlus. And – on Keith Warman's recommendation – a Mini-Maglite torch to supplement the head torch.

Just two more things to cram in. Most important is the drinking bladder, on which I spent shedloads in SweatShop during a last minute shopping expedition. Which means I've not tried it out yet, but the alternative is to have water bottles stashed in every available pocket so I'd be prancing along like a mobile drinks dispenser. Along with the drinking bladder I bought a pair of lightweight walking poles – and even as I was paying for them I knew I'd be doing what I am in fact doing now, which is to put them away in my halfway bag, along with the green waterproof trousers, another item I never use as when you put them on it's like wearing polytunnels. (A note of explanation here. The halfway bag is just that, a bag for extra items like spare socks and a change of shoes, which you leave at the start and which is transported to the breakfast stop, halfway.)

I hoist the rucksack over my shoulders. And it all starts again, the funk. Even supposing I survive Ingleborough, it's only going to be to perish by the river at 85 miles on the way to Bolton Bridge. The bit where three-quarters of the path looks as if it's been hacked out by a giant spoon. The bit which I'll be doing in darkness if things go pear-shaped and I have to go into a second night. The only handhold is a wizened strand of barbed wire, probably hung with shreds of dried flesh left by the last desperate scrabbling hand as its owner slid into the drink.

I want my mum.

Then the rational part of my brain takes over. Don't be an ass. It's only the Wharfe. It's not full of crocodiles. When did anyone get eaten alive by carp?

Think positively. Think of all the days and nights you've put in. All the rain and cold you've gone through. The seven o'clock starts in the dark. The endless limb-stiffening car journeys back to London from north, south, east and west, which took even longer because you had to pull into so many laybys to sleep, topped off with five-minute sideshows for the neighbours as you got out and waddled to the front door. Remember all the farcical scenes you've endured to get here: the pratfalls (six in less than a mile of Surrey mud); the occasion on which you ended up on top of a labrador when both of you tried to hurdle a Lake District stile at the same time; that Sunday afternoon you got so hideously lost in Kent you had to find your way back on route via a lorry-infested road tunnel on the A20.

And then I think of all the people I know who I'll be seeing today. There's Avril, who's going round with the partially sighted walker Ian McLeod again: 'Listen, if it all goes wrong and you feel crap, just sit and wait for us at the checkpoint and we'll take you through.' There's Keith Warman, aiming to finish his eighteenth Hundred, and Shirlie Gill, his partner, who's come along to support him and who, intuiting my knocking knees and quivering lower lip, envelops me in a sisterly hug. There's Martin Burnell, the Hertfordshire plumber, all sunburnt legs and droopy moustache; Brian Harwood, the lugubriously friendly walker I finished the Stansted Stagger with; Don Newman, a boyishly enthusiastic computer programmer from Surrey; Merv Nutburn, the spry, bespectacled sixty-something runner from Kent; Marie Doke, composed, dark-haired and graceful, waiting, like

Merv, for the runners' start; Garfield Southall, IT professor from the University of Chester, who seems to have more gadgets on him than the Electronics pages on Amazon. And there's Jill Green, the veteran racewalker who lives on the Isle of Wight and who has two courtiers this weekend, her husband Dave and a bloke she's taking round with her from the local paper.

Proceed to start in Aireville Park by returning to School entrance & turning right down road.

And there are even more familiar faces outside the school assembly hall where a huge, high-spirited crowd is gathering now. People mill about on the driveway. There are gangly men in shorts, warhorses, amazons, scudders, tall ships, wading birds, men with God beards, plus a few small nippy women like me. The weather is perfect, sunny without threatening intense heat later. I funnel out with them down the drive.

Pass car park & swimming pool to your right & enter Aireville Park through gateway & wait for start.

Somewhere beyond the wall of people is a rig, where a big plump Christmas robin of a mayor with a snow-white jabot and gold chains over her breast mouths words that come over on the PA system as *blarf-harf-harf.*

Once started continue down roadway on right-hand side of park exiting by another gateway.

The mass starts to shift, so I do too. I'm right at the back, penned in by codgers, unable to see anything but swinging buttocks. Ducking under flying elbows with a mad apologetic leer as the park spews an unending stream of walkers on to the Leeds–Liverpool Canal towpath, I arrive on a Martin Parr scene of gently heightened Englishness – canal boats, cotton bud clouds and a line of walkers lengthening and thinning like when you slowly pull on a wad of chewing gum.

You are now on the canal towpath for approximately 4 miles with the canal on your right throughout. The towpath is wide enough to safely allow overtaking if everyone walks/runs sensibly & with consideration.

The fast walkers are already half a mile ahead. I break into a little jog. It's a lovely sunny day. Ahead of me are two whole days and a night with nothing else to worry about except getting back here. After eleven years, I'm on the Hundred.

Checkpoint 1: Gargrave (Car park of Fred Green & Son) SD 934 546

Opens: 0945 Saturday; Closes: 1330 Saturday

Total distance: 5.02 miles; Total ascent: 184 feet; Total descent: 244 feet

Manned by: Dave Green

Outdoor checkpoint with cold drinks and biscuits only

FOUR

A Long Day's Journey, and Then Some

THE SOUTH OF ENGLAND, MAY 2005. IN the distance, a glimpse of hills, of patches of pea green, lime and viridian, below the blurred dark topline of woodlands. In a postcard-blue sky, the sun eased itself above the well-heeled Buckinghamshire town of Chalfont St Giles. In the college campus car park, checkpoint marshals rammed crates of food into a minibus: bags of pasta perched on cans of rice pudding, cartons of custard made room for towers of quiche, sliced loaves seemed to peer out of the windows.

The event was the Chiltern Landmarks Hundred, three years in the planning and the work of local LDWA group Beds, Bucks & Northants. Invisible from the car park were the eponymous attractions, Coombe Hill with its huge view across the Vale of Aylesbury, Burnham Beeches, Marlow Bridge, Ivinghoe Beacon, the Chequers estate, the Hambleden Valley, the windmill on Turville Hill that had featured in *Chitty Chitty Bang Bang* and the countryside in which *The Vicar of Dibley* was filmed. Inside, the college dining hall had turned into a vast, noisy check-in area, the floor a weird terrain of chairs and rucksacks forested with people's legs. Walkers pored over maps, exchanged jocularly nervous banter, queued for the free tea and toast. As ten o'clock approached, they formed a herd on the playing fields and filtered down to the country lane at the back for the start.

A dog-walker had stopped to watch. 'What on earth are they doing?' she enquired in Margot Leadbetter tones.

That was, in fact, a pretty good question. What were they doing, exactly? Described baldly, the object of this exercise was to walk a hundred miles. It seemed too idiosyncratic, though, simply to classify it as an endurance event, or even a massively attenuated bog-standard long distance walk. Interviewed in the April 2004 edition of *Strider*, Adrian Moody, designer of the Chiltern Landmarks route, spoke of the difference between a normal challenge event of 20 to 30 miles and a Hundred:

> Size. Five times more of everything. Number of walkers, distance, checkpoints, things that can go wrong. Night-walking – generally two lots of it . . . The second night particularly gives you the problem of entrants who are dead on their feet . . .

Not only bigger and grislier, the Hundred possessed much more of an air of festival than a normal event. It was an annual rendezvous in an older England of beautiful villages and countryside. You could have compared it in that respect to the Tour de France, without the commercial exploitation. It was also like deep sea diving in that doing it exposed you to an esoteric condition peculiar to the activity. Divers risked the bends. In the later miles of the event, some Hundred-ers tilted. The official term for it was Leaning Over Sideways Syndrome: acronym, LOSS. While not potentially fatal, it did make you look like a walking Anglepoise lamp.

Saying what the Hundred was like, though, moved you little closer to defining it. Even the people who took part could talk only in terms of why it appealed. If you asked them what the

Hundred was, what you received were contributions to a mood board.

'It's the atmosphere,' said Ken Falconer. 'Everyone knowing that you're all going to go off together.'

'A Hundred means enjoying the countryside by night and day,' was the offering of Tom Sinclair, a former LDWA chairman.

'A Hundred is the ultimate test of fitness, stamina, navigational ability and downright stubbornness,' said Keith Warman.

'It's a Zen-like experience,' said Chris Dawes.

'I suppose the Hundred is really a celebration of Britain and Britishness in a very old-fashioned sense,' said Bobbie Sauerzapf. 'Britain because whatever part of the country you're in, the countryside is at its finest in May. Britishness because it's about being eccentric in a harmless way and also being single-minded about being different.'

'Foreboding,' said George Foot. 'Evening. Fading light. A mystical feeling. Slightly threatening. You know you're going to walk through the night. The 1996 Yorkshire Dales, going up Wild Boar Fell. That stunning sunrise. When you're tired it heightens your sensitivity, awareness, all that kind of thing. To see a sunrise like that when you've walked through the night – it's a different dimension. You perceive and feel things quite differently when you're in that frame of mind. It's sheer magic. Special.'

In short, you could come up with lots of different takes on it. But to come up with one single encompassing definition reminded me of Edward Lear's nonsense poem: 'Who, or why, or which, or what, is the Akond of Swat?'

The way the Hundred took place in a different part of the country each year – that merely added to the indeterminacy. It wasn't like the Grand National or the FA Cup final, in which a permanent venue was synonymous with the event. One year it could be the bleak moors and stiff-treed forests of the North-east, another year Wales's lush hills and coldly rippling reservoirs, another the chalk surfaces of the South Downs Way. The Chiltern Landmarks route was based originally on the mildly hilly Chiltern Way, with plenty of tweaks when the Way passed too close to civilisation for comfort. 'They change every year because of the conditions,' said Merv Nutburn. 'How can you compare a Hundred in Dartmoor and one in Northumberland?'

The indeterminacy was increased by the weather roulette. The 1992 Invicta in Kent was so hot helpers at the breakfast stop were defrosting sausages on the car roof. Floods in the same county made the 2000 Millennium Hundred almost a swimathon. 'I was marshalling at Kentmere on the 2002 Lakeland and it was red hot,' said Northumberland walker Philip Powell. 'I was wearing sandals and my feet were sunburnt. There wasn't enough water. There was a cistern for the hamlet – we drained it. No mobile coverage. We had to send a message by car asking for bottled water. No one in Kentmere could flush toilets. We'd drunk the Lake District dry.'

A further variable had to be factored in – the quality of the instructions. 'On the 1985 Yorkshire Dales the conditions were awful, it rained most of the time and it had one of the lowest finishing rates,' said Ken Falconer. 'I was looking at the route description for that the other day, it wouldn't be tolerated now. Five sides of banded, very brief description. I remember going over Wild Boar Fell in the night, looking back across the valley and there were torch lights all over the place. They should have been in a straight line but they were just covering the hills.'

'The 1990 Chilterns was a total shambles,' said George. 'There were a lot of problems with the route. It was very badly planned and there were a large number of considerable short cuts you could take. You went round in loops, visited three checkpoints twice. I remember turning up at one of the dual ones, at seventy miles and seeing some chap sitting there eating a banana. I said, "I'll have one of them," and was told, "Sorry, it's a ninety-mile banana."'

This essential variability meant there was no yardstick by

which to judge individual performance. Usain Bolt's 100 metres in 9.69 seconds would have been a record whether he'd done it in Beijing or Basingstoke. But with few stiles, good track all the way and no steep inclines, Downsman Hundreds (there have been four) were famously fast. Mark Pichard finished in 16.52 on the 1986 Downsman. It's still the record time for a Hundred. But was it better than Mick Cudahy's 21.45 finish on that 1985 Yorkshire Dales with its route over Pen-y-Ghent and Ingleborough in mist and almost non-stop rain? And what about the people at the back of a Hundred, the ones who Keith Warman called 'warhorses – people just happy to plod round'? Some argued that it was the unathletic end of the pack, facing down pain, exhaustion and confusion through a second night to finish, who put in the really great performances.

A further barrier to comparison was that a Hundred was a round number rather than an exact measurement. 'A cross-country walk is very different from a circular athletics track where you can be very precise about what the distance round is,' said Ken Falconer. 'But you can be certain that the distance is at least a hundred miles.' And then some, on one occasion. The actual length of the 1993 Cleveland worked out at 109 miles. 'Annie and I took forty-two hours,' said George Foot. 'The route description was incompetent. Cocked up. It just went on and on. I thought it was never going to end.'

At other times, the add-ons were intentional. 'In the 1981 Cumbrian, the first Lake District Hundred, they shoved on another twenty-five miles for those who didn't think a hundred was long enough,' said George. 'Seven did the extra, six finished. For the 1982 Pilgrims Hundred, along the North Downs Way, Guildford to Canterbury, Ernie Bishop, the organiser, devised a Pilgrims Plus – forty miles optional extra before the start, beginning at Winchester. There were fifty or so starters for that. Most of them recanted a hundred miles down the road, but Roger Cole did the full hundred and forty.'

As if to confuse matters further, effectively two Hundreds took place every year. The tradition of the marshals' walk evolved from two or three people making a final check of the route and description into a regular event, held normally over the first Bank Holiday weekend in May and giving helpers on the main event the chance to walk it (it counts as an official completion). One Hundred, the 1983 Snowdonia, offered two routes: Standard Route and High Level Route. 'That was a really tough one with much more climb – it went over Snowdon,' explained George. 'On the day it was cancelled because of appalling weather conditions, so the only one who ever did it was Ernie Bishop, who completed it as the sole participant on the marshals' walk. That was the last time there was anything but an ordinary Hundred.'

Except, of course, that it wasn't. In 1990 two official Hundreds were held, the Chiltern in May and the Shropshire, also known as the Marchesman, on the August Bank Holiday weekend.

'There was quite a history of Hundred problems,' George continued. 'People were getting anxious about the event filling up after the LDWA brought in the five hundred entrants limit because of sensitivity to possible environmental damage, so in 1990 it was decided to have a go at having two Hundreds. They said you weren't allowed to do both. Then the Shropshire one wasn't very full so lots of people did both anyway, but they could only count one towards their ten Hundreds badge.'

It was also becoming clear that a Hundred wasn't like the marathon, where abundant advice was available. 'There are no easy Hundreds,' was about as specific as it came. That and the caution not to think about the total distance, but only the mileage to be covered to the next checkpoint. The vagaries of weather and route meant there were few predictable eventualities, like hitting the wall at 20 miles. Head-lolling despair could take over anywhere. 'Think of the average emotions of a forty-eight hour period in your life, exacerbated in a Hundred because of your physical and mental state,' said John Walker. 'They're up and down like a bride's nightie. It doesn't take much. Just lose your way with fifteen miles to go – it's the end of the world, a catastrophe of cataclysmic proportions.'

The event also seemed to have two discrete shapes. One was topographical – paths, climbs, location of checkpoints. The other was temporal. It took the form of the Start, the Finish, and a hundred-mile middle, which was known as 'going round' and was subdivided into the First Day, the Night Section, the Second Day and the Second Night, on which was predicated a condition known as Second Night Fear (i.e. people didn't want to go into it). In that vague middle were several notorious dropping-out points. 'Thirty miles for the burnouts,' said Keith Warman. 'Then the checkpoint around forty miles or wherever you are when night starts getting a grip. Then the breakfast point at fifty or sixty miles. You get so comfy it can be hard to get up and go.'

'On the 1997 Downsman, I was too cocky,' agreed Garfield Southall, the IT professor. 'I ran the first forty miles, burned up and blistered my feet on the hard surfaces and had to retire. My (now ex-) brother-in-law lived quite close – I'd stayed with him the night before and I'm sure that had a psychological impact, knowing I could say, "Come and get me".'

'People say a Hundred starts at seventy-five miles, and I think that's true,' said runner Marie Doke. 'On my first, the 2003 White Rose, that was when I dropped out. If you feel really lousy at seventy-five, if someone says to you, "There's twenty-five miles left to go", it's an extremely long way.'

'I know someone who retired at ninety-two miles on the 1994 Dartmoor because he was late meeting his girlfriend,' said Keith Warman.

I realised, too, that because of this inbuilt indeterminacy no specific training schedule applied. Some people took part in an event every week, some one a month, some half a dozen a year.

'I basically don't do any training,' said Ken Falconer. 'I believe in just keeping myself at a general fitness level. I try to get at least half an hour's walk throughout the day and that makes a lot of difference. Really I like to get out on a reasonable walk – twenty miles or a hillwalk – most weekends. It's a good idea three or four weeks before an actual Hundred to do something slightly longer. My standard walk since I've been in St Andrews is thirty-five miles of the Fife coastal path – it's quite rugged. It tells the body, "Soon something's going to be expected of you."

'On the Hundred itself, no two people have the same approach. I know some people who completely bandage their feet. Tony Rowley wraps his feet in plaster beforehand. I've always got to the start with a pair of boots and a pair of trainers and I've chosen depending how dry it's been underfoot.'

'Towards the Hundred, I'd get up my 10k running speed,' said George Foot. 'The key on the day is being well organised. Have things in place, know where you're going. Stick to your plans. Don't start off too fast. Lots of food at the first checkpoint. Don't bugger around in the other checkpoints. If you're feeling depressed, go and have a kip.'

But it wasn't just a matter of being fit enough to do a hundred miles non-stop. You had to find your way as well.

'I've always wanted to know exactly where I am,' said Ken Falconer. 'I have my double-sided map case, route description on one side, 1:25,000 map on the other. When walking a Hundred you don't just look at the current instruction, you look at the next one. OK, you read *Continue down the road for half a mile*, but you've got to realise you have to read the next sentence *and turn right by house*, otherwise you're not thinking ahead and you'll get lost. I've actually come to enjoy solo nightwalking, it's better than sex any day. I do enjoy the route-finding and finding my own way at night.'

'The temptation is not to focus on the route description but look around,' said Merv Nutburn. 'But you know damn well you've got to read the instructions. Especially at night. One line at a time. In daytime – "Oh, I can see that tree over there." At night, you can't. It helps if you have someone with you, so one reads out loud while the other looks and can say, "Hang on, that doesn't make sense," if you're reading the wrong line.'

That gave rise to another question. Was it acceptable or bad form to recce the route beforehand?

'The old ethos was, you didn't recce,' said Jill Green. 'Some people still feel it's cheating and shouldn't be allowed. But I overheard some men saying, "We were going all right and then this lady joined us on the night bits, and we couldn't go on, because we couldn't dump her." I thought, "Chivalry is not dead! But nobody is ever going to say that of me." That was when I started to recce. It doesn't mean that you won't go wrong, but you'll know you're wrong, very quickly.'

'My second Hundred was the 1984 Dartmoor and I said, "Right, I'm jolly well going to recce the night route",' said George Foot. 'Made an enormous difference. I overtook loads of people. But on the second day, on South Dartmoor, there was a bloody great tramline track and towards the end you had to set off down into a valley and go west to meet it. I failed ever to find it. I wandered across open horrible Dartmoor for miles and found the bloody thing eventually, just when I had to leave it. So in the 1985 Yorkshire Dales I recce'd the night section *and* the following day. Then on the first day, going up Ingleborough, the mist came down. Some people got lost and ended up five miles up the road. After that I said, "Right, I'm going to recce the whole lot." To be confident, to know where I'm going makes an enormous difference psychologically. I wanted to avoid the anxiety. It saves me two hours on a Hundred over the people who get lost. If you know the way you don't have to think, "What do I do now? Where do I go afterwards?"'

Where you hoped to go eventually, of course, was back to the finish. In a sport whose purpose wasn't victory but arrival, no matter what state you were in, the arrangements for that were regarded as crucial. 'If you come into the hall and there is the finish desk and everyone who is in the hall can see you, you feel part of it,' said Ken Falconer. 'If you get a finish desk in the lobby separate from the main hall you don't get the same applause and atmosphere. It is important.

'The 1996 Yorkshire Dales was based on Settle and started and finished at a school, and it was a wonderful place because you looked up on to the hillside and you could see people coming over the ridge and making their way down. That was a perfect finish.'

BACK AT THE CHILTERN Landmarks Hundred, it was Monday morning. The sun climbed high over the University of Buckingham campus for a third successive day and in the finish hall a clock was ticking towards the cut-off time, ten o'clock.

The arrangements didn't quite conform to Ken's template of perfection. Sagging walkers, tidemarked with sweat, eased themselves through an open door and shuffled on bloated, hammered feet into a large lobby with a lounge bar at one side in which students partied obliviously. Most people were flaked out behind the dark double doors that led back into the dining hall. Still, there were enough of us around to applaud the final finisher at 9:52. It was Gerald.

Reports in the following issue of *Strider* dwelt on all the defining preoccupations of long distance walkers – the route, the nature, bizarre sleeping arrangements and that special joy of occupying a parallel universe: 'The route description was one of the best we have had'; 'Specific recollections include a magpie with a slow-worm by the roadside, the strong smell of wild garlic, and the pink sunrise on Sunday, to say nothing of walking into the wedding party as they emerged from Hambleden church'; 'One of the highlights was eating potato wedges with tomato ketchup'; 'During the first night I came face to face with a hedgehog trotting down the path towards me'; 'I went astray only once during the second night – I was asleep on my feet at the time and walked past a right hand turning.' One first-timer, Phil Thornton, wrote of being all but dragged out of a checkpoint by a weathered stranger called George when he was on the cusp of giving in:

> Without a second thought he said that we would continue together, and this we did, for the rest of the event. He didn't leave my sight despite clearly being able to move much quicker than me. Seeing my inexperience, he made it his task to get me through . . .

That sense of fellow-feeling was emphasised time and again as I asked people what defined the event. 'We look after our own,' said Bobbie Sauerzapf. 'We'd always stop to lend anyone a hand if we came across them in trouble.'

'It's the spirit of the Hundred,' said John Walker. 'It's so British, so eccentric, the fact that it is *not* a race. You get hundred-mile events in America, for instance, but they have winners and losers, whereas everyone here is really helping everyone else.'

I didn't find John and Bobbie's view completely convincing. Not everyone on a Hundred, surely, was an exemplar of *agape*. Even so, what they said was affecting. And they were right, the Hundred did seem to be a very British event with its emphasis on courtesy, fair play and stoicism. As far as most of the entrants were concerned, the normal rules of competition didn't apply. That feeling of connectedness and *Weltanschauung* of 'do no harm' was contrary to the ethos of almost every other sport I could think of. It was certainly one of the Hundred's essential qualities.

Even so, I was no closer to the one-word answer I sought. There probably wasn't one. The proper noun 'Hundred' was itself a kind of caterogem, a term capable of standing alone as subject and predicate of a logical proposition. Only 'Hundred' could signify the combination of ritual, pilgrimage, emotional rollercoaster, interdependence and entrancing absurdity of walking a hundred miles in one go.

'It's a ridiculous thing to do,' said Martin Burnell. 'I'm sometimes walking along and I start smiling and chuckling and thinking to myself, this is mad.'

Which is appropriate, considering how long distance walking started.

YOREDALE HUNDRED 2008

2: Gargrave (SD 934 546) to Kirkby Malham (SD 895 610)
Distance: 5.73 miles; Ascent: 583 feet; Descent: 321 feet

Continue on road for 950yds passing entrances to Gargrave House, Home Farm & Gargrave House Gardens to reach somewhat hidden Pennine Way sign on right (approx 200yds after footpath sign on left). Leave road to right in the direction indicated & cross wall stile into field...

This is pretty much like the first section – flat and fast. Except the scene-shifters have taken away the canal towpath and replaced it with sunny, breeze-blown fields. We're tracing the River Aire, alongside Eshton Moor, a blur of walls and grazing land with that faintly toothless-old-man air that solitary tree stumps lend to a landscape. Kirkby Malham's Bovine Massive lounges truculently against stiles, barricading escape routes with their steaming backsides.

Anyway, here's the plan. I'm going to do the first day on my own because I want to jog. For me this is a sort of middle-way, Lib Dem of gaits made up of running bits and walking bits. To put this in some kind of perspective, it's a pace at which I can keep up with fast walkers, though not necessarily the whole way. But the target is to be on top of Ingleborough by seven tonight. Hopefully, I'll manage that. Then I'll be able to leave Horton-in-Ribblesdale while it's still light and be halfway up to Kidhow Gate before night gets a grip. The route is obvious – most of it has been surfaced and it's like a wide, sandy forest track.

With luck I'll find someone who's going at my speed and who I can tag along with so I don't have to drop down from Kidhow to Hawes on my own in the dark. Let's be more specific here. I want to get myself a man for the night. And then, stage two. I'm aiming to arrive at the breakfast stop before it gets light – Hawes, the furthest north we'll be. Once you get there you're halfway. There'll only be another fifty to go – just another day's walking. I've never gone further than fifty before but with luck I'll find a group I can leave Hawes with, and we'll finish the Hundred together. Obviously, there's a few things that could go wrong on route. There's a tough section within two miles of the finish where you leave Addingham and climb on to Draughton Moor, over a very rutted track. The steep descent to the road by Jenny Gill is gruesome even when you're limber and wide awake. But what I'm aiming for is to reach the finish before midnight on Sunday so I don't have to walk through a second night.

Go up steps onto road & turn left over Hanlith Bridge (You have just left the Pennine Way). Once over bridge continue on road for about 600yds (passing seat on your left & then round right-hand bend) to reach cross roads. Turn right with the Victoria Inn on your left for about 30yds to reach checkpoint on right.

I file into the village hall behind a line of walkers as another line of walkers files out. A weird thought ensues. Autonomously I'm doing the Hundred, following my plan. At another, quieter level, I'm a small component in a mechanism. We're all going round together. We're part of some greater whole. Or maybe we're just luggage on a carousel, but I suspect it's more meaningful than that.

Checkpoint 2: Kirkby Malham (Village Hall) SD 895 610

Opens: 1030 Saturday; Closes: 1430 Saturday
Distance: 10.75 miles; Ascent: 767 feet; Descent: 565 feet
Manned by: Vermuyden Group
Indoor checkpoint with hot / cold drinks and food

FIVE
The Cradle of the Game

THE LDWA WAS INSPIRED BY A MADWOMAN.
OK, there was more to it than that. Organised long distance walking as it developed in Britain in the sixties and seventies was the convergence of a number of traditions and activities that can be traced back to Regency times. But the immediate catalyst was a Russian-born woman, Dr Barbara Moore, who spent most of 1959 and 1960 walking from Edinburgh to London and from John O'Groats to Land's End.

It wasn't the kind of thing anyone, male or female, did at the time. Marching alone through the drab towns and along the car-light roads of post-war Britain, Dr Moore was a novelty. The fact that she lived off nothing but nuts, honey, raw fruit and vegetable juice – or so she claimed – made her seem even more exotic. Her walks caught the public imagination to such an extent that holiday camp entrepreneur Billy Butlin, quickly spotting a publicity opportunity, set up a John O'Groats to Land's End walking race open to all comers. Suddenly the whole of Britain was riveted by long distance walking.

That was how it seemed, anyway, as 725 competitors set out from the top of Scotland in February 1960. Nine hundred miles and 15 days, 14 hours and 31 minutes later, Jim Musgrave, a 31-year-old glass blower from Doncaster, staggered into Land's

End followed in due course by another 112 survivors, including the inevitable 'granny', 62-year-old Maud Nicholas. They were all that was left of the original 725.

It was obvious why so many had been prepared to put themselves through what was for most an epic passeggiata of non-stop pain. First prize was £1,000 – almost enough in those days to buy you a house. Just why Dr Barbara Moore was doing it no one was sure. Did she want to be a celebrity? Was she selling some kind of health programme? Could she have been anorexic?

'No, she was just a madwoman,' snorts Barbara Blatchford, a little, sturdy woman with a no-nonsense hairdo and an aura of brisk competence. 'Barmy. But it started a discussion in our YHA group about how long it would be sensible to walk in a day. Thirty miles seemed the answer, and out of that came the Tanners Marathon.'

The Tanners, as it's usually known now, is a key part of LDWA folklore. And as a teenager Barbara, now widow of the LDWA's co-founder Alan Blatchford and based in Oxenholme in the Lake District, was one of its organisers. The first, in 1960, simply called the Marathon Walk, was 30 miles long, and based on the tracks, footpaths and bridleways of the Surrey countryside around Leatherhead. It started at a small, remote youth hostel, Tanners Hatch, in the woods in the middle of Ranmore Common. What singled it out was that it was open to all comers, on a set date, with a time limit, checkpoints and a route description. The setting was rural, the course virtually tarmac free. Participants could run or jog if they wanted, but it wasn't a race. As such it's recognised as the first challenge walk ever.

Examine the components of the Tanners Marathon more closely and you begin to sort out the ragbag of activities that converged in the LDWA. For one, you have to look at the rambling enthusiasms of the Romantic poets. 'Wordsworth was a terrible poet but a very good walker,' says author and long distance walker Ronald Turnbull of the man who set the Lake District to verse.

Coleridge, who wrote 'Kubla Khan' in an Exmoor farmhouse, had a 40-mile walk around the area on which he used to take guests at night. Keats wrote *Endymion* on Box Hill in Surrey. But for another of the modern challenge walk's antecedents, you have to go back to the Footman racing of the seventeenth and eighteenth centuries. That was when aristocrats and gentry bet wagers on whose carriage footmen could 'walk fair heel and toe on the turnpikes, heaths, downs and racecourses of England' the fastest. Races could last up to 24 hours and even take place over six days and out of them evolved the nineteenth-century craze for professional pedestrianism – foot travel over unfeasibly long distances, the forerunner of both ultramarathoning and long distance walking.

By then the growth of the popular press had ensured that particular feats caught the public imagination, strange though it is to think of long distance walking as a crowd-puller. Peter Radford's excellent book *The Celebrated Captain Barclay: Sport, Gambling and Adventure in Regency Times* tells of the wager walk that drew thousands to Newmarket Heath in the summer of 1809, when Captain Robert Barclay Allardice, 6th Laird of Ury, 'The Celebrated Pedestrian', walked one mile every hour of every day and every night, without a break, for 1,000 hours – just nine hours short of six weeks. The wager was for 1,000 guineas, but with side-bets success was probably worth more like 16,000 guineas to Barclay (one guinea at the time amounting to the average weekly wage). It was, writes Radford, 'an athletic event that challenged the very limit of human capability', and the equivalent of £40 million today was placed in bets, the Prince of Wales being among the punters. It's a nice irony that so much money was at stake when these days long distance walkers make not a penny.

Barclay was an interesting character, too. Born in Scotland in 1779, he was the son of a Scottish laird – Robert Barclay senior – who became a Westminster MP. His mother, Sarah Ann, was an

Allardice from Allardice Castle; Radford records that 'she had the blood of ancient Scottish kings running through her veins', and in exchange for the land that she brought to the marriage the 5th Laird agreed to couple the surname Allardice with that of Barclay. The family owned extensive estates near Aberdeen.

An inch short of six feet tall and with a slightly receding hairline, Robert junior was not the first long distance walker, but he is certainly the sport's first icon and seems to have exhibited many of the qualities – and experienced the same plights – of today's 'special breed': 'it was in walking, and the weariness that went with it, that he found who he was. In the open air, buffeted by the weather, he felt alive and powerful.'

A free-spending laird devoted to the Fancy and an officer in His Majesty's Army as well as an obligatory walker, he was noted for a strong, imposing physique that featured the muscular, well-formed arms and shoulders of the prize fighter rather than the stringy frame common to today's long distance athlete, but also had 'unheard of physical strength and endurance, and an almost frightening determination and mental toughness'. He had no need to walk for money – he was a man of means and education – but as a schoolboy, he 'had already developed a dislike of being confined indoors for too long, and preferred to be "out in the air"'. He successfully completed his first wager walk at seventeen, walking six miles of the Brixton to Croydon road inside an hour; subsequent performances included walking 110 miles in 19 hours 27 minutes and completing 180 miles of rough, steep Scottish roads non-stop over two and a half days. 'There were times,' writes Radford, 'after hours on the road in heavy rain or hot, dusty weather, when he looked more like a vagabond than an army officer. He lived in two parallel worlds.'

By the time of the ultimate wager walk, for which Barclay planned 'with the detail and precision of a military campaign', he was a few weeks short of thirty years old. He set out each hour on a line across the heath to a point half a mile off and back, on a route lit at night by gas lamps on poles every 100 yards, encumbered not by a rucksack but by a brace of pistols as a deterrent to those who had money invested in his failure to complete. John Gully, the former champion prize fighter, acted as his bodyguard at night. Barclay was benighted variously by a strained knee ligament, toothache, torrential rain, scorching heat and extreme tiredness from accumulated disruption of sleep. During the fourth week, when he was taken to the starting line for the 607th mile, he was asleep standing up. Even so, 42 days after he began, at 3.15 p.m., he set out for the last time, completing the 1,000th mile at 3.37 p.m. Afterwards, he slept for nine hours; eight days later, after 1,000 hours of physical effort and broken sleep, he was able to take his place in a fighting force and go off to war.

Nearly fifty years later, Newmarket Heath was the setting for Charles Westhall, 'the first real racewalker', to do 21 miles in under three hours. Walkers organised the first English amateur walking championship and began to compete in 100-mile, 24-hour races for enormous cash prizes. The betting at events like these was impressive: one writer referred to seeing someone 'cash up a £100 fresh bank-note, which I thought might have been more usefully invested'. The spectators were 'of a class of society we may denominate rough and ready'; the competitors, meanwhile, 'slowly walk up and down the course, wearing long great coats, beneath which we may see their naked legs, and feet encased in light laced shoes'; the food concessions included 'a peripatetic vendor of sandwiches of a mysterious origin'.

As far as the sports pages were concerned, though, the biggest event of them all was the Long Distance Championship of the World, instigated in 1878 by MP and sports buff Sir John Astley. Held over six days, the Astley Belt Races, as they came to be known, were 'go-as-you-please' events; distances of over 500 miles were recorded. Not just walking, but trotting, jogging and running were allowed. In that way they diverged from other walking races; from the middle of the nineteenth century the latter were subject to the 'fair heel and toe' rule, by which the toe of one foot was not permitted to leave the ground before the heel of the other foot touched down. This was the basis for the racewalking rules codified in 1880 at the first championship meeting of the Amateur Athletic Association.

With the advent of go-as-you-please, professional pedestrianism faded out. Long distance racewalking went one way, with the founding in 1911 of British Centurions; the qualification for membership was to walk 100 miles, on road or track, in 24 hours or less within competition. Go-as-you-please evolved into distance running and in due course into the type of event pioneered by the Tanners Marathon.

How we reached that point from the Astley Belt Races is by way of Britain's Industrial Revolution, which left ordinary people with free time and what had once been the preserve of the leisured classes – fell-walking – now within their reach. The same went for hiking, mountaineering and peak-bagging. Events initiated by Manchester's Rucksack Club (founded in 1902) strongly prefigured the Hundred's night-walking and epic mile-eating: in 1908 Munro-ist John Rooke Corbett, the club's Convenor of Rambles, inaugurated the 'Moonlight Ramble'; in 1926 Fred Heardman and John Firth Burton were first to complete the 70-mile Colne to Rowsley Walk. The Rucksack Club was later behind the gruelling Tan Hill to Cat and Fiddle walk of 1952; going from the Yorkshire/Westmorland border to the Cheshire/Derbyshire border, it was 120 miles non-stop between the eponymous pubs, at 1,732ft and 1,630ft the two highest in England.

Britain also had an informal network of footpaths and routes that over the centuries had grown out of people's needs – driving cattle, going to the village, getting to work. These days, rambling is regarded as the last activity before senescence. In the mid-twentieth century, the age profile of participants was much lower. With the establishment of the Youth Hostelling Association (1930) and the Ramblers' Association (1935), what had been a means of transport now provided leisure and social activity for young people. Footpaths were generally good; because they were in normal use as short cuts from place to place, other transport not being available, they were well trodden and needed no other maintenance as they do today. Bulls, however, were a hazard; there was no legislation against them and in fact farmers were not averse to using them as a deterrent.

Jill Green, the racewalker and Hundred-er, showed me the copy of a speech given to Croydon Rambling Club by her mother, Rosalie Saunders, who joined the Ramblers in the mid-1930s at the age of twenty. Rosalie, who died in 2007 aged ninety-one, told of walking in boys' boots with three-pronged studs hammered into the soles to give a grip, stockings with seams and woollen ankle-socks to help fill up the boots and stop the blisters:

> Waterproofs were either that yellow oiled-silk and weighed a ton, or else rubberised mackintoshes which tended to perish and stink of rotten rubber. I had a hand-knitted woollen skirt which got longer every time it rained, so the hem was turned over and over as the years went by. It was so thick it rubbed the backs of my calves raw. Crocheted woolly hats kept out the wind and the rain hat was a sou'wester, tied under the chin.
>
> Most people worked a five and a half day week so weren't available until midday on a Saturday, so to get the mileage in we walked until after dark. On Sunday you took a packed lunch to eat in a field, or a barn if you were lucky, and then the leader had to find a teaplace to book in advance. These usually accommodated the party at trestle tables, with a huge teapot and lashings of bread and butter and jam.

It sounds idyllic, even with the bulls. And rambling had one very important thing going for it. As Rosalie pointed out, it was about the only way the sexes could get together, naturally, away from home, without raised eyebrows: 'Parents knew it was all respectable.'

The same sense of youthful wholesomeness pervades Barbara Blatchford's account of the first Tanners Marathon some thirty-five years after Rosalie's walks with the Ramblers. A teenager about to go up to Oxford to read for a degree in botany, Barbara was running the Epsom & Ewell YHA Group's newsletter, *RAA!*, so called because its three committee members lived within three roundabouts of each other; the initials stood for Round And About. Alan Blatchford had been doing his National Service in Cyprus: 'I'd heard of him because he was always sending letters to the magazine.' What did he look like? Barbara pauses. 'He was . . . not bad looking. He'd got that Celtic darkness, he never tanned. He had a slightly broken nose, not because of anything very heroic – he'd fallen off something.'

The young people measured out the route with a map wheel. ('You couldn't get it *as* accurate as you can now,' says Barbara.) Most of the marshals were on bikes because in 1960 young people didn't have cars. The checkpoint signs were made of hardboard, and people strapped them on their bikes and pedalled over the lanes and tracks through chalk and greensand hills to put them in place. They obtained water supplies from farms: 'I remember going down to one near Tanners and borrowing a milk churn for a water container, and having to wash cow shit out of it,' says Barbara.

Within five years, the event was so popular that Tanners Hatch youth hostel was too small for the start, which was moved to Leatherhead; by the end of the sixties, the entry was close to the thousand mark. More germane to the LDWA, though, is its role in connecting Alan Blatchford with co-founder Chris Steer. About this there's a folk tale: it involves the old post office in the Surrey village of Peaslake where, legend has it, Steer, a recreational runner and keen walker some years Alan's senior, first set eyes on a poster advertising the Tanners Marathon. The story is actually a little more windy than that. 'I think Chris had just finished the Tanners when he saw something Alan had written on a poster, asking if anyone was interested in helping him with the planning of other walks,' says Barbara, 'so Chris got in touch and found himself on the Tanners Marathon Committee.'

By then Alan and Barbara were married and living in Guildford, with Alan working as an aircraft design engineer at the British Aircraft Corporation in Weybridge (he ran to and from work twice a week) and organising orienteering events in his spare time. He was also gaining a reputation as an ultrarunner, as well as doing 100 miles in the Brighton to London and Back Walk in 22 hours 10 minutes to qualify as a Centurion. In 1966 he set up the 30-mile Punchbowl Marathon with Guildford & Godalming Atheics Club, following that up in 1971 with the Guildford Boundary Walk, a 20-mile event with a massed start from the Hog's Back ridge.

He was by now something of a victim of his own excellence, having become by default a one-man long distance walking information service. 'People kept writing to him,' says Barbara. '"What do you know about McGillycuddy's Reeks walk?" etc. It took a long time to find the answers. He thought it might be a good idea if there was a magazine giving details of those walks.'

In 1971 a letter from Blatchford appeared in *Climber & Rambler* magazine, asking if people would be interested in a newsletter listing challenge events and giving details of long distance paths. There were some two hundred replies. Chris Steer, who ran a plumbing and heating business, owned an elderly Roneo that lived in his attic; he was roped in to print the first Newsletter, together with Margaret his wife, who, says Barbara, 'did an awful lot of typing'. Newsletter 1 was sent out free, but enclosed a membership form advising that the subscription was '35p minimum which will allow those more affluent to donate a few extra pence'. Right from the start, the LDWA was prepared to trust in people's better nature.

It's only as I look through these early Newsletters that I begin to realise the paucity of what was available to long distance walkers at the start of the 1970s. Twenty-six events were listed in the calendar of organised walks in the Diary, virtually for the entire year. Compare that to August 2008 *Strider*, in which twenty-four events were advertised for September alone. There were no group social walks because there were no groups. It's a nicely perverse touch that the Newsletter predated most of what are now the defining aspects of the LDWA. Things happened almost back to front, as if *Wisden* had been started up before anyone got around to organising the county cricket season.

Over the next few years, the events calendar began to fill up: the hand-drawn map of challenge walks, marches and races in England in the first *Long Distance Walkers' Handbook*, published in 1980 and largely the work of Barbara Blatchford, shows more than double the original number. One telling point was the agglomeration in Surrey: Tanners to Hindhead, the Surrey Inns Kanter, the Surrey Summits, the Tanners Marathons (winter and summer), the Guildford Boundary Walk, the Weybac Walk. That makes Surrey indisputably the cradle of the game. But of all the events created by Alan Blatchford and Chris Steer over the first few years, one stands out. In fact, because of the sheer size and duration of the challenge, it's not so much an event as a feat. The Hundred is the opportunity for everyone to discover their inner Captain Barclay.

YOREDALE HUNDRED 2008

3: Kirkby Malham (SD 895 610) to Settle (SD 818 639)
Distance: 7.40 miles; Ascent: 1480 feet; Descent: 1540 feet

Aim for solitary tree in wall up hillside. Your path should take you about 25yds behind the tree & reach a gateway & gated wall stile in the wall about 100yds beyond the tree . . .

Straight out of Kirkby Malham, you reach the first of several forsaken-looking spots on the route. The map is scattered with names that sound as if you're eating a gravel sandwich: Fair Sleets Head, Grizedales, Great Scar. The track is lined with barns: Burns Barn, Field Barns, Great Heads Barn, Butterlands Barn. If I had time to think, I'd make a feeble joke about there being one barn every minute, but I'm too busy climbing Pikedaw Hill, a giant crazily tilting bulb covered in grass carpet that bulges in places as if that's where the bodies are buried. The path over the top is ankle-wrenchingly rocky, sole-bruisingly stony. It's blowy up here, too. But the wind drops with the plunge down to Stockdale Lane and a trek through a boggy area, with scree slopes to the right. To clamber over, there's a fine selection from Yorkshire's wall stile archive. Then you breast another grassy top and see Settle spread before you, the route descending on the steep wide path that led to the finish of the 1996 Yorkshire Dales Hundred.

I'm still on my own. I don't want the chore of having to interact with other people till I'm desperate for someone to take charge of the route-finding. Thing is, I've never been good at the kind of small talk favoured by walkers. My social skills were moulded by the bygone Fleet Street pub culture in which a good chat included foul and abusive language, leching, bitching, weeping, back-stabbing and punch-ups, culminating in someone singing 'A Scottish Soldier'. Most definitely not the kind of stuff that plays well on LDWA events.

Back in civilisation, it's ten to two. I consume a Penguin, five digestive biscuits, an energy gel, two mugs of tea and more ProPlus. Eighteen miles done. This is more or less the point at which on a marathon I would be plunging into almost suicidal despair, at the thought of having another eight miles to run. Here, it feels as if I've barely started, though not in a bad way. I think, actually, I've discovered the key to dealing with this really long distance stuff. Once you've done a couple of thirties and fifties, miles seem dramatically to minimise. Ten miles telescopes into pretty well zilch. It's like saying 'Pff!' to a minotaur and watching it shrivel before your eyes to the size of a gerbil.

Checkpoint 3: Settle (St John's Methodist Church Hall) SD 818 639

Opens: 1200 (noon) Saturday; Closes: 1730 Saturday
Distance: 18.15 miles; Ascent: 2175 feet; Descent: 2105 feet
Manned by: London Group
Indoor checkpoint with hot/cold drinks and food

SIX
We've Started, So We'll Finish

IT TOOK ME ELEVEN YEARS TO MAKE IT TO the start of a Hundred. That something is all in the mind might be a motheaten platitude, but in this case it was true. Ann Sayer, holder of the women's world record for walking from Land's End to John O'Groats, said that provided your body was 'fairly functional' the difference between doing a Hundred and doing a twenty was largely mental: 'If you can do a twenty, you perhaps could do a Hundred if you put your mind to it, but you've got to want to do it. If you don't, as soon as you get a bit tired or it gets a bit dark or wet you'll think, Oh, that was a nice walk, I've had enough.'

Keith Warman, who has been taking part in Hundreds since Margaret Thatcher's first government was in power, said virtually the same thing: 'You've got to *want* to do the Hundred. As well as being fit, you've got to have a desire.' And the mantra was repeated in various forms by almost all the Hundred-ers I talked to. The Hundred takes place ninety per cent in the mind. It's not simply about being fit.

Take the 1997 Downsman, the Hundred I entered in a flurry of rash enthusiasm after the Three Forests Way back in November

1996. You can sometimes, in fact, get a place on the Hundred even if you haven't previously finished a fifty. If they don't have enough fully qualified entrants by March they'll accept anyone they think is a fair bet, if not to finish, then at least not to do themselves serious, even mortal, harm. I did myself no harm at all, for the simple reason I didn't even bother to start.

I'd done my first London Marathon earlier that year, and spent the next few weeks basking in self-congratulation and resting a knee which had developed the habit of buckling underneath me if I ran further than three miles. Meanwhile, if I couldn't run, at least I could walk. As the Hundred weekend drew closer, I set out with some friends on a training walk around rural Hertfordshire. Thirty miles through fields, forests and along a towpath on a spring day, with a picnic stop in a churchyard serenaded by a cuckoo – idyllic, really. Bloody hell, it went on a bit. Bloody hell, I was tired. I traipsed further and further behind my friends. When they said at the end, 'Well, you should be all right,' we all knew it wasn't worth my even turning up.

But I hadn't finished with the Hundred yet. Eighteen months later I had another go at the Three Forests Way, where I learnt the truth of another whiskery adage – 'Never go back' – as I plodded on disconsolately further and further behind the field, breezeblocks of Essex mud clinging to the bottom of my trainers. That time I gave up at the third checkpoint.

How could I have failed so dismally to get further than 21 miles? In six – repeat, *six* – hours? Had I been walking in some different time dimension? I wasn't particularly unfit. Six weeks earlier, I'd run a ten-mile road race. I'd done it fast, by my standards – 1 hour 16 minutes. Why didn't I simply stick to running? To do a Hundred entailed days and weekends of training. I was a full-time journalist and writer with two school-age children. I was married to a sports journalist. He worked at weekends. The opportunities I got to participate in events were limited. I didn't need this.

But it was like being in the grip of some hopelessly unrequited passion. I knew it was never going to work out but I still kept hanging on. I persuaded my friend Avril to do the Poppyline Fifty in Norfolk with me. Whatever made the difference – I suspect being with a very good walker who was implacably determined that I was going to finish, as much as the warmth of the August weekend weather and the glorious lack of Essex mud – I made it back.

My first thought was, I've done it. The Fifty. I can do the Hundred now.

My second thought, as I took off my socks and a lot of bloodied skin with them, was, There's no way I could walk another fifty miles on top of this.

That was just rubbish. It was all in the mind. I was most definitely going to do the Hundred. As training, I entered for an October 100km event in Kent, the Wealden Waters. The night before, it was called off. The route was flooded. I quickly stifled the feeling of relief.

And then it all went badly wrong, not just for long distance walking. In February 2001, an outbreak of foot and mouth disease was confirmed at an Essex abattoir. By the end of that month, cases had been confirmed in Northumberland, Devon and north Wales; by March it had spread to Cornwall and Cumbria.

The foot and mouth epidemic effectively closed the countryside for a year. No way could the 2001 Hundred go ahead in the Lake District. I did what a lot of walkers did – drifted away to other sports. In fact I probably wouldn't have come back if it hadn't been for a phone call early in 2002, asking if I'd be prepared to edit *Strider*.

I look back on the *Strider* years fondly. The job put me in touch with a wildly interesting bunch of enthusiasts. There was the feature Merv Nutburn sent me about the Marathon of Britain. He'd just got married and for him and Fiona it was their honeymoon. They spent it in separate tents. There were handwritten articles from Martin Burnell: infused with cheerfully scatological humour, they usually had 'PRINT THIS IF YOU DARE' across the top. Garfield Southall contributed a marvellous piece about his particular passion, nightwalking; I had witty, lyrical, erudite copy and photos from Ronald Turnbull; Ken Falconer wrote the definitive guide to surviving a Hundred; while any number of other equally enthusiastic and interesting people chipped in with work that was always a labour of love but hopefully gave them as much satisfaction writing it as I had publishing it.

Being editor of *Strider* also gave me my first exposure to what I'd only previously read and heard talked about. The Lakeland Hundred, held over from the previous year, took place in 2002 on the usual late spring Bank Holiday. It was like the first time I went to the USA, which I'd only seen on TV as a child before – nothing prepared me for the hugeness of it. From the body count (four hospitalised) to the tilters lurching back after sun-up on the Monday, everything exceeded my imagination – the exhausted people stacked against the outside wall at the breakfast stop; the 70-mile checkpoint in Braithwaite, where several walkers, confused and sleepy as they came off the high ground, joined the church service next door by mistake; people throwing up, people with sunstroke, people crashing out. It was a really hard Hundred, with a staggeringly low completion rate – 455 starts, only 260 finishers. Instead of being put off, I was spurred by the applause as each walker finished. I wanted it. I *had* to do the Hundred.

A year and two months later I was back in Sheringham for another Poppyline Fifty. It was obvious I wasn't going to find it easy – I hadn't walked further than 20 miles since that March. And there was a further complication. Who you end up with on the later stages of a walk is often a matter of chance. The wheel of fortune turns, you spend a little too long chatting at checkpoints, you get lost and have to backtrack, you aren't fit enough to speed away if you don't fancy the company. This time

I found myself with an elderly couple who walked along heads together, murmuring to each other in a faintly sinister way. You could imagine the newspaper headlines the next day: 'There was nothing about this quiet, respectable couple to suggest that they could have hidden three dismembered ramblers under their patio.'

Additional company was provided by a hideously barmy woman with straggling hair who kept bleating every time she saw a sheep, which as we were in Norfolk was quite often. At two in the morning, as we trudged in the rain around a sheep field where we'd been marooned for three-quarters of an hour trying to find the way out, my left knee locked. It was the sort of pain that normally you ignore. This time, though, it wasn't an injury. It was a face-saving get-out clause. As I limped and winced up a road towards a village, miles off course, I saw a red telephone box, went into it and asked to be picked up.

And I can still see myself sobbing in the body bus in the early hours of the morning, as it came home to me that I'd thrown in the towel at exactly the same point, 43 miles, as I'd done seven years back on the 1996 Three Forests Way. This time there wasn't even the spurious glow of triumph that I'd got that far.

If there was any irony in my failure, that was it. I'd retired from an event because I'd allowed myself to get freaked out by someone whom I regarded as a loony. As I had voluntarily just spent an hour in a field of sheep in the rain at two in the morning, there was only one comment that could possibly be made about that, and it involved the words pot, kettle and black.

It's impossible to convey to anyone who hasn't been ensnared by these insane events how bad it feels to fail. They conclude, probably quite rightly, that to mind that much makes you a bit of a tit. But that I wasn't alone in this soul-searching became clear a few years later, as Garfield Southall and I sat in a Cheshire pub on a September day and he launched into his history as a Hundred-er.

'I remember that night so clearly. Midnight, absolutely

bucketing down, thick fog. It was on the 1998 White Peak and I'd retired at fifty miles, at a really cold little checkpoint in this place called Flagg. I'd got a rash on my bottom. I hadn't really learned the art of lubricating various parts of the anatomy and the friction and rubbing became absolutely intolerable, whatever I did to alleviate it.

'Then the fun started. I had to wait two hours for the body wagon. It was two in the morning when they got me back to HQ, a school in Buxton. What do you do at two a.m. in a school in Buxton? I tried sleeping across chairs but my legs and bum were too sore. The station was two miles away and I knew the first train out was at half-eight, so at seven a.m. I set off for the station. The line was closed for the day – there was a replacement bus service, the first bus was at ten. Next door – the Palace Hotel: big, grand, expensive. Me: wet, muddy, walking like a leper. I walked into this superfine restaurant and ordered the biggest breakfast in the place and ate it under the chandeliers, just to pass the time.

'So out of that came the loneliness, the complete desolation. You didn't finish. You should not have done that. I should have pulled my cheeks apart with Elastoplast. I should have *finished*. You're so completely demoralised, defeated.'

It was a huge relief to me that I wasn't the only one who'd felt that way. And what Garfield went on to say was even more encouraging.

He was in his mid-forties when he attempted – and failed on – his first Hundred, the 1997 Downsman. 'The event to me has changed its shape,' he said. 'When I first started it was Everest – something almost unfathomable – and you felt like in the early stages you couldn't conceive of finishing. It seemed so big and daunting.

'And then you think, OK, you've learnt a lot. The usual things come out. The next was the 1999 Durham Dales. That opened up to me a completely new side of myself as I pushed into regions I'd never gone before. I gradually started to realise the pattern. You've got to be patient with yourself, and that's what I wasn't. I'd tried to treat it like a 26-miler, dive into a checkpoint, grab a drink, whatever, go out again. So I started going through something like a flight check at each checkpoint – patching up my feet, etc. Once you've got into the stride of a walk, you can relax. My biggest problem is eating enough. The more tired you get, the worse it gets. It's a downward spiral – your blood sugar goes down. If you do have the patience with yourself and you eat and drink, it's not wasting time. You catch it up in terms of sheer confident speed afterwards.'

That took Garfield on to another point. 'It's the power of the power nap. I was coming towards the eighty-mile checkpoint. The place was quite a honey pot because of the Bank Holiday weekend. It was absurd, really. I remember walking down the high street, *pushing* idling tourists. Poor sods, only on holiday, relaxing, looking at shop windows. *Get out of the way!* By this time your blood sugar's so low you're living off one molecule. You've lost quite a lot of your basic control mechanisms. You're down to your basic primitive stuff. At the checkpoint I was so completely out of it, so shattered, I just put my head in my hands. Twenty minutes. Completely and utterly went under. Deep, deep. Afterwards I was absolutely fantastic. I went like a rocket. I was wide awake.'

Then Garfield's eyes lit up and his face glowed as he relived the moment he'd waited for so long. 'It was in the bottom of the valley. I was coming down off the moor, beginning to cramp a bit. Ninety-six-mile checkpoint, I tallied and carried on. Last four miles along the riverside, I picked my pace up. Get this thing over with, get finished. Consequently I missed the turning, ended up thrashing around in the undergrowth, feeling so frustrated. Two miles from the finish. Eventually I saw two head torches, the other side of a fence.

'As I approached the school, one of the marshals came along the road to meet me. I got emotional. Not a big full scale blub, but I was crying. You've come so far. You've pushed all these mental and physical barriers. And the marshal, she gave me a big hug. That was profound. That person was willing to put themselves out to greet me. That moment's going to stay with me for ever. That's the power someone has, to leave such a mark on you.

'And you begin to realise the resilience and the hidden strength you have. That you could go even further. That if at a hundred miles someone had said, "There's a Superbadge and Supercertificate if you do ten more . . ." I would have done it. I hadn't got anywhere near the limits of what I was capable of. I felt in awe of the resilience of the body, of what the body is capable of, and it was my body, the one I'd had for fifty years. I was finding secrets about it I never knew.'

Garfield wasn't to know it, but he'd put into words exactly what I felt one night in early August 2007 as I ran the last half-mile of the Poppyline Fifty – the night I gained my qualifier for the Yoredale and the night that a whole load of unfinished business was buried at last. But first, a backtrack in time.

After failing on the Poppyline Fifty in 2003, long distance walking and I went through a rough patch. It was like staying married for the sake of the children. I was only in there because I'd committed to *Strider*. There were no more thoughts of doing a Hundred. Over the next three years I changed jobs, wrote another book, carried on raising a family, and wore out several pairs of trainers doing road marathons. They were easy. To run, I just had to step outside my front door.

The downside was that I felt counterfeit. *Strider* wasn't a run-of-the-mill magazine. It was entirely possible to be the editor of *Woman's Own* if you were a man, or of *Stamp Collecting* without an interest in stamps. You couldn't be editor of *Strider*, I felt, unless you literally walked the walk.

In the spring of 2007, Ken Falconer took over as editor. By then my youngest child had gone to university. Suddenly I had the time to do . . . what? I'd applied for a London Marathon place but was rejected in the ballot and wasn't good enough to qualify for a 'Good For Age' place. But anyway, why did I want to run the London Marathon again? I'd done it five times.

There was only one way this could go. I'd give myself a year to train properly for the Hundred. If it was the last thing I did, I'd prove I was a long distance walker.

So it was that I found myself back in Norfolk for another Poppyline Fifty, on another warm August weekend. This time I did things differently. I didn't sleep in my car the night before to save money – I booked into a hotel. I ran some of it, because I was much fitter than I'd been four years before. The biggest difference of all was that I finished.

There were, obviously, the usual route-finding disasters – getting lost in the head-frying sun with a couple of walkers from Bristol on the way to the 16-mile checkpoint was just the start. I went ludicrously off course hunting for the right path out of a village and enjoyed half an hour of speculative trotting back and forth before arriving at the right spot from the wrong direction. Somewhere over the next ten miles I picked up three runners who were even more incompetent with a route description than me; they'd say hallo and pound off, and twenty minutes later I'd hear footsteps behind me and they'd be back again. Thirty miles in, I caught up with another walker; the poor man was in a terrible state, groaning and wincing, his face contorted like the victim of an atrocity. Every so often I'd try and make him get a move on, and then a hundred yards along he'd emit another harrowing whimper and I'd start to wonder seriously what the etiquette was about leaving somebody who seemed to be hanging on to life by a slender thread that might snap at any time.

Anyway, we made it to the 31-mile checkpoint. There were only a couple of hours of daylight left and, embarrassing though it is to confess this, I'm afraid of the dark. And because loads of people had given up in the heat, there was only one thing for it if I didn't want to be on my own in the night section. It was Groaning Man or nothing.

For a mile we edged along. I started to think pessimistically about my chances of getting to the 38-mile checkpoint before being timed out. But it was the only part of the whole thing where I had any doubts at all. Within minutes we were picked up by a couple of sweepers, one of whom stayed with Groaning Man while the other belted along with me to Bodham. The runners found us and we set off for Holt in high spirits.

Once we'd made it there, I knew we were going to do it. There were only eight miles left and I felt as fresh as if I'd just started. I remember guzzling three helpings of mushroom soup and two bowls of crisps in Holt Methodist Church Hall, putting off the moment when I'd have to leave that bright, comfortable place for seven miles of squinting at a route description in pitch-black woods with three exhausted runners who seemed to be relying on me – *me* – to navigate them home.

I sneaked a glance at Bill Anderson, the skinny, mischievous-looking marshal who was leaning against the wall, arms crossed.

'You don't fancy leading us back to Sheringham, do you?'

From then on, it was easy. I can transport myself back there now, feeling rather superior about one of the runners struggling desperately to make it over the last stretch, Bill walking and talking at a rattling pace. The rapture of knowing eleven years of hurt were about to end gave me extra energy. As I ran the last half-mile, all the blisters on the tops of my toes exploded in sequence. Revelling in the unfamiliar experience of not reaching the finish by body bus, I barely felt the pain. Garfield was right. I could have carried on for another ten miles without any problem. I just knew it.

All I had to do now was the Hundred.

YOREDALE HUNDRED 2008

4: Settle (SD 818 639) to Clapham (SD 744 694) *Distance: 6.92 miles; Ascent: 876 feet; Descent: 827 feet*

I'm in and out of the St John's Methodist Church Hall in fifteen minutes, and over a bridge across the River Ribble into Giggleswick. All the way from here to Ingleton it's pretty easy with not much ascent. There's only one minor problem so far: instead of water I'm taking draughts of air from the new drinking bladder. In short, it doesn't deliver, something that I might have discovered if I'd actually tried it out before.

Turn left in the direction of Clapham & Norber on enclosed track. (This enclosed track called Thwaite Lane is now followed for just over 1 miles.) In just over 200yds a track joins from the right at a corner of a plantation. Continue ahead (track kinks left & right) in direction of Clapham with plantation on your right. The track, rocky at times, descends steeply with numerous warnings to cyclists, to go through two tunnels.

The tunnels are dank and even in late spring they're dark, puddled and threatening. Then you emerge into daylight, past a church built into the hillside. And here it comes, the stuff I feel embarrassed about. What happened on the recce.

I just don't do God, or any high-flown stuff about the spirit of the hills. I wear the Richard Dawkins jersey. So I still can't work it out, why on the recce I felt such a terrific draw to go inside. Maybe it was the sheer enormity of what I was about to do. A hundred miles.

A rationally thought-through review of my training – two fifties, three thirties, two marathons and an average forty miles a week running – told me I was as prepared as I'd ever be. On another level, I was completely freaked out.

So on the recce I went in. Wasn't going to do the whole grovelling churchy bow-your-head, move-your-lips-silently thing. Stood on the very edge of the aisle. Sent a brisk series of thought waves like an old-fashioned telegram. WOULD LIKE COURAGE STOP AND A FRIEND STOP.

Now, emerging from the second tunnel, I nip back in there. Just in case. You never know. And then, because I don't want to lose time, I belt out again. It's the spiritual equivalent of a drive-by shooting.

Past the cinema club poster advertising *La Dolce Vita* and into the village hall. It's a quarter to four. I slurp a cup of tea and several pints of water, grab two Digestive biscuits and a slice of chocolate cake, swallow a handful of Haribo, two more ProPlus and a painkiller for luck, and head out towards Ingleton.

Checkpoint 4: Clapham (Village Hall) SD 744 694

Opens: 1330 Saturday; Closes: 2100 Saturday
Distance: 25.07 miles; Ascent: 3051 feet; Descent: 2932 feet
Manned by Nidderdale Group
Indoor checkpoint with hot / cold drinks and food

SEVEN
The Vanishing Station Mystery

THE MIDDLE OF ENGLAND, 2007. THE PLACE: an arable field. The time: mid-morning on a late August Sunday. The earth on this endless uphill path is rock hard and corrugated, and little desiccated wheat spears have mysteriously burrowed their way inside your socks; to speed you on your way, they're jabbing at your skin while thistles claw at your bare legs and parched brambles lasso your trainers.

Your rucksack is damp with sweat. It feels so heavy you wonder if a small dog has crept into it to sleep. The heat of the day is taking its toll in other ways: the skin under your arms and T-shirt is sore; the straps across your chest burn and chafe; it feels as if someone's set fire to your bum.

You hurry on to the next checkpoint. It's a table set out under a tree, and is a kind of English *Rubaiyat of Omar Khayyam* – a jug of orange cordial, a plate of biscuits and the bloke sitting beside you on the grass passing you his jar of Vaseline: 'Here you are, luv. Bit of grease for the back axle.' There's a great big finger-shaped gouge in it already, but you're beyond caring about personal hygiene.

Back on route, you skim along, a breeze taking away the

fiercest of the heat. You run down a shady, enclosed path lined with sorrel, buttercups, vetch; you cross a chamomile field, intoxicated by the sweet, soporific smell. In a paddock behind a line of trees, horses gallop alongside you. There's nothing, not a sound, absolute peace but for the padding of hooves on grass. This is what you come for, this is what makes it worthwhile. All the getting up at five to drive to remote, bucolic dots on the map. All the blisters and bruises and scratches and stings, the thirst and the exhaustion, the wrenched knees and sprained ankles, the way tiredness plays tricks with your perception of time so when you think you're going terribly fast – practically jogging – you're actually doing less than one and a half miles per hour. All the . . .

. . . All the standing in the middle of a field peering at a route description. What is going on here? *TL by ladder and thru gap in hedge*, that's what it says. Hedge, yes. Gap and ladder, no. One out of three – not good. You look around. People patrol the field edge, peering into the hedge for anything that might conceivably qualify as a gap, debating whether 'ladder' might be local dialect for 'rusting water tank' or 'dead rabbit'. Half an hour passes. This madness can't continue. You attach yourself to a group that leaves by climbing over a barbed wire fence. The idea proves successful, in that you're now going somewhere, not simply hanging around in a field. Contrary to pessimistic expectation, you find yourself back on route. On the other hand, now you're dying to go to the loo. Furthermore, it's another five miles to the next checkpoint.

There's only one thing for it. You'll have to go behind a bush.

Oh no. No. No, really. There are limits.

You plod on, teeth clenched, everything clenched. Not exactly the stuff of which Empire was built, are you? Bloody hell. Do you think Lady Mary Wortley Montagu would have baulked at an al fresco comfort stop when she was exploring Turkey? Would Mary Kingsley have been too embarrassed to drop her knickers behind a tree when she was journeying alone in the unknown regions of the Congo jungle?

There's a good spot. A leafy path leading into a little glade. Plenty of ground cover.

You veer swiftly down the path.

'You're going the wrong way! It's this way!' someone bellows helpfully.

You're too embarrassed to tell them why you were going that way. You carry on plodding, dropping further and further behind them and then, after a furtive glance behind you to check no one's following, dive into the bushes. It's the last of your inhibitions to crumble. As you emerge from the foliage, you hear the crunch of footsteps. A walker with the same intent greets you cheerfully and disappears into the Men's Foliage on the other side of the path. You go your way rejoicing.

And, of course, at the end of every long distance walk, eating your cheese ploughman's followed by strawberries and cream, you immediately overlook the hideous bits. Otherwise no one would ever do it again, in the same way that if women were to remember the pain of childbirth the world would rapidly become depopulated. You look back fondly on the mistakes, all the choices that, for reasons you will never understand, you – no, I – thought made sense at the time, such as running the Tanners Marathon with a piece of glass embedded in my foot because I assumed it would work its way out (instead it worked its way further in, and had to be removed by the podiatrist at a cost of £75); believing that a lightweight running jacket would be warm enough at night on a rain-lashed weekend in the Lake District; thinking that the way to stop my toes blistering across the tops was to wrap them in sticky-backed padding (there are few agonies more excruciating than ripping adhesive padding off well-pounded toes, accompanied by several layers of skin).

Then there were the weeks when I wanted to look away every time I took my socks off, weeks of raw flesh and yellowing, flapping skin: of corrugated toenails, toenails that fountained pus when I tried to remove the blood beneath, toenails that moved sideways and could be lifted from the nail bed like a car boot lid, toenails various in hue from the colour of cheese and onion crisps to deepest blackberry, toenails that simply weren't there any more. But in the end it was not unlike Quentin Crisp's observation on his New York apartment – after four years the dust doesn't get any worse. My feet were still a gruesome sight, but I stopped noticing.

And anyway, this isn't simply a diatribe on the hazards wrought by long distance walking. Along with all that came the treats. There was being able to indulge the particularly famished feeling that comes from long active days in the fresh air, the ravenous, cheek-bulging, eye-popping greed you had as a child after playing out all day, the liberation of knowing that you could eat absolutely anything and you still didn't struggle to fasten your jeans. There were what people writing in 'Past Events' in *Strider* termed the views: the Devil's Punchbowl, a dent pressed into a common like a giant's thumb, up which swarmed lines of walkers; Welsh reservoirs as small as hand mirrors below you; empty moorland and sky tenanted by a single heron; matchbox-sized villages.

But it wasn't only the views that I did it for. It was for those occasions when I was actually within the landscape, in places where I felt at the core of England, not observing it from a hilltop. Eating hot cross buns in June outside a village church where the congregation was singing a Christmas carol; surrounded by the precision of Kent orchards, lines of trees hung with apples, a riot of pale green, red and rose; glimpsing a dipper perched on stones beside the River Dove; climbing grassy slopes in the Peak District, a tableau of black-faced sheep, staring cattle the colour of Chris Evans's hair and big dimples in the earth. Grassed over and ringed by grey stones, they were filled-in mine shafts. They reminded me of healed appendectomy scars. There was that path through a small common just before Ilam, where the grass was pea green and covered in fallen purple-black leaves. There was the

Happy Valley walkway – the Poppyline Fifty's *haute route* – rising gently along the seafront at Cromer alongside a tatty chain of fairy lights. In Essex were dog roses like screwed up handkerchiefs in hedges; abandoned farm implements rusting in field corners; old trees wearing choker necklaces of ivy; a muntjac deer bolting across a bridleway. In Surrey were cows ambling pungently in my path; a horse so stiffly recumbent in a field that it might have been dead, till it stood up and wandered away.

Being inside the landscape in this way felt intimate and mysterious. It was like being in England's underwear drawer. It was exactly the feeling I had as a child, playing in the bedroom of a friend's mother, knowing that something went on in that bedroom which I was one day going to find out about.

THEN, OF COURSE, there were things walkers saw that didn't actually exist. Over the year of training for the Hundred, I met people who had encountered John Major on traffic control, Roman armies on the march and slugs the size of handbags crawling up the walls of village halls. I was told by others that they had observed faces appear on the moon, green-eyed cats perched in trees, a mother and daughter in 1950s summer clothes sitting in the sunshine in an orchard – at midnight – and an old-fashioned railway station with wooden buildings and platforms that unaccountably disappeared within fifty yards of approaching it.

'On the 1999 Durham Dales I saw a car being driven high in the sky through fog,' said Geoff Deighton. 'And a human face on the track, which I apologised to after I stood on it.'

'I was on the second evening of that one,' said Bill Anderson, 'heading across a heather moor when I saw my girlfriend riding a bike with a basket on the front towards me, which was totally impossible because we'd driven up there.'

'It was on the 1995 Yorkshire Dales,' said Roger Winterburn. 'Near dawn on the Monday morning, I was followed by a woman on a white horse.'

'That was the Hundred when I walked a long stretch under an iron frame covered with roses,' said Tony Farrell. 'Then when we went down to the finish in Settle, there was a Belisha beacon walking towards me. It was my wife.'

'As I was walking out of Ambleside at one in the morning on the 2002 Lakeland, there were clowns dancing on the flat roof of a pub,' said John Jennison.

'I was with a walker called Ken Wiley and we'd been forty-four hours with no sleep,' said Alan Hindmarsh. 'It was on the second morning of the 1993 Cleveland, somewhere near Rosebery Topping. Ken said, "Which way now?" and I said, "Just follow the guys carrying the bales of straw." Thirty seconds later, Ken says, "Which guys?" "The four guys down the bottom of the hill." So Ken says, "What guys?" They were yellow gorse bushes.'

'On the second night on the 1994 Dartmoor, something happened to me that I've never been able to explain,' said Reg Kingston. 'At ninety miles, down near an old porcelain works – which was a few slag heaps, not beautiful countryside – I was walking away from the checkpoint when I thought, "Oh, I've been here before." Everywhere I went, I knew where I was going. I thought, perhaps there's a secret part of my life I don't know about.'

'I saw buses and waving seaweed on the 1988 White Peak,' said Chris Dawes. 'On Tunstall Edge.'

John Walker, the chemical engineer from Wiltshire, had a fantastically florid time on the 1995 Shropshire. Tramping through a quagmire, eighty miles in, he was staring at a mass of mud in front of his feet when it turned into a prehistoric fish, all popping eyes and grotesque fins. 'After that, there was no stopping it,' he said. 'Crabs, whales, shrimps – every kind of fish and crustacean.' He went down a lane where the stones were ghost-pale on a background of black mud and pairs of animals smiled at him insistently – gerbils, rhinos, even nonsense animals, for one and a half miles: 'They couldn't have been more friendly.'

Five miles to go. It was the dead of night by then. In the light dispersed on the track by the head torches of the walkers in front, television programmes were being screened in colour. He watched avidly, completely ignoring where he was walking till the final stretch after Ironbridge, a crossing of the Severn at Coalport. 'I saw three footbridges quite clearly. None of them were real.'

Other Hundred-ers came up with similar stories. Shirlie Gill, Keith Warman's partner, experienced three distinct types of hallucination on the 1997 Downsman. 'You know the way a head torch leaves a ring of light? Mine was full of little black outlines of Walt Disney characters – Tom and Jerry, Dumbo, Donald Duck, Mickey . . . hundreds of them, all happily wiggling and moving, like a can of maggots, inside the ring. I watched them for quite a while. Then as we were coming up to stiles, I was looking ahead seeing a big tiger sitting there waiting for us. Then a lion and a giraffe, at consecutive stiles. All waiting on the side we were about to climb over. They were friendly. They weren't wanting to do anything, except see we got over all right.' Later came the third set of visions. 'At the edge of a track before we came to some trees there were white haciendas half sunken in the ground. It was as though I was walking in Spain. Every building was different. I wished I could have photographed them all. I wanted to share them because they were so amazing. It was like a trip.'

Buildings seemed to be a consistent feature of hallucinations. Before the 1981 Cumbria Hundred, John Westcott and his friend Dan Hadfield, along with his sister Olive and her husband Roy, camped near the start at Kendal. As John recalled, 'During the event, I was walking with Dan – it was before the breakfast point, but in the early morning twilight – and I noticed a pub. There were lights blazing. I mentioned it to Dan. He said, "Ooh, yes. Let's go back when we've finished."'

After they'd completed the event, John suggested to the others that they should move their tent out to where they had seen the pub. 'We set up the tent and went down to the pub. It wasn't there. I can't even say where it was. Just a row of houses somewhere.' Something similar happened to him on a 100-mile Centurion race in Holland. 'It was daybreak on the second day and I was walking by this avenue of trees. Crikey, I thought, I didn't notice that castle before. When I came round on the next lap it had disappeared.'

'It was my first Hundred, the 1985 Yorkshire Dales,' said Don Newman. 'I was five miles from the end and fading fast. At the top of the hill I saw these people from St John's Ambulance. Now when I was a kid I was in the St John's Ambulance Brigade and in those days they wore a grey military-style uniform, and it was these people in sixties-style uniform coming out to get me, not in present-day dress. But I thought they were real. I was looking for something to boost myself and it wasn't a blonde in a bikini that was being laid on for me, it was them.'

Hallucinations could start towards the end of a fifty, but they were a good deal more common on Hundreds, any time from just before dawn on the second day. Often it was the sheer monotony of long stretches of track that set them off, especially at that stage of head-hanging tiredness when it took a gigantic effort of will to raise the eyes from the toecaps. Discount the runners and very fast walkers who weren't out there long enough to get them, and those whose brains didn't reward sleep deprivation with private cinema, and you were left with a hundred or so people along the route experiencing some form or other of benign derangement. The details would vary but the entertainment was the same.

Because when I thought about hallucinations, I realized that entertainment was what they were. They weren't to be regarded as one of the hazards of long distance walking. They didn't give you blisters or swollen knees or a jack-knifed back, or make you throw up or faint or walk like a crab. 'There's nothing negative about hallucinating,' noted Don Newman. 'It's positive, it helps you.'

There was obviously a proper, scientific explanation for the way that, on a Hundred, the terrain became a giant box of tricks.

OUT ON YOUR FEET

It was the combination, maybe, of prolonged sleeplessness and intense physical effort. In the interests of literature and psychology it was probably something I ought to investigate. But I knew I wouldn't. Hallucinations seemed to be part of the mystery and magic of Hundreds and as far as I was concerned that was how they would stay.

YOREDALE HUNDRED 2008

5: Clapham (SD 744 694) to Ingleton (SD 695 730)
Distance: 4.66 miles; Ascent: 270 feet; Descent: 386 feet

Pass entrance to Clapdale Way & Eggshell Lane both on your right.
Continue for another 280yds to reach bridleway sign on left. Here go
left through the left hand of two gates into enclosed track . . .

The next few miles to Ingleton don't present any serious
difficulty on the face of it. They're flat and fast – fast enough for me
to run. I want to get ahead of those people younger than me. And
that effortlessly walking pair who are proving annoyingly difficult to
catch up.

Every so often I come to my senses and slow down, telling
myself that it isn't a race, it's a personal challenge. And then half a
mile further along, I've forgotten everything I've told myself. I ignore
the warning voices as I half kill myself to pass a doughty old Surrey
biddy with stout boots and a little shrivelled rucksack – how did
she get ahead of me? Yes, it's pointless. Yes, it's tragic. Like Sir Alex
Ferguson v Rafael Benitez, with added HRT.

We're going down Laithbutts Lane. An enclosed track, a long,
dull, gentle slope of pocked concrete bordered with wild garlic. I can
see Ingleborough out of the corner of my eye, a misty, inflated grey
whale. I can hear the clatter of footsteps; the real runners are coming
now. For a while I join in, tracking their slowly disappearing backs
across a field.

Through gate & ahead for 10yds to go through a further gate back into an enclosed path. Follow this uphill going through gate to pass to the right of Laithbutts ...

And then it just happens – *phut*. All the optimism drains from me. It's not even as if I'm tired or out of breath. Nothing hurts. I haven't got lost. Very suddenly I'm just glum. I feel clapped out and past it, with a dodgy ankle and manky bits of cartilage hanging off my patellas, and scabs on my knees from ten months of tripping over. Every feature on the map seems to amplify the dismal mood. Cold Cotes Waste. Bleak Bank. Scale Mire.

And I'm lonely. I've been on my own since the start. And why am I on my own? Because I'm an ageing short-arse who can't keep up with the real runners and who doesn't want to walk because it'll take so long and I'll get so bored. I'm always out of step. I'm not a real long distance walker. I can't talk about maps and GPSs and grid references and all the other things they seem to like. I just fell into this by doing a newspaper story, got roped in to edit their magazine because I felt flattered and made a bit of a cack of it. So I took on this thing out of defiant, wounded amour-propre. God, this is horrible. Huge, huge bloody hell.

And then, just as suddenly, it's all right again. I'm over the bad patch and heading downhill towards Ingleton Community Centre. I meet Garfield, the IT professor, coming out. He seems to be welling up. 'Amazing,' he says, taking out his earpiece. 'Amazing. Hull are in the Premiership.'

Off he goes, up the hill out of the village.

It's just after five-fifteen. The plan is to be off the top of Ingleborough by seven. I'm not only on time, I'm ahead of time.

The checkpoint is in a too-small room, where walkers girdle a table on which is laid out a fabulously overstuffed buffet: tuna rolls, quiche, four kinds of sandwich, three kinds of cake, mixed biscuits, sausage rolls, vegetarian options, rice pudding, jelly, fruit salad. I squeeze into a chair against the wall and eat ravenously. I'm just accepting a fourth sausage roll and another handful of cheese straws when in comes Martin Burnell.

'If we're still going at the same pace can I tag along with you up to Kidhow Gate?' I say.

A sort of 'Oh God' look flashes across his eyes before he composes his features into a gallant smile. 'You can spend the night with me any time you like,' he says.

He eats and leaves rather quickly. I think I've added an extra mile an hour to his pace.

Checkpoint 5: Ingleton (Community Centre) SD 695 730

Opens: 1500 Saturday; Closes 2330 Saturday
Distance: 29.73 miles; Ascent: 3321 feet; Descent: 3318 feet
Manned by: West Lancashire
Indoor checkpoint with hot/cold drinks & food

EIGHT
Quite a Nice Weekend

WHEN THE FIRST HUNDRED TOOK PLACE IN 1973, I had no idea such a leviathan of an event existed. I'd just started my first job as a sportswriter on a Sunday newspaper; all that interested me was that Leeds had lost 1–0 to Sunderland in the FA Cup final a few days earlier, Ilie Nastase was about to win the French Open, Ray Reardon had just beaten Steady Eddie Charlton in the final of the World Snooker Championships and the flat racing season was about to reach its peak with the Derby. My colleague Chris Brasher, the athletics correspondent, who wrote in addition and with far more enthusiasm a weekly column on the outdoor life called 'A Breath Of Fresh Air' (under a photo of him wreathed in smoke from his vile-smelling pipe), might have been expected at least to nod at the Hundred in passing; he had, after all, the previous year, refused to follow up the rumours of doping in East Germany (men with breasts, women with beards) after the Munich Olympics, because he was off to the World Championships of another dotty outdoor sport, orienteering. But the Downsman Hundred might have been taking place in Middle Earth for all anyone, even Brasher, cared.

The only records that remain are in the painstakingly typed pages of the LDWA's own magazine. Still known by its pre-*Strider* name, Newsletter 3 announced a meeting at Arundel youth hostel on 21 October 1972 to discuss the feasibility of a 100-mile walk, provisionally called the Downsman Hike, on the 1973 spring Bank Holiday, starting in Winchester and finishing at Beachy Head. By the end of 1972, what was now the Downsman Hundred had been given the go-ahead. That left five months to organise what subsequent Newsletters called 'the greatest test of endurance open to walkers since the John O'Groats to Lands End Walk of 1960' and 'the superwalk'.

There's a seat-of-the-pants quality about the arrangements that would be unheard of in a modern event. The route description was worked out, along with the location of checkpoints, in the space of a few weekends. There were no route directions issued to entrants but, as the event rules put it, 'a sketch map would be an asset'. Navigation was to be by walkers' own one-inch OS maps; four would be needed. Entrants were advised that the way was generally easy to find and waymarked to some extent: 'Also the Y.H.A. publish a booklet which gives full route directions.'

'The South Downs Way at that point stopped and started in the middle of a wood on the Hants–Sussex border south of Petersfield,' says Barbara Blatchford. 'It was just a post on the county boundary, with the acorn long distance route sign. Petersfield was the nearest railway station. The least they could have done was decide a route to the nearest railway, but they didn't, so we did our own route, using the Old Mill youth hostel at Winchester as the checking-in point – just across the road was the riverside with some weirs on it. It went over old Winchester Hill, meandered round The Means, then Butser Hill and across the A3, using the underpass.' The Blatchfords' caravan provided one checkpoint. The others were in tents or someone's garage, apart from the breakfast stop (cornflakes and a fry-up) at the headquarters of Steyning AC. At the finish, walkers were promised a hot meal – tinned stew with Smash, tinned peas and carrots. 'THIS IS A TOUGH EVENT AND SHOULD ONLY BE ATTEMPTED BY THOSE WITH COURAGE', thundered the instructions to entrants.

'Though there had been people who had done 100 miles or more there'd never been an organised event across country,' says Keith Chesterton, the LDWA historian, 'so they didn't know how it would go.'

I've come to Guildford to visit Keith at his rather splendid house, which is in a winding uphill residential road, and boasts a gravel driveway and garden well stocked on the foliage front; this is Surrey *profonde*. Keith is in his early seventies – 'I don't want to do Hundreds any more' – and is an imposing figure, tall and straight-backed with white hair that sticks up slightly. He is a Cambridge-educated mathematician and a Centurion (he once solved a work problem mathematically to pass the time during a 100-mile event). A King Charles spaniel and a black cat fuss around his feet, as if he's a grandee about to have his portrait painted, though actually, in Surrey terms, Keith is practically a leftie fire-eater; one-time Labour parliamentary candidate for Guildford (he didn't get in) and still chairman of Guildford Labour Party: 'There were three years when we had a loose alliance with the Lib Dems. I got the first solar panels on the roofs, and cycle tracks.' He is also a school governor and chairman of Guildford Ramblers, and a former chairman and treasurer of the LDWA. To steal a phrase from Angela Carter, he is someone who sits on committees a lot.

He is also member number 81 of the LDWA, so pretty much a lifer. 'I was one of the first to respond to Alan's ad in *Climber & Rambler*, so I was out walking with him and Chris in the very beginning.' By that time Keith had already been long distance walking for some years: 'Mathematicians are meant to be unsociable and long distance walking can be an unsociable activity. I just liked it. My family never went anywhere, so I signed up to the NUS walking tour of Austria, and then in 1960 I walked the first half of the Pennine Way. I liked the idea of the challenge to yourself. I recognised that runners would always be faster than me. I felt as someone who wasn't particularly athletic that this was something I could do. Then when I was in my first job, living in Northwich, I used to do a lot of walking on my own around Saddleworth. I saw an ad for a walking group called the Kindred Spirits in the local Ramblers magazine. It had been formed by Len Chadwick, who contributed a column under the name of 'Fell-Wanderer' to the *Oldham Evening Chronicle*, where he was employed as a male typist. I contacted Chadwick and arranged to meet him in Saddleworth.

'When I got there, no one was there, so I thought, "I'll go round the moors anyway." Halfway through I met this one rather disreputable-looking bloke and said, "What's the time?" At the end of my walk I dropped into a fairly seedy place called the Yellow Cat Club, and this same guy turned up. It turned out he was Len Chadwick. "Ooh," he said, "nobody ever comes so I don't bother to wait."'

Chadwick was, says Keith, 'a strange character. A prisoner of war, not many teeth, dreadful straggly hair. He couldn't dye it very well. The Kindred Spirits did trips to the Lakes, Peak District, overnight walks. They weren't challenge walks. You could have called them social walks, except they weren't very. He had a programme of walks. Short walks – under thirty miles. Medium – thirty to fifty. Long – over fifty. So he didn't get many members.'

There was shortly to be one fewer. Keith moved down to London in 1965. He took part in his first competitive long distance walk in 1968, the Lake District Four Three Thousands: 'About forty-six miles in twenty hours, out from Keswick at two a.m. Saturday, finish by ten p.m. Sunday. When I got to the top of Skiddaw – which I thought I did reasonably quickly, and by which time I'd done several thousand feet of climb in two hours – I was fourth from last.'

The second long distance walk he did was the first Tanners Fifty – he dropped out at 30 miles. By the time the Downsman Hundred came around he was better prepared. Training walks were held across Surrey, the first two within three weeks of each other, one at the beginning of March and the other three weeks later. The first, from Frensham Ponds on the Hampshire border to Tatsfield on the Kent border, was supposedly fifty miles. On the later one they walked the same fifty miles in the other direction. One of their company was a girl called Sue Rayner who lived in a caravan at Box Hill, and she walked from there to Tatsfield before the start as well. 'She was a meter reader, and became the subject of a complaint from her workmates because she whooshed round so fast all the time, and showed them all up.'

When he reached Frensham Ponds he carried on walking back home to Guildford, which made ten miles extra. The next training walk was the Ridgeway, there and back, a total of 80 miles. He walked from one end, Streatley, to the other end, Goring, overnight. It rained heavily all the way and on arriving at Goring he set off immediately on the return journey with Chris and Alan, who were very fresh. 'After fifteen miles I was distinctly alone. I saw a bus stop and there was only one bus a day. So I only did fifty-five miles on that one.'

About the Hundred itself, Keith's recollections seem much sparser. Maybe that was because he was going so fast; he got to the 80-mile checkpoint in 23½ hours. 'I was walking at more than four mph to get to Butser Hill.' He finished in 31 hours 50 minutes, was 'pretty tired' and, hobbling and bent double, was given a lift home by Chris Steer. 'I must have slept somewhere,' he says. 'I didn't feel wrecked. I felt quite cheerful.'

The weather was, from other people's accounts, blisteringly hot. Sweltering under a bright orange anorak for maximum visibility, Alan Blatchford led at the beginning because nobody knew the way. He walked at what he said was a moderate pace, which left a lot of entrants having to jog to keep up. In a later article in *Strider*, Roger Cole wrote: 'One chap looked very old and walked at the same rate with jacket and trousers pleated, ex army I think. He actually stopped at a B & B in the Devil's

Dyke area and still finished within the forty-eight-hour time limit.'

Colin Saunders, another early joiner of the LDWA, is able to fill in more detail. 'It was quite a nice weekend. I don't remember any rain.' In his early twenties at the time, Colin, author of *The Capital Ring Guide* and *London: The Definitive Walking Guide*, was part of the support team that weekend for a London-based group called the Vanguard Ramblers which originated with the old Ramblers Association train excursions in the mid-sixties. 'We called ourselves that because it was founded in the guard's van with the aid of a bottle of Drambuie.

'Being the first Hundred – well, it would be too much to say it was chaotic but things weren't entirely smoothly organised. But we all had a sense of being in on something groundbreaking. I was the driver of the van, trying to keep tabs on the Vanguards, which was difficult because they were spread so much on route. Dave Wright did the night section in his pyjamas for a joke.' Two of the Vanguards decided to camp overnight and Colin and the support team were deputed to pitch their tent. 'It didn't do them any good – they gave up at the breakfast stop. Edith Sharp lay down in the middle of the road. She was hallucinating, she thought she was in bed. We found her, retired her and put her in the back of the van. We all had to sleep in there too.'

As for the stats, 138 entered, 123 started, 66 finished. According to Newsletter 6:

> 22 hrs and 20 mins after the start David Rosen, aged 20, arrived at the final checkpoint to become the first qualifier. 66 year old Wynne Evans was recorded as finishing last, 'closing the door at 48 hrs 25 mins'. There were seven female starters; three finished, with Dianne Pegg the first in 38½ hours. Too fast an early pace, the continuing hot weather, and the hard walking surface led to the retirement of 58 people. Most gave up before the breakfast stop . . .

After the walk several enquiries were made about 'next year's Downsman' but it is not proposed to hold another until 1975. If support continues it could become a regular biannual event.

But they did hold a Hundred the following year after all. On its 'Future Events' page, Newsletter 8 (May 1974) advertised the Peakland Hundred, on the same spring Bank Holiday weekend, organised by the LDWA's first local group, High Peak, with a start/finish at Hayfield and a route including Bleaklow, Black Hill, Derwent Valley, Lathkill Dale, Upper Dove Dale and Goyt Valley. The Hundred was launched as an annual event, and the Newsletter rechristened after a competition to come up with the best idea for a name. Suggestions included 'Footslogger', 'Wanderlust', 'Mercury', 'Shanks's Pony', 'Pedometer' and 'Trekker'. In the end Mac MacArthur, a Bristol & West walker, came up with *Strider*. It was the name of a character in *The Lord of the Rings* and, bearing in mind the sport's air of occupying some parallel unworldly universe, pretty damn perfect.

Over the next few years the membership built up in eclectic fashion, too. At one end of the spectrum were fell runners like Boyd Millen and champion orienteers like David Rosen. The other end was typified by a pair known as the 'Galloping Grandmas', Phyll Jackson and Molly White, who both went on to participate in several Hundreds. 'Phyll was in her fifties and came from the local Ramblers group,' says Barbara. 'She was a good word-of-mouth recruiter; she carried membership forms in her rucksack and whipped them out at the opportune moment. She did talk an awful lot. And she was a hopeless map reader, finished several things quite late. She was quite cheerful about it. I did the Fellsman with her and before the start she was reading a "How to Map Read" book. We went across a bit of bog in the middle of the night and she was fading. I said, "I'm going to leave you behind if you don't hurry up." That got her going.'

Alan Blatchford still hadn't run out of ideas. In 1975, he organised the unofficial road marathon Masters & Maidens. The only people excluded were good male club runners; anyone who had done under 3 hours 30 minutes was ineligible. Masters & Maidens was for slow, old and very young men, and for women. Some female athletes entered but they were told by the Women's Amateur Athletic Association that if they went ahead with it they would be thrown out. It beggars belief now, but that really was the mindset of sport in the early seventies – a rigid distinction between amateur and professional, men-only clubs and events, and a chronic lack of opportunities for women.

I knew nothing of this at the time, of course. I was too busy trying to get the Press Club and the front bar at El Vino to lift their bans on women so I could smoke and drink along with the men. But Alan Blatchford delivered Sport for All at least three decades before anyone else had even come up with the phrase. 'It was because he was really interested in encouraging people,' says Barbara. 'He expected the athletic ones to finish. It was the not-so-athletic ones, people like the Galloping Grandmas, who interested him. Some people have to be at the front to prove they're the best, but that didn't matter to him. He was a very good ultrarunner and a ten-miler was a short race to him. He was very fit and could have been at the front, but if it was a social walk he wanted to encourage other people.'

John Westcott, his Surrey Group colleague, agrees. 'He was an amazing bloke – a workaholic for his fellow man. He had these ideas, and it didn't matter what time he had, he had to go and do them. It wasn't only walking. He was a scoutmaster and a football referee. He was very laid back and very unassuming. His big asset was that he was willing to get on with things. Delegating? I've seen him with a load of papers: "I wonder, can you . . . ?" You felt so sorry for him you'd say, "I'll do that, Alan."

'A few days before he died in 1980, I remember him ringing up and saying, "John, we've got the Guildford Boundary Walk coming up and I've only had two offers of help. What's happening to the Surrey Group?" So I had the job of ringing round and getting some marshals. He was forty-four when he died, six days younger than me. I suspect he had a bad heart and even though he knew it he wasn't going to compromise the way he lived. He actually died in bed. Barbara was sleeping next to him. They had two very young children.'

'About a couple of months before he died, after he'd been out running, he said, "My chest feels peculiar,"' says Barbara. 'He went to see the doctor, who sent him for tests at St George's Tooting. They couldn't understand what was wrong. When he had a check-up, they said he was fitter than any person there. In September 1980 he ran the London to Brighton. A couple of weeks later he ran to work, Guildford to Weybridge, which he did twice a week. The night before he died he helped our daughter with her maths homework. I think I can say without doubt it was the worst twenty-four hours of my life. The worst thing was telling the children. The Guildford Boundary Walk was that weekend and everyone said, "What do you want to do?" So I said: "Carry on, carry on."'

You wouldn't, of course, have expected any other response from a long distance walker. But I don't think Alan Blatchford's story finishes there. When I happened on the obscure sport of long distance walking in the late nineties, I had no idea of quite how important his contribution was. The fact that everybody in the LDWA made such a fuss of celebrating him and Chris Steer in events like the Founders Challenge – an event whose route visited various founder-related shrines, such as the old post office in Peaslake – merely seemed quaint, a little sect-like. It's only now, writing this book, that I really come to appreciate what Alan Blatchford did to bring sport to everybody – not just the fast people but the slow, old and very young men, and all women. He gave opportunities to people like Keith Chesterton and me, who weren't particularly athletic but who liked the idea of a challenge to ourselves. That was something that simply didn't happen before 1971. And if you still need convincing about the importance of what Alan and Chris did, you only have to look at the walkers and runners, young and old, fast and slow, male and female, charging across the green hills and footpaths of Britain on the Hundred. So important to one man, in fact, that he's done every single one.

YOREDALE HUNDRED 2008

6: Ingleton (SD 695 730) to Ingleborough (Trig Point/ Refuge) (SD 741 746) *Distance: 3.47 miles; Ascent: 1963 feet; Descent: 38 feet*

Note: The distance to a checkpoint with facilities is 8.59 miles

Going up out of the village, I trot past Don Newman. 'Bit windy, isn't it?' he says cheerfully. I hadn't noticed before, but it's the cue for a loud whistle to start emanating from the gaps in everything.

After another 200yds, when road swings left, bear right onto track, initially with wall on right. This well walked track is now followed to the summit of Ingleborough . . .

It's not a full scale gale. It just feels a bit gusty. Shouldn't give me any problems. After all, I ran up this thing on the recce.

After another 230yds, bear right at track junction as indicated by signs, passing Crina Bottom boundary wall on your left . . .

Actually, I think I'm going to have to take it steadily this time. Just along this bit, where it's really starting to blow quite hard. It'll probably ease off once I'm past the farmhouse.

Continue upwards on obvious path, through rocky areas . . .

I catch a blast of scratchy, stinging dust full on. Immediately it lodges behind my contact lenses. I crouch sideways on the sheep track, shouting 'Fuck!' and rocking back and forth like someone in a locked ward. Having stuff in my eyes always makes my nose run, so now my face is covered in snot as well. And now I'm climbing I can't shield my eyes any longer because I need my hands to hang on.

Suffering shagbags. This wind is malevolent. Even Goya's Colossus would have trouble keeping his feet. As for me, I'm just an annoying midge. It's going to bat me off the mountainside without a second thought. People beside me climb in slow motion, past others sitting catching their breath. Up the stepped path I'm bent so low my chin is practically rubbing against the slabs. It's like trying to break down a door while someone throws sand in your eyes. Maybe doing it backwards wouldn't be such a bad idea.

Yes it would. I'd be able to see how far I was from earth. The further up I get, the more I can't stop thinking about the instant oblivion below. I've become obsessed with the feeling that I'm about to be whisked into empty space. I can't even look sideways. I can only keep my eyes on the stone slabs that mark the final twenty feet of steep curving climb. It's worse than being in the same room as someone who's just dumped you, trying resolutely to ignore them while being aware of them non-stop. Shoulder clamped to the wall of stone, I belly-crawl the last of the shirred rocks on to the plateau. I haven't climbed Ingleborough, I've grovelled it. But I'm there. I yank myself up and sprint towards the refuge. The surface is randomly scattered with rocks as though Colossus had just chucked down a game of jacks and wandered off. A marshal muffled in fleece clips my tally. Five past seven. Target more or less achieved.

What would fill the bill now is sandwiches, a thermos of tea and a chair. Instead I snatch a quick drink and head for the path down.

There's a straggly, flapping roadmenders' tape wound around stones on the plateau to guide us to the steps at the start of the descent, but a fat lot of notice I take of it. In the euphoria of successfully negotiating the narrow ledge off the plateau without freezing I step away from the steep drop and launch myself towards Horton.

At least, that's where I think I'm heading.

Checkpoint 6: Ingleborough (Trig Point/Refuge)
SD 741 746

Opens: 1600 Saturday; Closes: 0200 Sunday

Distance: 33.20 miles; Ascent: 5284 feet; Descent: 3356 feet

Manned by: Andy Ward and friends (if he has any) (West Yorkshire LDWA)

NINE
King Cole

GREAT GLEN IN LEICESTERSHIRE LOOKED TO
be one of those mystifying places middle Britain seems to specialise
in, somewhere you couldn't quite identify as either a wannabe-
suburb (it was a few miles south of Leicester) or a village grown
and exploded over the surrounding fields like a bolted lettuce.
There seemed to be no centre; what might have been the village
green was a big triangle on its edge, veined with roads. There were
pubs, churches, a youth club, a recreation ground. The backdrop
had the tamed emptiness of arable land bisected by an A road.

The street where Roger Cole lived was a pleasant suburban
development, with family saloons parked on driveways or under
car ports, and neat shrubs in the front gardens. The summer air
hummed with the sound of motor mowers. Roger's house was out
of the same mould as the rest, comfortable and unremarkable.
There wasn't a hint that it was the home of a sporting giant.

But that's what Roger was. He had a unique record, that
of completing every Hundred since the first in 1973, when he
finished in 35 hours, blood leaking from his socks and vowing
never to do another. It was something that was hard to get your
head around if you didn't have the mindset of a collector, if
you didn't comprehend immediately the single-minded sense
of purpose that drove someone to maintain that awesome but

extreme and fundamentally pointless record every year, come what may.

One other Hundred-er came close. Martyn Greaves was one behind him and at some eighteen years Roger's junior might well overtake the total in time. But Martyn hadn't done the lot in an unbroken chain. To bastardise the old football chant, there was only one Roger Cole.

On the way up from London, I'd been looking at Roger's cuttings. Perhaps they would give me the key to what made him tick. As ever, it was a frustrating haul. As far as the rest of the world was concerned, the Hundred and its greatest exponent may as well not have existed.

He had been written about only once in a national paper, and that along with half a dozen other Hundred-ers in the Saturday *Telegraph*'s two-page spread previewing the 1995 Shropshire Hundred weekend, where he was featured alongside the likes of Chris Dawes and Ann Sayer. The Shropshire was his twenty-second. The *Telegraph* quotes him as saying, 'I've got more to do than I've done already.' In the article that went with it, Denis Herbstein wrote: 'We ramble, stroll, bird-watch and plant-watch for the exercise, for relief from work, car, family. But these are home-for-tea afternoon strolls . . . A hundred miles is some other, very British tradition, that of the explorer – Dr Livingstone, Mary Kingsley, Sir Ranulph Fiennes – where physical attainment comes second to an inner bogeyman that has to be conquered.'

The other cuttings were photocopies from old *Striders* or thank-you letters written to organisers. Mostly they were no more than Roger's good-humoured accounts of Hundreds completed. Reading of the cat-and-mouse game between them on the 1999 Durham Dales, I gained an insight into his rivalry with Martyn Greaves: 'I caught him and went straight past . . . he didn't come into the following checkpoint having his card clipped outside and so stole another march on me while I relaxed eating inside . . . eventually I caught him again and pulled away from him over the closing stages to finish one place and thirteen minutes ahead of him . . .' There was an element of roguish twinkle in Roger's comments on checkpoints ('those delicious fleshpots'); there were his thank-you letters to the organiser of the 1993 Cleveland: 'What about those girls in their fishnet stockings and low necklines at Glaisdale!', and to Kent LDWA for the 2000 Millennium: 'In my hour of need the fair young damsel thrust two hash browns into my hand.' But the one from *Strider* for August 1992 caught my eye:

> It's great that the event still caters for all sorts and speeds, just as the initiator Alan Blatchford intended.
>
> I would just like to say to the runners, don't feel elitist and expect any special treatment, for until you've been through two nights you don't know how hard the event is for some of the slower walkers. And to the walkers, please sympathise with the runners and us 'in betweenys' as I was called in this latest event (made me feel like a transvestite), who have to push ourselves towards the limits to satisfy some inner masochistic urge we are plagued with.

But there was no time to ponder whether Roger was a Victorian explorer *manqué*, plagued with some inner bogeyman. There was the man himself, coming out to meet me wearing shorts and his latest Hundred sweatshirt. His legs were slightly bowed, his feet splayed. He was by no means skinny and his grey hair was sparse on top. A smiling, friendly man, his first words were, 'I don't know how much I'll be able to tell you. I've forgotten most of it now.'

I responded with some pleasantry about how I'd forgotten most of the walk I did last week, and followed him along the side of the house to the back garden. There was a reception committee: his wife, daughter and daughter-in-law were waiting for us at a patio table laid for afternoon tea. Were they here to stick their oar in? Then gradually the penny dropped. They were there to fill in the gaps. When Roger said he'd forgotten most of it, he was speaking nothing but the truth.

To explain why necessitated a trip back to the end of 2004, when the family thought he'd had a stroke because he couldn't speak properly. By the time he was diagnosed, he couldn't speak at all. The tumour had been there for at least five years, possibly fifteen. It was now the size of a satsuma and pushing his brain from left to right. After surgery anything he said sounded as though he was speaking German. He had to relearn who everybody was, and read up about what he'd done in his life so far.

But he still knew enough about who he was and what he wanted to take the Hundred entry form round to Tracey, his daughter, so she could fill it in for him. Three months later he showed up at the University of Buckingham campus for the Chiltern Landmarks Hundred. I was in the hall when he arrived at the finish. I had no idea at the time about his illness. I don't think anyone did. I just saw a shy, self-deprecatory smile on the face of a dazed, blinking but happy man with his trademark walrus moustache, wearing a jersey of multicoloured stripes and the boots for which he'd swapped his trainers halfway round. His legs were slightly buckled under a pair of baggy shorts. His time wasn't far off the one he'd recorded for the 1973 Downsman, even though he had 32 more years on the clock and, unusually for him, he'd got himself lost two miles from the end. He asked for directions at a pub and two hours later found himself back at the same place.

Many people, on learning all that, would probably have thought: 'He's bonkers!' And they'd no doubt have followed it up by thinking, 'How tragic for a man to be so in the grip of a fundamentally pointless sporting endeavour that he's prepared to put his life on the line so as not to break the chain.' But they didn't know Roger – or Hundred-ers in general. And as I listened to him and took in what he'd achieved, a far different picture emerged.

He was born in London in 1938 and grew up in Ealing – 'Mum and Dad never went further than to watch the cricket.' When he said that, of course, I was reminded immediately of Keith Chesterton's remark that 'My family never went anywhere.' I wondered if, for young men of that generation, doing the Hundred was the one way to satisfy their craving for adventure and experience beyond the boundaries of town. As a boy he was a climber and cyclist; later he ran for the Air Force and then took up road marathons, doing all the early Londons – 'Never got in under three hours' – and one Paris marathon during which they all went the wrong way: 'Ran through 40k thinking, This is the best I've ever done – and it took us two hours to do the last 2k.'

So he was not, never had been, a top class athlete. On Hundreds, the highest he had ever come in the finishing order on the main event was eighth out of 200 in the 1975 Downsman. By the time I met him, he was arriving back in the middle of the pack. But his idiosyncratic achievement meant he would be remembered far longer than those who finished in front of him.

For a lot of his working life, he was a sales rep at a water treatment company. What he did when in 1990 they decided to boot him out shows the mettle and bloody-mindedness beneath the good-natured exterior. 'It was a terrible shock,' said June, his wife. 'When his brain tumour was diagnosed, the consultant said it might have been due to a trauma. Well, what that company did to him was a trauma. He was incensed. I've never seen him so angry.'

He channelled his fury into starting his own company, which I was happy to hear outstripped his former employer in due course. But in a sense his life's work was the Hundred.

He did the first with his friend Roger Maher; the pair of them turned up outside the Old Mill youth hostel in Winchester for the noon start. Weighed down with boots and rucksacks, they were amazed to see a few of the entrants in singlets and shorts, preparing to run the event. They had severe blisters by the first checkpoint at 13 miles, when they were given water – 'Cor, did I need that water,' said Roger. They ran till they couldn't run any more, and then they walked. He remembers, too, that the other Roger had to borrow a walking stick because his knee had gone.

'I had blood coming out of my laceholes by the finish. We said: "That was silly, doing that. We'll never do it again." The next day – "Well, if we trained a bit, wore trainers, carried less gear etc . . ."'

After that one and all those that followed he made succinct notes on dog-eared sheets of paper from an exercise book. For the Downsman, they read: 'Number of starters 125. Number of finishers 66. Fastest time 22:20. My time 35:10. Position 44. Comments – Walked in boots.' And so on through the decades. He did the 1982 Pilgrims Plus, the one with an extra 40 miles tacked on the end for anyone who hadn't had enough: 'I had to go through a second night, without sleep again,' he said. 'Keith Arnold, who was in the military and very fast, did it in 29:05. He beat David Rosen by fifty minutes. Martyn Greaves did 33:10.' Roger finished in 45 hours 3 minutes – seventeenth out of twenty-six. Under 'Comments' was written: '100. Also Plus. 142M. Too long.'

He got his Ten Hundreds badge in Bristol, after the 1983 Snowdonia Hundred. Mike Harding gave a speech and played his guitar before presenting Roger with a cup. 'And we didn't have to pay for our meal,' said June. In 1990, the year there were two Hundreds, he completed both. The 1992 Invicta ('Very hot. Beat 1st girl') was his twentieth and the National Committee bought him a special one-off trophy, then argued about getting it engraved in advance in case he failed. He finished. As he did on the 2004 Exmoor after he tripped running downhill and crashed into a tree, at which point the marshals tried to make him drop out because so much blood was pouring from his head and arms. 'I've never felt that we wouldn't finish,' he said. 'Best not to think about it, really. I've never wanted to give up.'

In fact the closest he came to breaking the chain had been much earlier, in 1986, one of the Downsman years. The day before, he'd moved house and, leaving June with the unpacked tea chests, he made the start at Winchester a few minutes before the off. As soon as he completed (in his fastest time ever – 22:26), he took the train back home and carried on unpacking. The next day he went off to work as usual.

A while back I happened to be interviewing a London Marathon ever-present, one of a gradually diminishing bunch of people who had been there in 1981 when Dick Beardsley and Inge Simonsen crossed the line together, and had not missed one since. What struck me was his comment that, far from being a source of pleasure and pride, the pressure to keep up the record had turned it into a burden. Was it the same for Roger? Poor bugger, can't give up and let the side down? He shook his head. 'No, it's no burden. The only thing that's right for me is that I've always been able to do this. I've always been OK to run.'

That was the only explanation I was going to get. But then, even the people closest to Roger found his obsession difficult to explain. 'We don't know what drives him,' said June. 'I think he'd crawl on his hands and knees to do it if he had to. He would never cut a corner. He'd rather walk six miles longer than cut a mile off. He never took a day off work afterwards. He's come back from a Hundred with his water bottle still full, with the muesli bar he set out with, plus another he picked up on the way round. He never goes out on LDWA walks. His idea of training is to get me to take him out in the car and when we're fifty miles from home he says, "Right. Drop me here." Then he finds his way back.'

The surgery Roger underwent hadn't left him in perfect nick. It was not just memory that had been affected; his speech seemed brusque, a distilled version of what he wanted to articulate. Yes, he would have liked very much to have been a Victorian explorer, 'but that time's gone. It's a different way of thinking now.' So what did he like best about the Hundred? 'Seeing the people each year, the friends. You look for them. I can't remember their names. Last year I wrote them down.' And did he like company or solitude? 'On my own, two or three around me at most. Finding my own way. Everybody gets lost except me.' And no, he never walked out any of the route beforehand. He walked on his own in the night. 'Don't wait for anybody.' And the way he got through it? 'It's to be done. It's toughness of mind.'

As for how he managed to navigate, he answered with the same no-nonsense succinctness as he did every other question. 'You know where you want to go. You can see the hills and the map in your mind.' That was apparent when you watched him in action, when the easy-going smile was gone and instead you saw a man intent and completely focused. His gaze fixed on a distant point while some highly efficient, instinctive spatial skill operated within, he was as alert and majestic as a stag.

From time to time he seemed impatient, especially when people answered for him and words were put into his mouth that he didn't hold with. But when I asked him about the old days his eyes lit up. He was in almost at the very start of the LDWA. Newsletter 8 recorded his name and address under 'New Members'; he was number 564. He ran the Tanners Marathon with Alan Blatchford and Chris Steer, remembered all the legends: Ernie Bishop, David Rosen, Keith Arnold. Fondly he relived being on the 1993 Cleveland with Boyd Millen: 'We talked and talked. We'd gone wrong. The others had kept on route. Boyd and I got back on course by doing a couple of hills that were in the way.'

When he spoke about Alan Blatchford, there were almost stars in his eyes. 'Brilliant chap. Fastest forty-miler in the world. He was *so* fast. The Peakland Hundred was a bad one – communications were poor, long distances without stopping, louts back at the finish. We were trying to finish inside thirty hours. Alan did it in about twenty-four hours. Most people sit down, put their feet up, then go home, but he got rid of the louts and came back out on to the route, helping us in the last five miles.'

He still ran as much of the route as he could, because it made it easier. 'Though I probably enjoy them more now because I'm not running so much of it.' Over the years, June said, his feet had gone a funny shape. As I'd already noticed, they were somewhat splayed after all the miles, and had bunions. But he was still pretty fast. On the 2007 Mid Wales he did 36:43; out of 487 starters, he placed 165th. On his first Downsman, at half the age, he'd finished in 35:10.

Just once or twice I sensed a hint of melancholy. It was apparent when he said, 'It seems strange that it's gone on this long and Chris and Alan aren't there,' and when he remembered how he used to shake Boyd Millen's hand and say, 'See you at the end.' I suspected that every year when he set out on a Hundred, a part of him was back outside the Mill at Winchester, a young paterfamilias with June and the kids watching, wearing boots, carrying a rucksack, overawed by the guys in running strips, turning to his friend Roger Maher and saying, 'A hundred miles? And they're going to run it?'

But it would be wrong to end Roger's story on an elegiac note. That's not what it's about. Here was a man on the brink of his seventieth birthday who was strong and physically active; who possessed a sporting record that could never be beaten and to which he still hadn't finished adding. That was clear from his parting shot, spoken with a grin: 'It's only another year to wait and I'll have to do it again.'

As I drove away, I pictured the scene that the neighbours must have been treated to if they'd poked their heads over the back garden fence. They'd have seen Roger, seated in splendour like a potentate, with four admiring women gathered around him, attending to his comfort and hanging on to every word.

YOREDALE HUNDRED 2008

7: Ingleborough (Trig Point/Refuge) (SD 741 746) to Horton-in-Ribblesdale (SD 809 720) *Distance: 5.12 miles; Ascent: 78 feet; Descent: 1664 feet*

This is the big one. The bit where you have to grope your way round the boulder while descending on a path the width of a scribble. Where you mustn't look over to the left and see the thousand-foot drop.

Descend through rocks on stepped/surfaced path & at base of extremely steep section, at fork in path, take the right-hand paved path (110) soon passing a very small pond on your left . . .

Just get down it. Don't think about DEATH. Think of what's on the route description. DEATH. Remember the fork in path. DEATH. Find the pond.

Where is this bloody pond? Has someone moved it? I press on for a while, waiting for it to materialise. Over to my right, descending on a distant track, on a parallel hump, is a line of walkers. Maybe there's another event going on.

No there isn't. That's my event. That'll be my pond, over there. I've picked the wrong path, because I'm a henwit who follows blokes in the belief that blokes know what they're doing. And if I keep following them now I'll be following them all the way to the B6255 and the Ribblehead Viaduct.

What I ought to do is turn round and climb back up again. But I can't. Not back up the scribble-path. No way. It's time for desperate measures. Between me and the path I should be taking is a forty-foot grassy drop, which is peppered with sheep shit and almost perpendicular.

There's only one thing for it, the arse toboggan. Here goes.

Back on the right track, the first person I see is Don Newman. We pass the time of day again and off I go in the evening sun, periodically blinking grit out of my eyes, hurdling stones and lumps of rock, finding grassy verges where I can, over the short-cropped grass and limestone pavements around Sulber Nick. The wind's dropped here but it isn't as quick as I hoped. The surface is all tufts and bristles. It's like running across the face of a warty old aunt.

It's twenty to nine, and still just about daylight, as I hurry past the Pen-y-Ghent café towards Horton-in-Ribblesdale Village Hall. A terrible high-pitched howling is coming from round the back. Either someone's harpooned a cat or there's a runner throwing up. But inside, it's cosy and steamy, like a rollickingly overcrowded transport caff. And now it's time for some serious eating. I eat as if I'm paid per bowl. I stuff myself with ravioli in a paper bowl, then ravioli with baked beans, then a thing with custard over it, then another custardy thing. I even eat while I'm pulling on my fleece. I feel I've staggered away from a battlefield. I'm not tired, just relieved. The wind madness – it's over. I've escaped off Ingleborough alive. Nothing else on this Hundred can possibly be as bad.

Which reminds me, I've got six hours of darkness ahead. And I'm not planning on doing it on my own.

My gaze settles on a quiet, lugubrious-looking figure in the corner. Brian, that's his name. The guy I finished last year's Stansted Stagger with. We go at around the same pace. He seems a pretty chivalrous type.

I pipe up.

'Brian, will you spend the night with me?'

Checkpoint 7: Horton-in-Ribblesdale (Village Hall)
SD 830 720

Opens 1730 Saturday; Closes: 0400 Sunday

Distance: 38.32 miles; Ascent: 5362 feet; Descent: 5020 feet

Manned by: Mid Wales and Marches Groups

Indoor checkpoint with hot/cold drinks, food

TEN
The Stuff of Which Empire Is Made

'IT WAS JUST SOMETHING TO DO. A SPORTING endeavour.'

I'm waiting for Ann Sayer to tell me more about her record-breaking walk from Land's End to John O'Groats. I want her to tell me what it felt like to walk 60 miles a day for nearly fourteen days, about the teeth-gritting fatigue and the relentless, lonely miles, about the euphoric moment of finishing, knowing all the pain was worth it, knowing she'd made sporting history.

But she doesn't. Instead, she seems almost casual about it. I don't think it's false modesty, nor boredom with telling a story she's told many times before. It's more that she is a naturally matter-of-fact person who can't be bothered to elaborate or philosophise. And anyway, it's obviously not in her nature to bang on about herself. The perversity of it is that in a sport that demanded she be solitary, she was a team player by nature. When she does talk about her achievements, her chief concern is to acknowledge all the people who enabled her to make them happen.

Yet, however prosaic Ann is about what she's done, she is one of the best walkers Britain has produced and without doubt one of its greatest female athletes. Chris Brasher called her 'the stuff of which the British Empire was made'. What she embarked on in 1977 was not simply an epic series of achievements. She was a mould-smasher.

It was in October that year that she became the first woman in Britain to break the barrier for racewalking 100 miles in 24 hours to become a Centurion. That vindication will mean nothing now to a public who can barely remember a period when female athletes were regarded as trespassers on male preserves. Even at that time, when resignations were advanced over the decision to admit her to what had been till then an all-male club, no one outside that close-knit world would have known something phenomenal and pioneering had happened. But it had. She did it at the Bristol 100 with a time of 20 hours 27 minutes 14 seconds. Soon after that she broke 20 hours for the same distance.

That isn't all. In 1979 she completed the 420-mile Three Peaks in 7 days and 31 minutes, breaking the record held by Arthur Eddleston, a London policeman, by 11 hours. Naturally she immediately points out that Eddleston came back the following year and beat her record by a whole day. But Ann holds another record, set in 1980 and still unbroken; that for the fastest ever Land's End to John O'Groats walk by a woman. Her time – 13 days 17 hours 42 minutes – was beaten by Sandra Brown in 1995; in 2006 Sharon Gayter went even faster. This is not to detract from either of those performances, but both women ran at least some of the way and so these were running records. Ann Sayer walked the lot.

And how she walked, striding on massively long legs, a Valkyrie with flying blonde curls who was given the nickname 'Metronome' because of her relentless, unremitting pace. She even looked magnificent in people's hallucinations about her; on the 120-mile Tan Hill to Cat and Fiddle walk in North Yorkshire, one of her fellow walkers, Chris Dodd, who held the record for the Coast to Coast, thought he saw her in a white ballgown walking amid broken loo pans.

We're in a restaurant near Ann's house in Twickenham, having a ladies' lunch. Well, lunch, anyway. Ann Sayer never did 'lady'. In her early seventies, the once blonde hair grey but still untidily rumpled, she's a little stooped now but still seems to me immensely tall. We've walked here from Ann's small, elegant modern house in a nearby side road, me at a normal brisk pace and Ann considerately employing the mimsy little half-shuffle she has to use in order for people like me to keep up. I have memories of scampering alongside her on events, legs going round like those of Jerry trying to get away from Tom. I've thought, God, I'm really improving, I'm matching Ann Sayer step for step. Then she'd say, 'Anyway, must get on now,' and without apparent effort she'd be a hundred yards up the path even as 'Bye, nice to talk to you' was escaping from my lips.

It would be pointless to ask for advice about doing the Hundred. My ambition – to finish without going into the second night – is so footling it's too embarrassing to mention. As is our first encounter in 2001, the year of the foot and mouth epidemic, when with the countryside closed for business I led a group of long distance walkers, Ann included, around the course of the London Marathon. As we reached the halfway point, I asked her blithely: 'I'm not going too fast, am I?'

Ann's sporting background was rowing. At London University, she wanted to do something active that she hadn't done at school. Having gone swimming once – 'I decided I didn't like being damp and cold' – and not attracted by fencing, she opted for the river instead. She loved it, rowing for the university and carrying on after her graduation – she worked for BP ('I was a geologist. Didn't do much geology') – with United Universities. 'The highest we came was fourth in the European Championships. We won minute pots or tankards in domestic regattas. I rowed in an eight. I liked eights. I can safely say I would work my heart out for the crew, but not for myself – I'd have been a hopeless single sculler.

'It was great.' Empowering? 'Occasionally, when we were

on top form. It was nice to overtake men's crews when we were practising (they had to be quite bad for that to happen). But I can remember doing it once to the University of London's second crew. They must have been on particularly poor form.'

There was no women's rowing in the Olympics in that era, the early sixties, but she was selected for Great Britain in the European Championships. The crew had to pay virtually all their expenses themselves, and to sew all the letters saying 'Great Britain' on the back of their tracksuits. 'Some of the sewing was rather uneven,' she says.

And after that?

'I wasn't pioneering in the Hundreds sense. I wasn't there at the first one. On the second one, the Peakland in 1974, I was a complete novice. I'd only done one challenge event, in 1973. I had joined the Rockhoppers Mountaineering Club in central London. Two friends suggested they knew a walk I'd like to do – the Long Mynd Hike, fifty miles. At the end I was more tired than I'd ever been, but as I left someone handed me an LDWA membership form and I was intrigued. I thought, These people are mad, but I want to see what they're doing.'

And she liked what she saw. 'We were doing something unusual and in the case of my racewalking something we shouldn't have been doing,' she says. 'There was never any sexism. It was never like cricket where the attitude was "women should be making the teas". Rambling and hiking had always been a mixed-sex social activity. In the LDWA there was never "women shouldn't do long distance stuff". That's why it was surprising to find the opposite view held in the athletics world. I wasn't aggressive women's lib. I was more bolshy. If men were allowed to be daft and do twenty-four hour walks, why not us? Why shouldn't a woman do this?'

No sexism in the LDWA at all? Well, maybe a little. There was the time when she walked into Fangdale Beck breakfast stop checkpoint on the 1976 Cleveland, on her own because she'd inadvertently left everyone behind at the 50 mile mark. 'It was early on Sunday morning. I'd already caught up with Boyd Millen, who'd really bitten the dust, at Bransdale Beck – fifty-eight miles officially, around sixty-two miles actually. There were five men in the checkpoint. Their jaws dropped. They leapt to their feet, knocking over chairs, and rushed out. I suppose at that time they couldn't believe a woman was there. They were enjoying their checkpoint and in bowled this woman. I wasn't even a runner.'

By that time she was building up to the glory years, and these are clearly powerful memories because she can still repeat thirty-year-old dialogue word for word: 'There didn't seem to be any great fund of knowledge one could draw on, so you had to make it up as you went along. It was just necessity. The whole thing was a progression. A couple of LDWA Hundreds. Then, let's try something different. I'd heard of this bunch of people called Centurions who had walked a hundred miles in twenty-four hours on the road – I'll give that a try, I thought.'

That must have caused a stir.

'There was a certain amount of bemusement. Some anti feeling. And a lot of support. I phoned up Alan Blatchford because I knew he was a Centurion and had done the London to Brighton run. There was a slight pause at the other end of the line because I don't think even he had thought of that. Then he said, "Basically you'll need to join an athletics club."

'"Oh, is there one near me?" (I was living in South Woodford.)

'"There's Woodford Green AC. But that's men only." But Essex Ladies used the same facilities and they didn't come any better than that. Alan knew that Tom Richardson, the captain of the Centurions, coached walking at Woodford Green track at the Ashton playing fields. So I went down to the track. I had to go about five times before I managed to encounter him. I was really so shy that I wouldn't have asked anybody – like when was the best time to find him.'

She found Richardson eventually and told him she aimed to be a Centurion. He seems to have failed to appreciate the strength of her ambition and suggested she simply try racewalking. Then in March 1977 he happened to mention he was going to the Netherlands in June to officiate in the Dutch Centurions. She knew the Dutch were less hidebound than the British and in April she reminded him what she wanted to do. A somewhat bemused Richardson said, 'How long do you think you can walk before you need a rest?'

She told him that on the recent 100km Surrey Summits she'd had her first sit-down at a checkpoint after 28 miles, so on the Centurion event in the Netherlands they arranged that she would sit down and have a rest after 50. When she reached 50 miles, she didn't want to stop but felt rather diffident about mentioning it: 'But I plucked up courage and asked him if I need not stop. "Carry on," she was told. So I carried on to the end without stopping.' In fact, you might say the next stop was Bristol.

At the time the top distance in women's racewalking was 5km, though they were experimenting daringly with twice that distance. Ann wanted to go further – 20km, 20 miles, 50 miles. Some of the attitudes she encountered beggared belief but she seems to have accepted them with a kind of wry humility. 'When I contacted the organiser of the Essex Championships and asked if I could do the 50km, he said, "You're very welcome to come along but I'm afraid you won't figure in the results." I knew I was a ghost. When the prizegiving took place I thought, If I weren't a ghost I know I'd get an Essex County medal, because I was third.'

Some ghost, you might think. Then there was the time she wanted to do the 54-mile Manchester to Blackpool, and the organiser said, 'Well, we can't stop you walking on a public road.' When she reached the first checkpoint in Bolton, she was given water, which she thought was a promising sign. 'Then when I got to the finish I was handed a ticket for the Mayor's tea in the

Winter Garden and I thought, Crikey, I've really arrived. Then they gave me one of their gold medals, though I'd failed to reach the first class standard time by two minutes.'

An attempt on the Land's End to John O'Groats women's walking record, the thought of which had daunted her when it was first suggested, now seemed less of an Everest. 'I had a bit of sponsorship, too. A firm called Devon Conversions supplied a motorised caravan and BP – unusually, as they didn't normally sponsor employees – sponsored me for fuel. And Damart Thermawear got me modelling long-sleeved vests. Thick Double Force.

'The support was great. It was a case of, "How many miles would you like to walk a day?" "Well, I've literally walked the best part of a hundred and twenty miles in twenty-four hours and got really exhausted. Let's halve it and I should be able to keep that up every day."'

Originally Chris and Margaret Steer were going to be part of the support team, but Alan Blatchford died a few days before they started. Ann was ready to cancel the walk and go to the funeral but after talking to other members of the team the consensus was that Blatchford would have wanted them to carry on. 'They were obviously in disarray, though. Chris and Margaret, of course, had to go to the funeral so the support team was suddenly disturbingly short-handed. My main organisers, Jeff Ellingham and Mike Powell Davies, phoned around people they knew, mostly people in the LDWA.' A team of fifteen helpers was cobbled together. Some would be there for two or three days. Lilian Millen, Boyd's wife, was staying with her all the way.

'They were a wonderful bunch of people. It wasn't like a race. It was more like a time trial, a solitary time trial, so I could do what I knew I could do best – which was not bombing off at a vast pace at the start. Slowly slowly catchee monkee.'

And now I begin to learn what walking 60 miles a day, fast, over nearly fourteen days must have been like. I learn how she used to cry around tea time, because she was tired – 'struggling along feeling a bit feeble and weak' is how she puts it. And how none of the supporters wanted to walk with her when she was like that because it made them feel uncomfortable. 'They didn't really know how to cope.'

As she reached the last five or ten miles, all she felt was tired and a bit sleepy. It had become a way of life and to that extent she wanted it to go on. But that day she'd walked 76 miles. So – and it's with massive understatement that she concludes her account of the record-breaking journey – 'I was quite glad to get to the finish.'

What happened after that is strangely touching, though. The next morning, she got up and went outside. When she went back in, the house was what she describes as 'all quiet'.

'And,' she says, 'this is genuine, I thought they'd all gone off and forgotten about me.'

Sounds like the sort of thing that happens to you when you're a child.

She nods. 'I hadn't been part of their circle. They were having good times in the van when I was out on the road! I hadn't had the socialising. Only their care and support. I had been very dependent on them. That's when five-year-olds burst into tears, isn't it?'

There's still one thing that I'm curious about. Had the opportunity been available in the seventies, would she have gone where the fame and fortune was and become a marathon runner?

She shakes her head. 'I did one marathon – the Barnsley. I wasn't training for it. I only did it because it was something to do once my plans for what I'd intended to do, the Roubaix 28-hour race walk in France, fell through. But I was someone who did eight-minute miles, for a 3:30 marathon. I would never have got any faster. I would just have gone on longer.'

But anyway, why should she have been anything other

than what she was? She happened on long distance walking and it turned out to be the sport that she was made for. In 2005, at last, she did gain recognition – she was made an MBE for services to sport. Even that she plays down. 'Really I don't think I've done a vast amount. I've been part of a continuum. Women's sport, because of the rowing side of things as well – when I was doing that, it was definitely a minority pastime. Bridging the gap between country/challenge walking and road/athletics walking.'

Just one of Ann's achievements should have raised interest in long distance walking. But even LEJOG didn't change its status as an eccentric pursuit engaged in by harmless obsessives. Does it matter? Not, by what she says, to her, though she would have welcomed recognition for the people who helped her, of whom Alan Blatchford and Tom Richardson were two of many. Even so, you can't but think it's a shame. 'One of the greats' is an overused phrase in sport. Said of her, it's true.

YOREDALE HUNDRED 2008

8: Horton-in-Ribblesdale (SD 809 720) to Kidhow Gate (SD 830 834) *Distance: 8.88 miles; Ascent: 1533 feet; Descent: 423 feet*

Note: The next checkpoint is only a tent & very exposed at 1900' but does have road access

It's past nine-thirty as Brian and I head past the Golden Lion pub to rejoin the Pennine Way. One minute we're walking into a tastefully designed sunset of pink and cream and dove grey, the next we're climbing the rocky track out of Horton in a manageably blowy wind. And now on the low slopes there are hideous, scalp-detaching gusts which transform themselves into a continuous howling onslaught the higher we go.

Ahead on enclosed track (wall on right broken in places). After 210yds go through gap in crossing wall. Ahead for another 530yds (along the way wall on right veers off) to go through gate at Sell Gill Holes...

What I can't work out is why I wasn't expecting this. It's not really a shock meteorological event, is it? Not exactly 'Volcano Erupts in Frinton'. How could I not have allowed for it? Will the Pennines be absolutely still and breezeless overnight? Does the universe tend towards order? Do bears use public conveniences in urban locations?

In 50yds track swings away from wall on left to climb more steeply...

Actually, I've become so used to being blown about that I hardly notice the gale any more. Brian and I simply plod uphill, heads down, blinking grit and dust out of our eyes. Landmarks I remember from the recce are invisible. Even the things the landmarks are on are invisible. It's just a great, swirling heap of blackness into which we carry on climbing.

But now there's something apart from blackness. It's a little light moving in the wind, like a glow-worm weaving home from the pub. It's the self-clip point, the clipper swinging from its chain while people blunder around it, trying to operate cutters that won't cut with weak wrists and fumbling fingers.

Stuff feminism. I'll let Brian work the clippers.

We carry on striding, up and up, in a kind of supercharged plod against the wind. Sometimes Brian goes faster than me. Sometimes I go faster than him. Then we ping back together, buffeted by the gale. We reel in another walker, a dark bulky labouring shadow who hangs on to us for a while before dropping back. I look round and see the light of his head torch on the point of his lolling head. There are more lights in a chain strung behind him in the black wilderness.

God, this is hard. Harder than Ingleborough because it's dark and because I'd normally be lying in bed now, reading a crime thriller before I turn out the light, and because I'm thirsty and my drinking bladder won't work, and because my eyes are painful and streaming and full of grit and the only vision I've got is through one half-open eye. The other one is closed.

Hang on. Way in front is a weird blurred contraption, red lights and yellow lights that all seem to be flashing and whizzing round, like a roundabout on the surface of the moon. That's got to be it. Kidhow Gate checkpoint. We're nearly there.

Except that every hundred yards we gain, the infernal fairground goes backwards. We're never going to get there. And when we do get there, we'll only have done 47.2 miles. I won't even be halfway. Time's getting on. And the next checkpoint is just a tent. Without toilets, so I can't take out my contact lenses in front of a brightly lit mirror and rid them of hideous gunk. I'll have to go on like this all the way down to Hawes.

And if I can't see properly I'll get lost. I'll have to take the map out. Which I can't bloody fold, let alone navigate by. I'll have to hunt all around the bottom of my rucksack – compared to which scientists' search for dark matter is nothing – for the mobile so I can howl down it for the rescue helicopter like an ignominious twit.

Calm down. If I can just sort my eyes out, I'll set off right away. Five and a half miles. Downhill most of the way. I've recce'd it. I'm not even tired. Just blind, ha ha!

But a little puncture of uncertainty has appeared in my confidence. What if I really can't see well enough to carry on? What if I have to give up?

That's OK. Plenty of people fail on their first Hundred. There's always next year's.

Except I won't come back next year. If I drop out, that's it. I'll simply accept that I'm destined never to get beyond 50 miles. There's plenty of people who sensibly realise that a Hundred isn't for them. I have to be mature about this. I'll never do a Hundred.

Oh, bollocks. I am going to make it down from here. This is not negotiable. I'll tape my eyelids apart if I have to. I'll get down on my knees and grope my way down.

KIDHOW GATE. The lights of the tent are agonisingly bright. I blunder in, eyes shut. I am shouting. '*I want a flat surface!*' Opening one swimming eye just wide enough to see where I'm going, squinting, weeping, crashing around like a zapped house fly, I stagger towards a table. '*Gimme a flat surface!*' I force myself in between the Raynet operators while simultaneously whipping off my rucksack and feeling around it. Crouching, I empty eye drops into my eyes and mop my face with the emergency loo paper.

That's a bit better. At least I can keep my eyelids apart. Through the streaky, grey film that has settled on my contact lenses I take a look around. The place is crowded out. There's barely room to back out again, let alone perform the movements necessary to sit down. And there's nowhere to sit anyway. All the seats are occupied by people who've given up. There are probably a few more of them underfoot. We're probably standing on our dead fellow creatures, like battery chickens.

I take myself outside, away from the piercing lights so I can open my eyes again. Out here is the overspill. More people huddle together. In my overwrought mental state it's a dystopian Tudor fantasy, a stinking encampment, full of papists plotting in whispers against the king.

Brian is waiting. I eat a cold hot dog in limp white Mother's Pride to an accompaniment of the wind whining over the Pennines, then follow him into the dark.

I'll make it down to Hawes somehow. I can do it.

Checkpoint 8: Kidhow Gate (Tent) SD 830 834

Opens: 1900 Saturday; Closes: 0800 Sunday
Distance: 47.20 miles; Ascent: 6895 feet; Descent: 5443 feet
Manned by: Guiseley Scouts
Tented checkpoint with hot/cold drinks & hot soup but limited food

ELEVEN
The Dark Arts

'I'VE SLEPT IN SOME VERY INTERESTING places,' said Keith Warman. 'In Yorkshire on the White Rose I was so tired I was wandering along, falling asleep on my feet and staggering. Thirteen miles to go. We'd had two miles along a lane. You need things happening, stiles, fields, to keep your mind going. This was never-ending. I knew I wouldn't get to the next checkpoint so I had to take a hedge stop. I've seen a baby elephant on the side of the path which turned out to be a bush. In a tree there's been an Indian squaw with a baby. I looked at it saying, "Why is that woman up there with a baby?" I've done one Hundred where I haven't slept, the Shropshire in 1995. But usually I get to the stage where I'm so tired I can't imagine anything else. I've got to sleep.'

If good walkers come in all shapes and sizes, they also go at all speeds. Keith, a short, self-contained man with a boyish face and determined chin, usually finishes in the last few hours of a Hundred, but taking his time seems to be choice rather than necessity. He even likes to start at the back: 'It's so crowded at the early stiles. Why stand in a queue when you can be having a cup of tea in the hall? Also I don't like being in a crowd. I was jostled at the start of one Hundred. The footpaths were narrow, people were wanting to get past. I sat down, let everyone go and thought,

I'll just go at the back and enjoy it. I've not carried a watch for five years because it adds to the pressure. Give your whole weekend to the Hundred. No worries. I can ask the time at the checkpoint. It's surprising how quickly time passes. Let the hares hare off, the tortoise always gets there in the end.'

He lives with his partner, Shirlie, a lovely, kind-hearted woman with brown bobbed hair and a warm impish smile, in a small, cosy house in a lane backing on to fields in a village outside Maidstone. His profession is quantity surveyor; one of his spare-time occupations is looking after the Hundreds database and the collection of Hundred badges – a copy of every one since the 1973 Downsman. He likes maps; he collects them and he draws them. His other passion is steam trains. In fact I think he likes timetables very much too; as soon as the Hundred checkpoint times are released, he makes a spreadsheet of them and plots his estimated arrival time at each.

Which is where the sleeping comes in. The subject had come up because it was something that concerned me – how on earth would I stay awake and on the move for anything up to 48 hours? But to Keith it wasn't a problem. 'If you need it, have it. We're all different. Some won't sleep at all. I find that fifteen or twenty minutes makes all the difference. I feel quite rejuvenated. On the 1982 Pilgrims, my second Hundred, I slept on the wayside at Wrotham. Early on the Sunday morning, before the breakfast stop, for fifty-five minutes. On the 1993 Cleveland I was with Neil Higham, the Kent Group treasurer. We slept three times during the Saturday night. It was heavy going. At one point he said, "I'm so tired" and fell asleep standing up, against a barbed wire fence. I slept on the wayside. You just have to make sure you're off path so no one treads on you. Later the same night, we found a circular sheepfold on the moors and propped ourselves up inside it.'

Keith was warming to his theme. 'The White Rose again. It was Sunday afternoon, about five o'clock, when I had my first sleep. Bolton Abbey checkpoint. Staffordshire Group were running it. A heavy shower had just started descending. I was with a friend, Jimmy Oddy, and the two of us wove in. "Sleep, please." "How long do you want?" "Half an hour, please." We were ushered into the billiard room. All around the billiard table were bodies. They had inflatable airbeds. Sleeping bags. Bliss. There was a violent thunderstorm going on – I was woken up by hailstones on the roof of the billiard room. We had to have another sleep at 91 miles, at Checkpoint Fifteen, which was two garages at the rear of an inn at Belford.'

But when you sleep on the wayside, how do you wake up in time to get going again?

'You get a bit cold. Shivering wakes you up naturally. Or I feel the rain on myself. It takes about a hundred yards to get going, to get your feet and legs going. Then I feel wonderful, so refreshed.'

But hang on a minute. What's to stop people doing the first day very fast, then sleeping overnight?

'You get retired if you stay more than two hours at a checkpoint,' said Keith. 'It's deemed not to be a continuous effort. The reason they brought that rule in was that runners used to run all day, be met by camper van for six or seven hours' sleep, then go again at first light.' Keith grinned conspiratorially. 'But what's to say you don't leave a checkpoint then sleep for three hours, then claim you got lost?'

Except if Keith claimed he'd got lost, no one would believe him. He's known for being an exceptionally good navigator. He spends a week before the Hundred recceing the entire route and goes round the old-fashioned way, with map and compass – no GPSs or Tracklogs for him.

He emptied out the contents of his rucksack and pointed to the Mini-Maglite torch he always carries along with the compulsory head torch. 'Because with a head torch you can't see stones so easily. Waterproof socks. Sealskinz. They've got neoprene in them. Gives them a sort of light, rubbery texture. I put them in my rucksack if I know there's a boggy bit at night. Pair of light trousers. I always wear shorts but I put them on at night when I get cold. Two laminated copies of the route description. Put one in the halfway bag so you've got a spare set. Dictaphone – I record the whole of the route description so I can listen to instructions rather than have to peer at them in the dark.'

Which brought him on to what was obviously a pet peeve.

'Limpets,' he said. 'Limpets are people who choose not to use their route description and use you as a navigational aid. They've no intention of navigating themselves. They follow seventy yards behind you in the background. You have to use anti-limpet tactics. Subterfuge. Mysteriously have to tie your shoelaces at frequent intervals. Develop a weak bladder. Get your clothes in and out of your rucksack. Phone home to check on a family crisis. Wait for a friend behind who isn't really there. Turn off your head torch, race ahead round the corner and lie in wait. That's a really mean one. If you like walking on your own you've got every right to,' he continued indignantly. 'Don't let on you've recce'd otherwise at checkpoints someone will say, "Follow them, they've recce'd."'

'We've come in with thirteen limpets before now,' interposed Shirlie.

'They sit and wait for you at checkpoints, watching for you to make a move,' said Keith. 'Solution – nip in and out of the checkpoint before they've realised it. You've got to have responsibility for your own well-being. Like you've got to know how to use a compass, you've got to know how to navigate at night.'

I could see being a limpet was bad form. And bloody annoying too, after all the effort Keith put in, like somebody plagiarising your work, or joyriding in your car. But Keith's stature as a walker is not simply down to his navigational skills. He is probably the closest we have to a Hundred chronicler and in 'Diary of a Common Man', his annual account of each one he's

Alan Blatchford, arguably the founder of the Long Distance Walkers Association's annual Hundred.

Ann Sayer, holder of the women's walking world record for Land's End to John O'Groats and pioneer of women's racewalking.

After finishing chemotherapy for bone cancer, Boyd Millen went up Low Man on crutches.

Jill Green and Graham Doke's purposeful stride and sunny demeanour suggest this must be the early stages of the 2005 Chiltern Hundred.

Thank you and goodnight: walkers on the 2005 Chiltern Landmarks Hundred leave a checkpoint and head off into the dark.

The stage of a Hundred when every single blade of grass is an assault on the feet.

The sheer melancholy of trying to force down a dry cracker, and the intense concentration required to insert a teaspoon inside the cup.

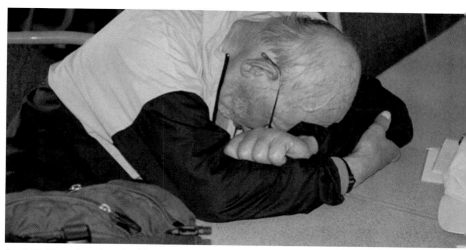

Post-Chiltern Landmarks Hundred oblivion.

Where Cole is king: Roger Cole proudly displays his badge and certificate for completing the 2005 Hundred.

Heaven is getting your boots off:
Ken Falconer rests his feet after the
2006 Northumberland Hundred
Marshals' Walk.

Groaning tables to feed the walkers at
Cleveland LDWA's checkpoint on the
Northumberland Hundred.

Exhausted
walkers find
a handy
Northumbrian
wall to slump
against.

Martin Burnell navigates stepping stones across a Northumberland river.

The later stages of a Hundred see many a walker's posture incline imperceptibly towards the horizontal.

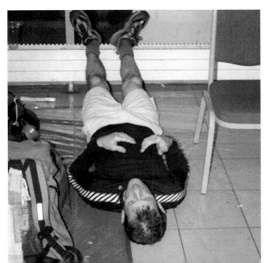

The Morgue – where Hundred finishers go to keel over.

Descending into Buckden on the 2008 Yoredale Hundred: our author Julie Welch is already in grimly determined mode, with thirty miles still to go…

Draughton Moor on the Yoredale Hundred: walkers set off in the gloaming on the last painful slog towards Skipton.

Still walking in the middle of the night.

A night-time checkpoint by a farm gate in the middle of nowhere. There are probably flying cars, a procession of nuns and a Shakespeare play being performed in full doublet and hose out there somewhere, for those semi-conscious enough to hallucinate them.

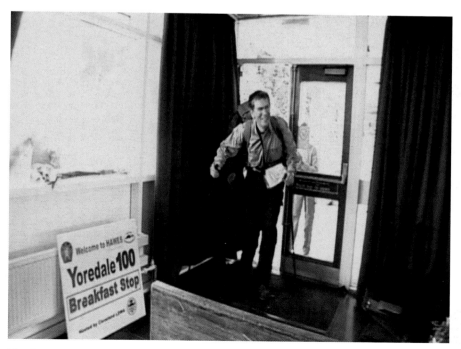

The finish of the Yoredale Hundred: John Walker is a curved but happy man as he makes it back into the Aireville School hall in Skipton.

A severely tilting Julie Welch, or is it Mrs Overall, completes the Yoredale Hundred in 38 hours 33 minutes.

Here's Gerald: the legendary Gerald Bateman impresses with finishing kick at the end of the Chiltern Landmarks Hundred.

Photographs by Steve Clark, Peter Morrill, John Cowburn and Martyn Hollingsworth.

done (nineteen at the last count), you get the whole experience, as viewed from the back of the pack, virtually mile by mile.

I really like these little records. They're unshowily written, but they give as true a flavour of what it's like to be on a Hundred as anything I've read. I like the mundane way they treat the extraordinary, and the way they make the ludicrous seem completely normal. Here's the 2006 Northumberland:

> 8 miles . . . Gorse alongside the College Burn was vivid yellow and smelt of coconut. Caught up the back of the field here . . .

> 12 miles . . . another steep climb to the Border Ridge. Very windy and nasty sleet shower for 20 minutes. Character building stuff! . . .

> 40 miles . . . Along Border Ridge to highest point on route at Windy Gyle (2030 feet). Very cold night.

It's the diaries that tell you most about Keith. He's not the demonstrative type. There's no exultation, no triumphant punching of the air when he arrives back at the hall. If you ask him what he feels, he says, 'Relief.' And in fact I don't think even Keith himself can explain why he puts himself through it, beyond describing it as 'an addictive but harmless habit'.

I took another look at 'Diary of a Common Man', this one for the 2003 White Rose:

> 29 miles, climbing up an enclosed lane from the hilltop village of Middlesmoor, following the dropping sun. Much bleating ahead as we caught up with a young man driving his sheep and lambs onto the fells. His Jack Russell was a bit wanting, so Jimmy and I assisted . . .

33 miles . . . Self clip point 2 (on isolated moorland) was manned by a young couple in a tent, happily listening to the Eurovision Song Contest . . .

75 miles . . . Just before arriving at Checkpoint 12, we passed a young girl playing with her scooter. 'Are you still walking?' she enquired. 'Yes we are.' 'Why?'

That seemed a pretty good question, in fact. Why is he?

'It's a great life experience,' says Keith. 'You see all facets of life on a Hundred. Including death. On the 2006 Northumberland someone died of a heart attack at forty miles. On the 1999 Durham Dales, someone dropped dead a mile from the start. But you can suddenly be ill just walking along the high street.'

And here's the Mid Wales Hundred:

32 miles . . . alone again on the most unremitting climb of the whole route . . . route diverted to avoid unexploded shell on original path up Harley Dingle . . . rumour was that the shell had been placed in an old tractor. What an adventure!

35 miles . . . Across the boggy moorland to the forestry plantation, caught up five more then, oh dear, four more torches way off to the left . . .

50 miles . . . Feeling very sleepy now . . . Skylarks started singing in Welsh . . .

67 miles . . . Rain had turned to horizontal sleet as I started ascent of Upper Esgair Hill . . .

69 miles . . . Managed to stay on my feet but was starting to shiver . . .

75 miles . . . The wind and sleet coming from the north was unbelievable. Such noise and turbulence . . .

81 miles . . . Arrived at checkpoint number 12, at Craig Goch dam. The wind was whipping up the water on the reservoir's surface and waves were crashing into the top of the dam's wall yet here, on the only piece of flat ground for miles around, was perched precariously close to the water's edge our refuge. It consisted of several sheets of white canvas lashed to a framework of scaffolding with ropes. Inside, the whole thing rattled and shook in the wind, which found its way in through all the joints between the sheeting. How did it not blow away down the valley? I sat quietly, trying to take in this absurd situation . . .

As I read this, I started to realise why I enjoyed Keith's Hundred Diaries so much. It wasn't just that they evoked the random absurdity, grimness and comedy of life, telescoped into an intense 48 hours. They also told me what was important to him. Then I thought back to something else he had said: 'When you're on the Hundred and get to the first night, there'll always be someone at your pace. You keep seeing the same people over the first ten, twelve hours, so by then you can gauge the people around you so you can choose who you want to walk with through the night.'

I think it's this principle of choice – deliberately walking at the back of the pack, stubbornly defending his right to walk alone, ordering his universe the way he wants it – that is key to Keith. He is not a misanthrope. Neither is he inconsistent. For all his inveighing against limpets, whenever I've seen him finish Hundreds he's accumulated two or three more late finishers, the difference being that he's in company of his own choosing. On the Mid Wales, a man he'd never seen before in his life came up to him in the tented checkpoint at Craig Goch, thanked him abundantly for leading him safely over the top, then disappeared out again. Shivering, Keith decided to visit the public toilet 100 yards away to warm up under the warm air dryer. It wasn't working. After two miles of extreme cold, following his torch beam as best he could alongside the reservoirs, buffeted by wind, sleet and rain, Keith caught up with the man who had thanked him. They exchanged names and details, such as which football team they supported, and walked together the rest of the way.

YOREDALE HUNDRED 2008

9: Kidhow Gate (SD 830 834) to Hawes (SD 870 898)
Distance: 5.34 miles; Ascent: 346 feet; Descent: 1411 feet

Leave checkpoint to follow Pennine Way on track (10°) (do not follow tarmac through gate/wall). This track across the hillside is now followed for just under 2 miles to near Ten End . . .

The first two and a half miles are relaxed and easy. The wind drops as we descend. Then we leave the main track to branch right towards Hawes and, within minutes, I'm a bungling liability. My contact lenses are smeared in a kind of grey paste again. I can't see clearly ahead and the route description is reduced to blobs on a page.

Ten End. I'm trying to recreate it from memory; in my mind's eye, on the recce, we found the faint path without much difficulty by aiming for some cairns. Pretty easy to spot a cairn even in the dark, you would have thought – pile of stones, yes? No. This is a nightmare, a descent booby-trapped with rabbit holes, boulders, mini-ravines and spilling becks. My head torch throws faint bobbing moons on piles of masonry mysteriously accumulated in waist-high tibia-threatening mounds. I plod behind Brian, stumbling and swearing, over and around outcrops, rocky bits, boggy bits and sopping grass. Half an hour seems like a year. He could be throwing in a detour via Leeds city centre, or a visit to Nora Batty's cottage, and I'd follow him slavishly. I'm a limpet. So what.

Anyway, I'm not the only one who's in trouble. Head torches and beams form irregular pulsing patterns across the descent as walkers become confused in the weirdly moonlit darkness. People hesitate in desperate isolation, separated from the route by black gulfs which could be simple grass and stones or yawning chasms that will eat them up within five seconds of sticking one trembling foot out into the blackness.

I peer ahead. Find the broken wall. Have the broken wall on your left. Count the yards. One hundred and eighty yards, go through gate in crossing wall. Another broken wall. Cross the sodding thing. And here's another gate. And another bloody crossing wall.

Oh, praise be. My distorted gaze picks out fuzzy lights. It's Hawes. Ten more minutes, then we'll be sitting down eating breakfast.

Only it isn't ten more minutes. The lane that I fantasised led directly down to Hawes doesn't exist. This has to be the worst section so far. It's not difficult. It's just cruel. I keep thinking we'll soon be there – surely to God – and then comes a sadistic series of zigzags involving fannying about around the sides of zillion-acre fields, interspersed with gated wall stiles served up as painful reminders of how empty my leg muscles are. Meanwhile my mind taunts me with random images of tea, Weetabix, hot milk, bacon and eggs, toast. And here's another bloody lane. And another gated stile.

But at last we're on the road at Gayle. As we pass Wensleydale Creamery and Car Park I start to cheer up. Only a school drive and another car park to weave through and we're there.

It's two in the morning. In the primary school dining room there are children's paintings on the walls and massive blokes with manly arses perching hazardously on mini-chairs at Lilliputian tables. My friends Edith Moran and Eva Bowes are helping at this checkpoint. Sorry if I sound a bit dewy-eyed here, but if you want to know what the LDWA is about, this is it – two people who've been awake for 32 hours so they can hug your grubby body and feed it breakfast. They're so friendly and welcoming I feel like I'm Jimmy Stewart at the end of *It's a Wonderful Life*.

The whole of the Hundred is like this – checkpoints stuck into the route like little field hospitals formed of sympathy, footbaths and rice pudding, where kind people are waiting to ease your aches and pains and bestow on you thousands of calories, all home made. And each is instilled with a uniquely English tone of understated empathy and affection. Together they are more than just a collection of tents and village halls and schoolrooms and weird shelters, more than the sum of their parts. Imagine a drawing of the route and you can almost see the little refuges of genuine warmth, of eagerness to send you on your way cheered and comforted and braced up. Excuse me for sounding soppy but I can't think of any other sport – any other human activity – where you'll be met with such care and attention and knowledge of what you need.

At a wobbling child-size table I gulp tea, eat eggs, beans and sausages, munch toast upon toast upon toast. I feel fine now. I can see Brian wants to be off but feels obliged to stick around for me. I release him from his role as my minder. Off he goes into the dark.

In the women's changing room a couple of people doze, heads back, but I'm too wired to snatch a nap. I glance in the mirror. My face looks like a party balloon that's been tied on a door knocker for years. My cheeks and chin are sprinkled with dust and grit like grey hundreds and thousands. I put in some more eye drops, pull on new socks and a change of trainers. According to Keith Warman, if you get up and leave from the breakfast stop, you finish. So I get up and go. To walk another fifty miles. Which is fifty more than I've ever walked before. Ultima Thule and all that.

All this profundity before daybreak. I'm out of here.

Checkpoint 9: Hawes (Hawes Community Primary School) SD 870 898 – Breakfast & Baggage

Opens: 2030 Saturday; Closes 1100 Sunday
Distance: 52.24 miles; Ascent: 7241 feet; Descent: 6854 feet
Manned by: Cleveland Group
Indoor checkpoint with full services including breakfast & changing facilities

TWELVE
Behave

Strider I've produced as editor drops through 6,000 letterboxes around Britain. There are misspelt place names, typos, gaps, wonky photographs with inaccurate captions, strange superfluous dots in the Events Diary. It is a pig's ear, and I receive a phone call from Ken Falconer, the LDWA chairman.

'Obviously there were a few flaws,' he says, with the most massive understatement I've ever come across. 'Did you mean to run that feature across a whole page instead of in two columns?'

NOOOOOO! No I didn't! I just didn't have a clue what I was doing. I had been given a cumbersome Stone Age computer running some creaking version of Quark Express on which, I was aghast to discover, I had to typeset this magazine as well as edit it. I give some kind of stumbling justification and we agree that the next edition will be better.

And of course I am indebted to Ken. In the first two years of my *Strider* editorship, not only did I make hideous mistakes, I redesigned the magazine quite radically. The changes were abrupt, imperfectly executed at first and highly unpopular, culminating in one harrowing AGM where various Father Times and doughty old boots were out to get me. And this clever, decent man with the air of a prefect pre-empted them by standing up from the floor to speak in my support, which shut them all up because he was Ken.

Ken's status in the LDWA has nothing to do with the walking he does with such effortless rapidity, but with the longevity and competence of his service to the organisation. This extends over more than two decades and includes a stint as chairman during the most challenging period in its existence. He is currently, for the second time around, editor of *Strider*, and as the magazine was the reason for the LDWA's existence in the first place and as its co-founder, Chris Steer, was the first to hold the position, the editor occupies a place on high. Precise, unflappable, dynamic, with the common sense to keep things the way they are because they are known quantities, he is just the kind of person you want running things. And I'd say that of all the people in the LDWA this makes him the most important to its future.

Ken is keen-eyed and finely built, with dark, wavy, greying hair and the upright posture of a Highland dancer. His job is that of Professor of Applied Mathematics at the University of St Andrews, and he has written a number of textbooks on fractals, at least one of which is a bestseller. But in terms of what they mean to his life, you get the impression they come a very poor second to the LDWA and Hundreds. This is someone who, during a sabbatical year teaching at Oregon State University, did his own 100-miler along the Red River Trail on the date of the Hundred. 'I was feeling withdrawal symptoms. I had to do something that weekend so I wasn't missing out.' He takes part in a Hundred every year, either the main event or, more often these days, the marshals' walk some four weeks beforehand, since on Hundred weekends he is usually to be found organising and coordinating things at event HQ, often going two nights with precisely zero hours' sleep, with no apparent neurological *ritardando*. Sixteen years on from Oregon, when foot and mouth disease closed most of rural Britain but Scotland, where he lives, wasn't so badly affected, he spent the late spring Bank Holiday walking 100 miles of the West Highland Way. This is not, you have to say, someone who adopts a take-it-or-leave-it approach.

'I suppose it's an addiction,' he says. 'I couldn't envision a year not doing one. If for some reason or other I couldn't then that week I'd feel utterly depressed. Even if I'd broken my ankle or something I'd still want to be there helping.'

So what is behind this compulsion to collect Hundreds? Ken's theory is that it's a product of the mathematical mind. 'One thing that I've always felt very strongly about my walking is that I like an objective. I find it quite difficult sometimes to have the enthusiasm to go for a walk just for the sake of it. If I feel I've got an objective or something to achieve – a mountain or completing an event or even walking a long distance path over several days – that's motivating. Possibly mathematicians and scientists tend to think in that sort of way – they like precision. You like to be able to say, Right, I've got something to do – and then you've done it.

'There are a lot of mathematicians in the LDWA, and more generally in the walking family. When I was a student I belonged to the YHA group and the vast majority were mathematicians, scientists and so on. All the people who did arts subjects, I got the impression they spent all their time running political societies and talking about the meaning of life.'

I, of course, am one of those people who did arts subjects, and the more I talk to Ken the more aware I am of the chasm between our outlooks. Ken: sensible, realistic, highly capable, accurate, brilliant walker. Me: imaginative, given to wildly impractical ideas, bloody useless at everything Ken is good at – numbers, navigation, forward planning, walking very fast . . . I could go on. Instead, I'll use the Hundred Algorithm as an illustration.

The Hundred Algorithm was my idea. My original plan was to go to Scotland to talk to Ken (he lives near the university in Fife). But he is also Publications Secretary of the London Mathematical Society. He was going to be in London for a meeting and helpfully suggested that, rather than drag me all the way to Scotland, he would come to my house in south London.

OK, so a brilliant, rather shy mathematician who walks sub-30 hour Hundreds was on his way to visit. It felt like when I was six years old, having a boy round to play. How on earth did I deal with him? Get out the Meccano?

I thought instead that we could have a bit of a laugh by creating an algorithm to optimise my chance of completing. We could factor in random effects. It would be a way of leading him in to talk about all the stupid slapstick things that might have happened to him on Hundreds, like falling asleep and walking into a hedge on some featureless track in the middle of the night, or having to ask a yokel the way at six o'clock in the morning.

But of course nothing like this ever does happen to Ken on Hundreds because he's too good. He never has to ask the way. He's never the wrong side of a hedge. Or raving incontinently or throwing up or seeing things that aren't there or mistaking boulders for cows. He simply starts off, walks very fast, and comes back again.

'You'd be far better off reading my "How to Survive a Hundred" guide on the LDWA website,' he barks when I tentatively put forward the idea. And now I come to think of it, Ken has been known to take things quite seriously. I have a recollection of him on the Chiltern Landmarks Hundred, walking down the driveway of the college campus to the finish hall, on slightly tender feet, tired, grimacing slightly, but immediately cracking a cheesy smile of acknowledgement when he saw all the people waiting to welcome him in (after nearly 30 hours on the move, his first impulse, as ever, was consideration for others). Once he'd handed in his tally, Ken and I sat by the finish desk. It was next to the bar from which staggered a girl student very loudly and clumsily on the lash. Ken and I exchanged glances and started giggling. Suddenly, he drew his back up, ramrod straight. 'Behave!' he said.

The longer I talk to Ken, though, the more I warm to him and the more I begin to understand what makes him tick. He was born in 1952; his parents, both English teachers from fairly modest backgrounds, were in their mid-forties. 'I was probably an accident,' he explains. 'My brother was much older so I was more or less brought up as an only child.' His childhood, then, must have been pretty solitary. And in a south London-based family without a car, he grew used to walking for hours. 'In the Surrey hills, so I got to know them. I got the bus there on a Saturday. That was important to me. I enjoyed staying in youth hostels, discovering a freedom I suppose. Getting away from my parents. It was an adventure.'

He was a prodigy, too – he'd been 'keen' (his word) on maths since the age of four. 'I never had to decide what I was going to do. I walked into Cambridge with a scholarship, with very little effort. In the early seventies it was a strange environment because it was ninety per cent male.' As an impoverished student he joined the YHA there because youth hostelling was cheap and he could meet girls. He stayed on at Cambridge to get his PhD and a college fellowship, moving to Bristol in 1980 to take up his first lectureship. By then he was married; he and Isobel spent their honeymoon youth hostelling in Scotland.

A couple of years later, he entered the 1983 Snowdonia Hundred with his friend Tim Ambrose. He remembers it vividly: setting out in very heavy boots, not really thinking about what he was doing, certainly never expecting to finish. 'I was with other people and maybe I thought it was a social thing, but I was actually making an effort to talk to them so they probably thought me a bit odd.'

He followed them through a forest because they seemed to know the route – 'I'd never do that now,' he says, horrified. There was an old railway, tented checkpoints dispensing a lot of jam sandwiches, the sight of Caernarfon Castle in the distance – 'As the sun came up it was beautiful. For some reason I remember humming to myself "Handel in the Strand" by Percy Grainger. I've associated that tune with Hundreds ever since.

'From about the first forty miles I had quite bad blisters, but Tim had told me, "Blisters can't stop you walking, just ignore them," and I tried to believe that advice. With hindsight my footwear was stupid but I didn't really think about that.' At one stage someone pointed out Ann Sayer, the LEJOG world record holder: 'I felt very pleased with myself as I went past. The tremendous feeling of finishing one's first Hundred, I'll never forget that. I got the train back to Bristol and the next day I hobbled around, reliving it and feeling very content. I'd never been like that before.'

He certainly doesn't do anything as uncontrollable as hallucinate. 'I cannot imagine walking into the second night,' he says. 'I admire people who are able to. It's different from getting a plane to the other side of the world. In a sense you're missing a beat of the pendulum rather than a phase of it and I think your body can adapt to missing a night's sleep much better than having to adjust your body clock to being twelve hours different from what you're used to. I'm sure that there's a research project for psychologists in the effects of loss of sleep.'

There probably is, but what I really want to hear about is the mystery and magic of it all. That's Ken for you, though. A man who in his early thirties was so square that he was humming something ancient from the days of the Light Programme, and who is so given to understatement that he describes how he felt after an experience quite possibly akin to first love – in the way that, a quarter of a century later, he can recall it in such detail – as 'very content'. It's a restraint that comes through whenever he talks about his walking. He makes it sound mundane when it's obviously one of the most important things in his life.

It isn't only the walking, either. It's hard to think of anyone who's given himself more willingly to the LDWA over the years. In 1987, after Chris Steer pleaded for someone to take over the editorship of *Strider*, Ken stepped in for the statutory five-year term of office. 'I've always enjoyed writing. *Strider* is something one can take some pride in. I've written a fair amount of mathematical articles, which are probably read by about ten people. This is something that gets looked forward to by six thousand.' Getting the magazine out in that era was a matter of typing out handwritten pieces on a battleship of an IBM typewriter, and sticking them all down with Letraset headings. Unlike me, obviously, he arranged the photographs in the correct places. The printer was in Swindon and the delivery of Ken's first manuscript coincided with the birth of his son Ben: 'I got a lift to the station in the ambulance taking Isobel to hospital.' Again, you see how much it all means to him. Editing what outsiders would regard as a tinpot house magazine is the source of some of his greatest joy.

Meanwhile, he and Isobel were among a bunch of enthusiastic thirtysomethings who put on the 1989 Brecon Beacons Hundred. The way he talks about it now, you gain the impression that they were among the best times in his life. The event was organized by two LDWA groups, Bristol & West and South Wales: 'There was an inner cabinet of about six of us. I think we discovered later that four of us had PhDs. Putting that Hundred together was absolutely great. We had some crazy ideas but everything went perfectly on the night and I still believe it was one of the best-organised Hundreds. Isobel, who by then was about to have our daughter Jennifer, organised the marshals' walk. It was a very happy time. And that, with *Strider* as well, really brought me into the LDWA family.'

You suspect it's because for a time in his life he was part of the fun, mixing with people who were comfortably on his intellectual level but doing something that wasn't intellectual. In the same way, you wonder if the LDWA has become the equivalent of a great, sprawling, populous off-the-peg set of friends and relations for someone whose high intelligence makes it difficult for him to connect.

The idea strikes a chord. 'Certainly when I was in Bristol it did. I'm basically a shy person when it comes to strangers.' In fact, it reminds him of an old joke: 'How do you tell an extrovert mathematician? When you're talking to them they're staring at your feet rather than their own.'

Later, after a move to take up the professorship at St Andrews, he became LDWA chairman, only for one of the biggest crises in the organisation's history to erupt on his three-year watch: the outbreak of foot and mouth disease at the end of 2000 and the subsequent closure of the countryside to the public. 'It was a grim time. There was a long list of cancelled events. I'd had one or two plans for attracting new members but there was nothing to attract them to.

'In some areas, canal banks, beaches and coastal paths were available and some ingenious local groups managed to put on walks – Merseystride made a Blackpool to Lytham St Anne's thirteen-miler using the promenade and taking the tram back – but anywhere there were sheep, it was impossible. The route of the Lakeland Hundred was in a major outbreak centre and it was put back to August, then cancelled. On the committee we were walking a tightrope. There were members on one side virtually saying all walking should be stopped and that it was irresponsible just to travel to another area because disease might be transmitted. Some people said even roadwalking was unacceptable in the countryside. On the other side were people saying, "Look, there's no evidence that the disease is carried by walkers." When one particular event was cancelled, some people decided they were going to walk it anyway. I got some very aggressive calls from both sides.

'Another unpleasant incident was the organisation of an unofficial Hundred on the Norfolk coast, by private invitation. About twenty people did it. A lot of the committee were upset about this – they thought it was setting a bad example. The committee decided – against my better judgement – that I should write a formal letter of complaint to the organiser. It caused bad feeling and was certainly a mistake. One or two still bear a grudge against me. I should have controlled the committee better.'

By the time the countryside reopened, long distance walking was in a slump. Numbers taking part in events had been decreasing even before the foot and mouth outbreak. Now a lot of the regulars had either found something else to do or decided they were too old. The trouble was, there weren't enough people coming in to replace them.

Being LDWA chairman might have ended in frustration and disappointment, but Ken was never going to be uninvolved for long. Such was his energy and passion for the sport, he was soon back in the role he had already held once, editor of *Strider*.

When Ken reclaimed *Strider* from me, I had a sense of him taking down the posters I'd put in my room, painting over decorations that weren't to his taste and moving the furniture. Some page layouts reverted to how they had been before my time. He changed a detail of the masthead which had annoyed many but that I was too pigheaded to drop. After all, when you move into a new environment, you automatically personalise it. What struck me, though, was that the first *Strider* in his editorship was much more like one of the old ones. And in some ways I think that's the LDWA Ken hangs on to, the one that existed when he took part in his first Hundred, organised the Brecon Beacons Hundred and was taken in to the LDWA family.

Which is still recognisable as the LDWA of the seventies. For all its flirtation with online entry to events, and gussying up its website, the old-fashioned, often baffling paraphernalia of LDWA life is largely intact; the rites and rituals initiated in the seventies and eighties which even then would have seemed quaint and batty to some. You only have to attend its AGM to see how little it's changed: the country dancing, the dinner, with speaker and slide show, the three grades of walk (long, medium and short) on the Saturday, and the Sunday morning AGM itself where the same people usually stand up from the floor as they've done since the eighties, the people who want to keep it exactly the same as when they started. And you mess with it at your peril, because that's where the soul of the organisation resides. At the time, I didn't get it. Ken does.

Over the years since foot and mouth, the LDWA's problems haven't gone away, though neither have they worsened. Membership is holding up; renewals are, says Ken, 'extremely healthy'; and the weekend social walks put on by local groups have a strong following. But no one's getting any younger. The average age on Hundreds gets higher and higher, though as Ken points out, it's not just walking that has been affected. 'The traditional things that people did in my youth – hobbies and societies for almost everything, from stamp collecting to going to church – it's exactly the same for them. At the same time, running is more fashionable because it takes up less of your day.' There's a touch of contempt in his tone when he adds, 'Younger people think running is cool and walking isn't. I did That's Lyth a few months ago. I'm not a slow walker but I came 184th out of 300.'

It's obvious why runners are there – trail running is a growth sport. And LDWA traditionalists have had to lose their disdain for them now that a lot of events need their presence to stay afloat. Even so, some resistance remains. I'm not sure that Ken was being completely jocular when in an emailed response to a query, he wrote: 'Don't you think that compulsory lead ankle weights for runners would be a good idea?'

'If you look on other websites,' he says now, 'they refer to our events as "races", which is annoying. I have heard one National Committee member suggesting we change the name to the Long Distance Walkers and Runners Association.'

It would be a more accurate name, surely.

'It would,' he almost spits, 'be over my dead body.'

YOREDALE HUNDRED 2008

10: Hawes (SD 870 898) to Bainbridge (SD 933 901)
Distance: 5.22 miles; Ascent: 332 feet; Descent: 403 feet

Turn right again on what is the main street through Hawes. On your left you will pass The Board Hotel, The Crown, The Fountain & The Bulls Head pubs. Cross road when safe to do so . . .

It's coming up to four o'clock. I'm in a little group heading along the main street out of Hawes. I've no idea who they are, but their birdsong chatter is very pleasant. I take in looming street furniture, shadows and silence. On the edge of the skyline is day.

I feel fine now. A wave of purpose moves over me as we leave the tarmac behind and head for Sedbusk. Dawn breaks as suddenly as the snapping of a biscuit. There are eight of us. Introductions take place. I forget most of the names as soon as I've heard them but there's Albert, who's Eva's husband, a compact, light-footed pit pony of a man; there's Albert's mate Dave, who's fair and lanky; there's Les from Hampshire, who is disconcertingly bright-eyed and coherent.

Turn left up lane for about 45yds to turn right through gate towards Cams Houses. Follow this tarmac track for about 1300yds (passing through four gateways as you proceed). When track turns sharp left towards Litherskew, continue ahead on the grass towards a power pole . . .

And on we go, ticking off the miles, the dewy grass brushing and cooling our feet, till we reach a stile beside a small gate I remember from the recce. This bit is easy. It's two thousand yards of swishing along the trackbed of the old Wensleydale line from Northallerton to Garsdale Junction, while the sun starts to come up and burn off the dew.

I said I felt fine. Which I do. But I also feel a kind of strangeness, almost a deracination. Like how I felt on the first day at boarding school, in a strange place relying on strangers to get me by. Every breath of air is strange air. The light falls differently.

Why has boarding school come into my mind? It's that intimacy you get from being thrown into proximity with people you barely know, and suddenly realising you've got to sleep alongside them.

After going through a rusty metal kissing gate continue ahead for another 60yds to go through a second kissing gate in fence on your right. Bear left on path to go through gap stile in left-hand buttress of bridge over river. Turn right on road, crossing Yoredale Bridge over River Ure and continue uphill into Bainbridge . . .

It's the miles that do it. Distance wears away reticence like the sea erodes cliffs. You need to accumulate at least a hundred for full disclosure. Over the hours they spill it all out, committing all their secrets and confidences across fields, along footpaths, the intimacy better and deeper for not entailing tissues and hugs, the privacy intensified by the wide open air. Tread, tread, tread. Out it comes, the whole sex-love-loss-death thing: the mating dances, the young couple arriving late at a checkpoint because they've been re-consummating their marriage at the spot they first met; the old man who wants to hold hands all the way down the final hill. A man on his deathbed tells his walking companion of thirty years that she's the only woman he's ever loved. All the private anguish borne stoically and soothed by the journey of the Hundred: first wives eaten away by cancer when barely out of girlhood; sons of eighteen killed on motorbikes; men with dying daughters. This, I think, is what doing the Hundred helps you come to terms with.

Bainbridge. Wake up. I'm aware of feeling slightly queasy. When I sit down opposite Albert and Dave in the Temperance Hall I can't face food. Just more ProPlus. More painkillers. Then I raid the bowl of sweets.

I leave at the same time as Albert and party. 'You're welcome to pop along with us,' he says.

'No, no, I'll push on from here.'

All this tagging on to other people has got to stop. I'm going to make my own way and reconnect to the route description.

Checkpoint 10: Bainbridge (Temperance Hall) SD 933 901

Opens: 2200 Saturday; Closes: 1300 Sunday
Distance: 57.76 miles; Ascent: 7573 feet; Descent: 7257 feet
Manned by: Northumberland Group
Indoor checkpoint with hot/cold drinks and limited food

THIRTEEN
The Sweetest Thing

EARLY SEPTEMBER 2007 BRINGS THE
Northern walkers to the low fells south of the Lake District.
Conditions on Boyd's Kendal Skyline Memorial Walk are perfect
– the weather mildly sunny, the ground dry and springy. It's a
25-miler, and time to get some hills in. Not that Potter Fell,
Benson Knott, The Helm and Scout Scar would count as hills
to people like Boyd Millen, first person to complete a double
Bob Graham Round (a feat that entailed running the eponymous
72-mile sequence of forty-two peaks of the Lake District twice
in succession) back to back and the man who responded to
complaints about the beautiful but unsparing route he'd devised
for the 2002 Lakeland by retorting, 'What do they mean it's hard?
There weren't any hills. You went over mountain passes, but not
one top. If you'd wanted it hard, we could have made it hard and
put some hills in.'

So the Kendal Skyline was probably a long morning's ramble
to Boyd. It was certainly one of his favourite walks. After he died of
lung and bone cancer in 2006, Lilian, his widow, started putting it
on as an event for Morecambe Bay & Bowland LDWA, the group
she and Boyd founded and which she carries on running now.

Predictably, there are comedy moments: being pursued by
cows; having to duck under a line full of washing that hangs

over a footpath (some of the walkers claim it's been personally arranged by Boyd from up above). But there are jelly babies at the checkpoints – always a treat – and a fine spread waiting back at the Burneside Cricket Club, where along with other returning walkers I embark on the sublime moment that ends every event – when, having built a sandwich mountain on your plate, you sit down with a mug of tea.

I've come here to see if I can put together an honest picture of someone I never got to know, being awestruck by him to the point of being too shy to say more than a grovelling hello. His death, the day after his seventieth birthday, brought tributes flooding into *Strider* – from Ann Sayer, whom he supported on her End to End and Three Peaks challenges; from Jill Green, whom he coached to international success; from Bill Smith, with whom he became the fourteenth person to complete the Bob Graham Round in 1973, beating the fastest time for the sub-24-hour circuit thus far. In 1977 he achieved his pioneering double circuit, in 52 hours 30 minutes. He was one of the great long distance walkers, completing 28 Hundreds, including the first Downsman in 1973, sockless in his trademark cheap trainers. His joint first finish, with Keith Arnold, on the 1977 Downsman, was for a time the record. But it was what he achieved when he could no longer run that truly shows you the measure of the man.

He had the unmistakable stamp of a fell-runner – a little, rugged, sinewy man, with striking silver hair and craggy features. By the time I met him he was in his mid-sixties, but it was eye-opening the way he could still shift, with the perfect balance that only the very best athletes have. And he was about as yielding as a prison wall. He would never, as I've seen other organisers do, stop the clock at 47:59 on a Hundred so that a crippled-looking tilter could inch his way to the finish to claim his badge and certificate. On the 2002 Lakeland, Philip Powell, who was marshalling for Northumbria Group, remembers sweeping a walker towards the 86-mile checkpoint near Wythburn. 'A forestry track came down to it and I was going along it with Boyd and the walker, who was taking it a bit too easy for Boyd's liking. Boyd was trying to chivvy him along. If he'd had a cattle prod, he'd have used it. And as soon as we got to the checkpoint, Boyd took a pair of scissors and cut his tally off: "You're out."'

Even Lilian, his widow, says he was 'an absolute bully'. A teacher at a local school, she is a former Great Britain international who at one point held the racewalking world record for 50km. Now in her early sixties, she may no longer be a lean, mean racing machine but any resemblance to a cosy, grandmotherly figure is strictly illusory; there's fierceness here, and passion and tremendous mettle.

The home in Oxenholme she shared with Boyd still evokes his presence. The dining table is cluttered with event paperwork; there are trophies on the shelves; and Murphy, the elegant lurcher who used to accompany him around the fells, and Molly, a small rescued dog, mooch around the living room. 'Molly's dejected without Boyd,' says Lilian. That she must often feel the same way as the dog remains, Britishly, unsaid.

He was born in Coleraine – on Burns Night – in 1936 and raised in Liverpool, where he spent most of his working life as a stonemason, serving his apprenticeship on the red sandstone of Liverpool's Anglican cathedral and not leaving it till his marriage broke up and he went round the country wherever the work was. In the 1950s, his hobby was cycle racing; the first long distance walk he did was the 40-mile Keswick to Barrow road walk. He moved to the Lake District soon afterwards and pursued his love affair with the fells.

He married Lilian in 1980; it was her second marriage too. He had five daughters, she had three. And it's impossible to write about Boyd and yet ignore Lilian's achievements. The year they married was the year she did a 27-hour Downsman Hundred and joined him as a Bob Graham-er: 'I wasn't a runner but I knew the fells,' she says now. 'It was just a case of head down and go.

Problem was that the pacer who went the first three sections with me didn't think I was going to do it. He wasn't very encouraging, he kept stopping to talk to people, leaving me to find my own way.'

When she got to Dunmail, the waiting Boyd worried that she would be out of time. She told him she no longer expected to get in within 24 hours but she was going to finish anyway. They set off together. He was amazed at her speed and energy. 'What have you been doing all day?' he said. 'You're going like a train, woman.'

'Well, I can go like a train with you.'

She made it back within 24 hours, only the fifth woman to complete the Bob Graham Round. The following year, with Boyd's help, she became a racewalking international. 'I'd been to a couple of Hundreds with Boyd and told him I'd like to do a Centurion 100 the next year. Obviously I trained, and he entered me for the Leicester 100.' She only managed 60 miles, but the organisers asked Boyd which racewalking club belonged to. 'He told them I didn't, that I wasn't a racewalker.' So he took her on holiday to Edinburgh, where he recorded her times at an athletics track. They were impressive enough for a coach in Keswick to agree to enter her in a race.

She went to Morecambe for a 5km event, was left behind from the start line, but carried on, gradually reeling people in. 'I felt strong, you see, from all the LDWA walking I did. I remember coming up to the finish line thinking, "I can't pass that girl, I really can't pass that girl." So I was second.' Six months later, in March 1981, she was selected for Great Britain at the age of thirty-six. She went on to hold the women's world 50km record for nearly fifteen years, till Sandra Brown, another LDWA walker, took it off her.

By the time Lilian gained her Great Britain vest, Boyd could no longer run. An operation at Easter 1981 to fuse part of his spine after a back injury at work put a stop to that. Even so, told that it would be six weeks before he could walk a mile, it took him half that time. Not long after, on the late spring Bank Holiday of 1981 – the weekend of the Cumbria Hundred, he disappeared. 'Somebody told me he'd set off from the start. I went flying out in the car trying to find him. Anyway, sense had prevailed. He'd got back on the bus to Oxenholme. He got the first three or four miles into the Hundred but he realised perhaps it was a bit foolhardy.'

Boyd wasn't on the sidelines for long. Unable to run off his competitive instincts, he turned himself into a racewalker. In 1995, he became a British Centurion and then Great Britain's oldest international debutant in athletics, in the 28-hour Roubaix in France. The *Strider* obituary written by his friend Jim Bispham recalls him beating 'all the French men half his age on their own ground'. In 1996 he completed eight 100-mile walks. The first was at the end of January, a week after his sixtieth birthday. He paused on his way out of the front door and said, 'I might be a while.' Lilian answered, 'All right. See you later,' and heard nothing from him till four that afternoon when the phone rang. 'Hallo, sweet. Can you put some things in the car and come and look after me?' He was doing the Cumbria Hundred he'd missed out on in 1981. It was his birthday present to himself.

'I mean,' says Lilian, almost in wonderment, 'there was snow on every footpath. I went up Mardale and it was shot ice. I met him at Grasmere and one of my memories is of putting the kettle on at Dove Cray. It was so cold there was no way the kettle would boil. It was cooling down as quickly as I was boiling it.'

Jim Bispham, no mean Hundred-er himself, joined Boyd part of the way through. 'You couldn't see him in the snow,' he says. 'He just disappeared. Part way, he fell to his knees. I thought, something's happened to him. But he'd gone to sleep. Five minutes and he went off like he was possessed. He could walk and be partly asleep. I've been with him and he's bumped into a barbed wire fence occasionally because he's asleep. He's got alongside somebody, just like he's put his arm next to them so he's got a bit of support, and he's just carried on walking though he's asleep.'

Lilian wrote about Boyd's birthday hundred in *Strider* for April 1996. The piece reads like a love letter:

> I felt on top of the world. He had done it. Yesterday, with the weather, I could not imagine this outcome. He had had no problems except the usual sleepy patch and going off his food. His feet were perfect and, as many people know, Boyd never wears socks, just bargain basement trainers. At the finish all the others were to meet him. I just waited by myself, I wanted that time. I saw them all come into view, and a lump came to my throat. I was so proud of my man. He finished at 2:04, 29 hours and 56 minutes after leaving Kendal Castle in atrocious conditions. As I looked up to the castle now, the sun was shining and the sky was blue even though it was bitter cold.

In 1999 Boyd qualified in Holland as a Continental Centurion, and in 2000 in Melbourne as an Australian Centurion. There are a multitude of stories, too many to elaborate here, of how he helped others achieve their goals, but he was often to be seen on a summer Saturday night helping Bob Graham hopefuls over Helvellyn, his favourite section. The picture is clear; it's of a human being of indestructible spirit and stoicism, hard as a diamond, exacting in the standards he demanded of himself and others but with a heart as big as the cathedral he once worked on.

Part of the way through his sixtieth birthday hundred, Boyd had changed his route due to the very heavy snowfall, so the next weekend he walked the original 1981 Cumbria route with a few mates. 'Boyd's Birthday Bash' became a fixture; Boyd, Jim Bispham and Tony Bland from Keswick completed a winter hundred every birthday up to 2004.

'They just used to go out and do a hundred miles,' says Lilian. 'From here up to Keswick, combining a couple of Hundred routes. In winter you don't only have fourteen hours of darkness – once they had twenty-three hours of rain. "We saw somebody canoeing through the woods," he told me when he got back. It was part of the year's calendar. He used to lead a fifty, first Saturday in December every year. They would finish in about fourteen hours. He was a cussed little man, that's all. He just used to get on with it. He always said, the more you did, the more you could do.

'He suffered dreadfully from sickness in his last few years. He used to do hundreds on milk. On one of our local walks, I had someone with me in the car and as we were going along, they said, "Can you hear that noise? I think an animal's been run over." I said, "No, it's Boyd coming. He's being sick."

'We just used to accept it. It made him feel pretty rotten. But it didn't stop him, not till the last couple of Hundreds. He didn't finish the 2004 Exmoor.' She pauses. 'I wonder if the cancer had started by then. They said he'd probably had it quite a long time but he was so strong it didn't show.'

That year, Boyd couldn't finish his winter hundred. In early January 2005, on the day storms ravaged Cumbria and thousands in Carlisle were moved from their homes overnight, he observed to Lilian that he had a pain in his leg and thought he must have torn a muscle. 'And that was it. He had a year left.'

The moment he was out of hospital after his first treatments, Boyd started training again. He took himself up Skiddaw on elbow crutches. 'With me walking behind him crying,' says Lilian. But Boyd didn't only go up Skiddaw that day. Off he headed, up Jenkin Hill. She didn't catch him till the south top. When they set off down, he said, 'We might as well do Low Man while we're here.' They'd got quite a way up when they met a friend with his daughter, so they climbed Skiddaw again, coming down over Low Man, before Boyd suggested that they climb the neighbouring fell of Lonscale too.

Five months before he died, he completed the 68-mile annual Audax bike ride from Arndale to the Yorkshire Dales. 'I never really accepted he was going to die, even though I'd been told he would,' says Lilian. 'I think he accepted it but he never mentioned it.' She stops to think. 'The thing is, he was the driving force behind a lot of what I did and sometimes it meant more to him than perhaps it meant to me. I think that's the same for a lot of people. The person who's actually doing the things – you're simply getting on and doing it. It's just part of your life – doing the work, going out there, getting your head down. Somebody said to me once, "Fancy having a world record." And I said, "I never give it a thought."' She pauses again. 'He was a very hard taskmaster. But . . . it was worth it,' she says finally. 'He was really, really proud of what I did.'

As I leave Oxenholme, the setting sun turning the slopes of the southern fells pale green and gold, I think back on Lilian's story about her Bob Graham Round, and the pacer who didn't believe in her. It strikes me that Boyd was the opposite kind of man – if a woman had the ability and was prepared to tough it out, he would do everything in his power to help. There weren't many of those about in sport during the 1970s and 1980s.

For most athletes setting out to break a world record, the spur that drives them is the prospect of prestige, fame and immortality. This one was different. It was a world record driven by love.

YOREDALE HUNDRED 2008

11: Bainbridge (SD 933 901) to Stalling Busk (SD 916 901)
Distance: 3.55 miles; Ascent: 648 miles; Descent: 306 feet

Continue uphill for almost 200yds & at end of small lay-by as road bends left go through gap in stile wall on right in the direction of Semerwater (if you reach a road junction you have gone too far) . . .

I stand staring at the route description like a Neolithic cave painter trying to work out how to use PhotoShop. I know this is right. I remember it from the recce. What am I buggering about for?

Then I start doubting myself again. How long is *almost* 200 yards? Is this the right layby? Did I miss another layby when I was charging up the hill? Have I reached and passed a road junction without noticing? I try to recall the route we took out of Bainbridge on the recce, but all the laboriously annotated and memorised landmarks – the tumbledown outbuildings, the flapping posts on dusty noticeboards advertising village hall aerobics and ancient arthouse movies, the grassy slopes with their sentinel fingerposts and the River Bain on the right at the bottom of a steep runaway hill, the climb up the banking on to a path to get out of the nature reserve – they've all tumbled into the oubliette my brain keeps specially for topographical detail.

This is all the result of hubris. I left Albert and party behind outside the Bainbridge Temperance Hall. I had fresh energy from raiding the bowl of sweeties and I used it to jog in a rather superior way out of the village. The air was cool and fresh, the sun warm on my bare arms, it was fantastic. And now it isn't. Nemesis has ensued. My punishment for showing off is that I'm completely alone. Six in the morning in bucolic Yorkshire.

All the times I've been lost pass before my eyes, like I'm drowning. Kent orchard, pinging up and down the rows of apple trees like a trapped pinball. Surrey, Puttenham Common, trying to block out a woman with strange floaty orange hair who was having hysterics because we couldn't work out the meaning of *In 700y ignore L fork and in 50y, before tall trees, TL (130°)*. Kent again, seduced by an Austrian pastry chef into turning *L* instead of *R* because he assured me he knew the way, blundering as a result up and down miles of forestry track, ending up at a barbed wire fence and having to go all the way back to where I started. Missing the turn on to a bridleway in Essex and ending up shouting like one of those crazies who have arguments with invisible people as they walk down the street.

And in a way I was having a crazy argument, with myself, about my inability to navigate. About how some people – probably just me, actually – are neurologically incapable of getting it, that after a few hours the necessary part of my brain goes offline and no longer connects what I read on the route description with what I see around me. The words themselves stop signifying. Layby-wall-stile might just as well be parsnip-drug mule-lederhosen. Bah!

'You all right there?'

It's Albert and his little flock, coming up behind me. They hop over the stile and I follow them. I follow them uphill and down across the dappled grass. I follow them past broken walls and stunted trees, making a show of keeping abreast of the route description. But it's no good, I've lost the will to consult it now. I'll just keep it rolled up in my hand in case I need to swat anything or blow my nose on something.

At Stalling Busk, Tony Willey, the LDWA chairman, is stationed outside as greeter. 'Did you have a lot of trouble with the wind?' he says bonhomously.

'No more than usual!' we holler.

Checkpoint 11: Stalling Busk (Village Hall) SD 916 858

Opens: 2300 Saturday; Closes: 1500 Sunday

Distance: 61.31 miles; Ascent: 8221 feet; Descent: 7563 feet

Manned by: North Yorkshire Group

Indoor checkpoint with hot/cold drinks & food

FOURTEEN
This Walking Life: December 2007–March 2008

Sun Dec 30: 7th Stansted Stagger

25ml in 10hr. From URC Hall Stansted, GR TL513249. Start 8.00 onwards (runners 10.00 onwards). Entry: £4 (non LDWA £5): late entries up to Dec 27 by phone & email, £1 extra. Incl cert, 1 Cp giving drinks, cakes & sandwiches. Mugs must be carried. Drinks & snack meal at finish . . .

Strider,

The Journal of the Long Distance Walkers Association December 2007

FOR MOST PEOPLE IN BRITAIN, THE WINTER holiday brought everything to a standstill. For long distance walkers, it was the chance to enjoy a combination of Christmas celebrations and their favourite activity. December 2007 *Strider*'s 'Groups Social Walks Programme' included Beds, Bucks & Northants' Tring a Ling a Ling of Xmas Bells ('starts at Tring Central car park, carol singing at churches on the 15-mile route'). Kent Group offered Graham Smith's 14-mile Christmas Cruise

Around Calais. Led by Peter Saw, London Group was putting on Peter's Christmas Walk, an annual 21-miler that visited the Brixton Windmill, 'the last windmill in central London'. Arthur Read of The Irregulars was to lead a 13-mile Boxing Day Walk around Haworth. For East Yorkshire Group, John Davis, the near-octogenarian journalist, was putting on his annual Twelve Dales to Christmas, a special off-footpath walk around Langtoft that, like many designed by John, eschewed the public footpath network in favour of private land over a route negotiated with local farmers.

'Farmers are the least Nimby of our population,' said John. 'As long as they know who you are, what you're doing and when you're doing it – that's it. They'll join you. We deal on a one-to-one basis, purely one chap to the next. As you talk to each farmer, word gets around. I do less walking these days than sitting around farmers' kitchens putting the world to rights. Farming's a lonely job, so someone who shares their interests is welcome.'

On other pages of *Strider*, 'News of Long Distance Paths & Challenge Walks' featured nine new long routes including the 105-mile Yorkshire Water Way, the 130-mile South Kesteven Round in Lincolnshire and the 60-mile Mid Wilts Way.

In 'Grit on the Hundred' John Walker wrote about Betty Lewis, the 74-year-old who had beaten Elaine Edwards's record to become the oldest female to complete a Hundred.

Other articles included one by Reg Kingston, *Strider*'s medic-in-residence, on 'The Hundred Breakfast Stop', and Ken Falconer's 'How Long is a Walk?', which dealt with measuring a walk using Von Koch fractals.

'Past Events' contained reports of the 62-mile Bullock Smithy Hike and the 45-mile Across Wales Walk (both on the first weekend in September), as well as an organisers' view of the 50-mile White Cliffs Challenge in Kent, by Graham Smith.

'Reports on Social Walks' included, from August, Essex & Herts LDWA's Onward Pilgrim Walkers, 45 miles of St Peter's

Way starting at Chipping Ongar at 4.30 in the morning and finishing the same day at the chapel of St Peter's, Bradwell, on the River Blackwater. Among the walks done by The Irregulars in July was the 20-mile Sherwood Foresters Memorial Walk from Matlock Bath station car park, visiting eleven war memorials to the Sherwood Foresters Regiment.

Also contained in the latest edition of *Strider* was the booking form for the annual AGM, which that coming March would take place at a hotel in Frodsham. As ever there were a choice of three walks on the Saturday, of 21, 17 and 10 miles. The form contained the promise: 'There will be barn dancing'.

In the Events Diary, Surrey LDWA offered two thirties and a fifty for Yoredale Hundred entrants – January's Winter Tanners, February's Punchbowl Marathon and, in March, the Surrey Tops. Marches LDWA's South Shropshire Circular, a phenomenally popular 25-mile hilly route based on Shrewsbury, had, as usual, EVENT FULL stamped over it. Northern walkers could look forward to Lilian Millen's Lunesdale Walks, '28, 17 or 6ml in 9 1/2hr from Arkholme C.E. Primary School, in the lovely Lune Valley by river, farmland, fps, tks & lanes. Afternoon tea & baked potato at finish, provided by school parents.' Norfolk & Suffolk LDWA were putting on the 27-mile Daffodil Dawdle, based near Newmarket and promising 'rolling countryside with studs, woodland, arable and pasture on Suffolk/Cambs border'.

Meanwhile, I'm one of some ninety walkers and runners setting off on a mild, light early morning on the cusp of the New Year on the Stansted Stagger. As ever, I get lost trying to find the right exit off the M11, the last five years flashing before my eyes in a compacted blur of pre-dawn diversions round Stansted Airport, the circulating of various roundabouts, a detour by mistake to Takeley or Bishop's Stortford. Shortly afterwards I get lost again, on the first 300 yards of the route. After rushing past Keith Warman, who has stuck to his habit of being last to leave the hall, I take the wrong fork and am half a mile up the lane before I realise my mistake. This, I hardly need add, is an event I take part in every year. I should know the first mile as well as I know the route to my local Tesco.

I keep going for a while, thinking there's bound to be a nick across the fields from where I can rejoin the track. There isn't, so in the end I go back almost to the start. I say hallo again to Keith. He lets my second coming pass with a polite nod.

I spend the second half of the event with Brian Harwood, who keeps up a steady pace and is good company. As ever, you find out more about a person in the peace and privacy of the open air. I learn that he was a water engineer until made redundant at fifty. 'It's sad your working life is cut short when you've trained for it.' Now he devotes most of his time to walking; in the run-up to the Stagger he's done the Burley Bridge Hike in Yorkshire (doubling that with the Steppingley Step the next day), the Gatliff Marathon and the Round Rotherham. The only weekend he hasn't taken part in an event is over Christmas. He has done seven Hundreds and completed six. His best time was on the White Rose: 33 hours 45 minutes. The one he'd failed on was his second, the Lakeland: 'I tried to go off too fast and I paid the penalty. I gave up at thirty-five miles. I used to work in Africa and there was a fight to get on the body buses just like the crowd surges they had there.'

I run the last mile in fading December sunlight, a new crop of toe blisters bursting in a sharp, searing sequence. Back in the United Reformed Church Hall I have baked beans on toast, half a dozen date balls and nine slices of tea loaf, weighed down with butter as if in an effort to stop them flying away. It's like coming home from school; you're given tea, asked about your day by people genuinely interested, not because they've been paid to do so, and you've got your friends around you. It's the only time in adult life this sort of thing happens to you. In a way, I'd like to freeze the frame right here.

YOREDALE HUNDRED 2008

12: Stalling Busk (SD 916 858) to Buckden (SD 942 772)
Distance: 6.87 miles; Ascent: 932 feet; Descent: 1220 feet

Leave checkpoint & turn left to retrace steps to road junction where fork right uphill. After 100yds turn right into enclosed track (Bob Lane). Proceed with care, it is quite rough in places . . .

This is the worst climb of the whole sodding Hundred. I'd rather be back on Ingleborough. It's not even a proper climb. There aren't any views, just yard after yard of foot-shredding crapness. First it's big cloddy stones the size of motorbike helmets. Next it's little shiny stones as glittering and sharp underfoot as broken trinkets. Then it's a long, long haul over Stake Moss, silver coloured and exposed, with a wide track bordered by green and grey nothingness.

Never mind. We've got a train going. There's Albert and Les and someone called John and Albert's friend Dave from Cleveland, and in front of us and behind us other little bunches of people. We're going too fast for some; they fall back. And I still don't feel tired. Not exactly. Except I'm not running now. I'm strictly walking. Technically I can still jog a bit – having a bit of bounce left, albeit fitful – but from this point on it's impossible to muster yesterday's pace. Frankly, I'm pretty desperate to pay a visit, too. I motor along, ahead of the pack, scanning the horizon, but it's completely bare of hedges and tree trunks. I can just about go fast enough to keep ahead of the pack. In the wretchedness championships, nothing beats mile upon mile of teeth-gritting, buttock-clenching awfulness during which you have to exchange small talk.

Look on the positive side. You feel so bad it's keeping you awake.

You could be . . .

. . . attending a timeshare presentation . . .

. . . assembling a bookcase using instructions translated from the original Chinese . . .

. . . fleeing through Canary Wharf pursued by giant Siamese cats with killer laser beam functions where their eyeballs ought to be . . .

. . . No, it's no good. I'd actually rather be at an Osmonds comeback gig than here. And now we're nearing one of the dodgy bits I remember from the recce: the crossing of a descending road with a sharp S-bend to reach a stile positioned at the exact middle of the S. So now there are two things for me to worry about: shitting myself and getting flattened by killer tractors. Great.

I stomp along the descending track into Buckden, heroically negotiating a gate in increasing gut discomfort. Another long, long hike to find Buckden Village Institute. But it's light and airy and welcoming once we arrive, and they're showing cartoons on the floor of the ladies' lav. Mickey and Donald and Goofy and Popeye and Bluto, all squirming and cavorting and jiggling about in old-fashioned black and white on the terracotta tiles. There's a whole Disney-themed programme going on. Amazing. How do they do it? Maybe it's some form of computer-generated image. From a projector cunningly embedded in the light fitting. I wonder if the village was awarded some kind of grant to install it, or whether the helpers brought it with them when they set up the checkpoint.

Back in the main hall, a man with a lovely kind face and a bright blue sweatshirt that says 'Staffordshire LDWA' brings me a warm, mildly salted bath flannel to eat. 'It's a Staffordshire oatcake,' he says.

I wolf it down. Just as we're about to go, my friend Julian Pursey arrives. Julian who I did the night section of the Surrey Tops with, back in March. My old mate, my brother, my comrade in the battle to find our way out of a ghastly black hole in the landscape called Jelley's Hollow! I greet him with reckless effusion, as if he's returned to the UK after months being held hostage by terrorists in some jungle hideout. Albert bustles us out into the day.

Checkpoint 12: Buckden (Village Institute) SD 942 772

Opens: 0100 Sunday; Closes: 1800 Sunday
Distance: 68.18 miles; Ascent: 9153 feet; Descent: 8763 feet
Manned by: Staffordshire Group
Indoor checkpoint with hot/cold drinks & food

FIFTEEN
The Winter Tanners Man

THE ONLY SIGN THAT AN EVENT WAS TAKING place was the man checking people in at a folding table under a street lamp. The place was devoid of any sense of occasion. Lights on the adjacent station platform were ringed with vapour. The walkers, hats pulled down over their ears, collars up, looked like a get-together of housebreakers, not participants in a famous old event. Someone rummaged furtively in the boot of a car.

The place was Leatherhead Municipal Car Park, the occasion the 2008 Winter Tanners, organised by Surrey Group. *Strider's* description of it – 'tough, with minimal support, no facilities at start and finish, not even toilets' – wasn't enough to stop 111 people from turning up on a dark Sunday morning in mid-January. Two of them, Keith Chesterton and Ian McLeod, were walkers of some eminence: Centurions, as was John Westcott, who was checking people in. John and Ian have more in common; they were born within six days of each other and educated at what was then known as blind school. Both are partially sighted.

I was filled with a sense of a vanished age as I stamped my feet to warm them in the dank, vaporous midwinter darkness. There were no cups of tea, no loos, nowhere to sit. The Winter Tanners is the LDWA in its time-warped glory – biscuits and cold drinks at open-air checkpoints manned by shivering marshals, a route across the commons and along the tracks of rural Surrey. The event is substantially unchanged since its origins in 1976 as a winter walkout of the route for the Tanners Marathon the following July; the people who walked it became the first Surrey Group.

Dawn broke through as we headed out of town into the countryside towards the first checkpoint, Friday Street. The route was undemanding, which was just as well as it was unfamiliar to me. In fact it was unfamiliar to everyone, because John Westcott devises a new route every year, but the others appeared not to share my incompetence at navigation.

Things were still going well when I reached Friday Street, behind the runners but in front of the walkers. But outpacing other entrants was one thing, going in the right direction another. A detour up the wrong track added an extra half-hour to my time. Back on route, I was now halfway down the field and so worried about getting lost again that I'd stop and pretend to hunt for my water bottle while sneaking an over-the-shoulder half-glance to see if people were still following. Then, because I didn't want them to think I was using them as a navigational aid, I would wait till they were out of sight before setting off again.

I wasn't last by any means when I reached the 24-mile checkpoint at Ranmore Common, but I was late enough for there to be no more tea in the pot for the shivering marshals to pour me, so I had to make do with very cold orange juice and a couple of dull biscuits that everyone else had rejected. And then, as the afternoon and the miles wore on, as the overcast sky turned to the faded grey of dusk and I found myself completely alone at the end of a bridleway, I came to the set of barriers I was looking for, checked again – don't be such a ninny, the route description does say *barrier*, followed by *cross RD* – and crossed RD. I found myself on a common out of which sprouted great tufts of knee-high grass and went thrashing over it to *Pass seat on your R and 100Y later, FR to pass next seat on your L*. And a whole

lot of other stuff (the light was fading) of which I could make out
SCULPTURE.

I wasn't completely sure of my bearings. Nor was I sure what
constituted SCULPTURE, but I found something I thought matched
the route description – a little grassy triangle with something in
it that might, I decided, strike some people as possessing artistic
merit rather than being a mere lump of wood. There was also
a wide track that I seemed to remember following with Merv
Nutburn two miles out from the finish of the summer Tanners.

Relief breathed fresh fire into my legs. I set off along it in the
rapidly falling darkness. I didn't remember the tall fence posts on
one side but that didn't mean they hadn't been there. Half a mile
further on, the fence posts ended and I was running between lines
of tall trees. I could see the lights of Leatherhead spread out in the
valley below. Great, I thought. Even if I'm off route there's sure to
be a track leading down from here.

There wasn't. I doubled back and trained the dimming light
of my head torch on the route description. Nothing had changed.
It still said the same thing. The wind had whipped up now. I
had to force myself to get a grip, remind myself that I was in
Surrey, not on Annapurna, that just because it was dark here and
a little isolated I wasn't likely to encounter the Dorking Yeti. I
took my mobile out to dial the emergency number. There was,
of course, no service available. I retraced my steps to the edge
of the common, staring at the barrier and peering at the sweat-
crimped route description again, wracked by doubt. Was that the
right barrier? How did I know there weren't other barriers up the
road? I mean, barriers – not what you'd call unusual phenomena
in rural areas.

I started thrashing my way back across the common.
Leatherhead. It must be over there somewhere. If I kept going,
I'd find it eventually. And if I didn't, there'd be another town
somewhere – they were all over the place in Surrey.

There's no point going on about the next hour of stumbling

backwards and forwards in the long grass, past the soughing trees, shivering and trying not to cry. I'll cut to the moment when something caught my eye – bobbing lights travelling in a parallel line in the opposite direction. Three more lost walkers. I lurched across to join them. And then, another hour and a half later, after a long, sheepish trek alongside the A24, we found ourselves back at Leatherhead Municipal Car Park. What a wonderful sight. It's not often you'll hear someone say that.

'I'm surprised you got lost with one of my route descriptions,' John Westcott said with mock severity some six months later, when we met in the genteel surroundings of the tea rooms at Greenwich Park.

John is tall and in his early seventies, though his curly black hair is barely streaked with grey. The big round glasses with heavy black rims he wears for the congenital cataracts that have meant lifelong partial blindness make him instantly recognisable. Never married, he still lives in the house in Chobham in Surrey to which his family had moved from East Dulwich when he was a boy, and in which he stayed to care for his widowed mother. But 'bachelor and retired civil servant' isn't, maybe, the most fun-filled way to introduce someone. I preferred my friend Avril's rather old-fashioned description of John as 'a super person'. He is that – courteous, gentle and drily humorous. And to get a proper handle on the LDWA, he is the essential person to talk to.

I'd contacted John to learn more about the first years of the LDWA, of which he is one of a gradually diminishing band of surviving early members. He didn't, in fact, take part in the first Hundred; it was November 1973 when he joined (he has the civil servant's precise memory), and that because the ad he saw in *Climber & Rambler* gave a Chobham address. 'I lived the other side of the village to Chris Steer. It was ten minutes' walk over the fields to his house.'

At the time it turned out not to be quite what he wanted: 'In fact I was in Edale on the Saturday of the 1974 spring Bank

Holiday – day one of the Peakland Hundred. I was about to embark on my first Pennine Way and I remember saying to my sister Olive, "There are some mad fools in the area who are doing a hundred-mile walk – walking overnight if you can imagine it."' But as he lived so close to Chris Steer, he ended up helping to prepare *Strider*, which was then a cottage industry. 'I used to monitor those entitled to receive *Strider*, address the envelopes and supervise the evenings when the local members came round to put the *Striders* and inserts in the envelopes.'

After that he began helping to organise Hundreds – the 1980 Downsman, the 1982 Pilgrims and the 1986 Downsman Marshals', for which he was overall organiser. 'I think I can claim to be the first one to organise anything which could be described as a formal marshals' walk before the actual event.'

He didn't walk many Hundreds; those in which he took part were mainly marshals' events, in the pre-1986 days when they were route-proving exercises undertaken by only two or three people and catered by one man with a frying pan halfway round. But he did participate in the 1977 Downsman, the 1979 Dartmoor and the 1982 Cumbrian: 'On the last two it rained like hell. It just seemed the thing at the time, although I can't say they were really what I wanted to do. I preferred the 100kms – the Surrey Summits, the Three Forests Way, the Wealden Waters. I also enjoyed the Centurion races I did in England and Holland, though for me it was definitely more the taking part than the winning. Perhaps it was just that a hundred-mile cross-country walk meant staying out longer than I like.'

He helped out at many other Hundreds. We expect creature comforts these days. John and his contemporaries did their Hundreds in an era before indoor checkpoints, where the walls are lined with chairs and there are warm, clean toilets and bowls of rice pudding and fruit salad from which you don't have to fish out fallen leaves or drowned midges before you eat. But it was when he talked about the innocent, bygone days of roughing it and making do that his eyes brightened and he beamed with nostalgic pleasure.

'The 1983 Snowdonia Hundred,' he said. 'Dan Hadfield and I were helping on the Pontnewydd checkpoint, which was in a nice little glade around the eighty-mile mark. It had rained, so one of our fellow helpers, a man called John Robinson, rigged up a tarpaulin. He was one of life's survivors – whatever the situation he could solve a problem. He was famous for his barbecues – he had a cast iron container and he built a fire around it, using wood he'd gathered. He tried to provide, even if it was dried-out teabags. It was the sort of checkpoint I liked. It was going most of the day. We had our little tents that we slept in over two nights, and that were made available for any walkers who wanted a sleep. It was really lovely.'

'But anyway,' he continued wistfully, 'by the time of the next Snowdonia Hundred, in 1987, things were already different. Our checkpoint was half a mile away from the glade, in this filthy old sheep pen. We had a radio, which was Only Speak If You're Spoken To. Interrupting wasn't allowed. But halfway through it was obvious other checkpoints were having difficulty getting HQ, and I interrupted: "I can hear both of you." We became a relay station. Everybody at the checkpoint wanting to talk on the Radio. People busting to go to the lav wouldn't go because they didn't want to let go of the Radio.'

He could still reel off where the checkpoints were on the 1977 Downsman, too. They varied from the tables out in the open to the glories of Checkpoint Three: 'HMS *Mercury*. Shore-based. The navy did us proud with a big marquee.' The breakfast stop was at Steyning AC: 'That was the only one that was under cover. At Ditching Beacon, it was very windy. The Essex & Herts tent nearly hang-glided away. Southease – Itford Plain, a lean-to at a farm. British Airways Walking Club helped out there. Bo-Peep Farm – an old glider hangar at the end of a road leading down to the A27. Jevington checkpoint, the last, was in somebody's garage.' He smiled. 'I'm from the old school. The pioneering days. Tents and tarpaulins.'

But John's longest spell in the LDWA's service – and, a lot would say, his most worthwhile – has been spent with the Winter Tanners. That came about, John said, because Alan Blatchford had over-committed himself; less than a month before the Tanners Marathon, he would find he hadn't yet walked out the route. 'So he decided that in January, come what may, he'd do it with a few friends, and that became the Winter Tanners.' Blatchford also thought the Summer Tanners was becoming a little too easy – 'so he suggested doing it in winter conditions'.

John has been devising the route and producing the route description for both events since 1978, and for thirteen years after Blatchford's death in 1980 he also took on the organisation of the Winter Tanners. 'When I took over, my attitude was to leave it in a time warp. But Alan would look round, see who had entered, and write their names down on a piece of paper on top of his car, whereas I did introduce a bit of formality, in the shape of entry forms.'

John would draft a route description, give it to his checkers, then check the route again himself a month before the event. While Alan Blatchford was in charge, he asked John to waymark the summer Tanners Marathon route with yellow markers, another job he had been doing ever since. He used to do it by himself the Saturday before the event, 'when I was good', starting at four in the morning and finishing at nine in the evening. The next day, after the runners' start, he would set out and take the arrows down, catching up the slower walkers for whom he would act as sweeper. It takes him a couple of days now, and his sister helps him. 'Still, we don't have to go to work any more.'

My first reaction was that there was something touching about the way John keeps the flame burning by his efforts. Here's a man, I thought, who is the living history of the LDWA. Then I realised that any sentimental attachment to times past was irrelevant. It wasn't nostalgia but necessity. The only way people like me could enjoy the Tanners and Winter Tanners was because, when the cold was biting, the ground was sodden and the sky was bleak, an elderly man was prepared to make a route for us and spend two days putting up and taking down waymarks. He isn't a larger than life character, this self-effacing, sweetly droll bachelor. But he is a lionheart in winter.

YOREDALE HUNDRED 2008

13: Buckden (SD 942 772) to Kettlewell (SD 969 723)
Distance: 4.48 miles; Ascent: 334 feet; Descent: 434 feet

Follow riverside path with the River Wharfe on your left. Continue for 1020yds going through gates where necessary & observing the notices to keep to field edge path (be warned – cutting the field corner is a deviation from the rules of the event) to reach finger post . . .

It's coming up to ten-thirty. I'm on automatic, trotting along with the group, nodding and saying, 'Yeah, that's right,' when they consult the route description. We're meant to be on the Dales Way, following the river. There's something with water in it on the left, so I guess we're going the right way.

The path is attractively scattered with miniatures. There are men in bouffant periwigs, women with big white hair. I tread carefully, trying to avoid stepping on mini-barristers. A dream trove spills open. Ancient coins glint and melt, stones writhe and crawl, melting like pale tar, tree roots turn into copper piping which dissolves into snakes. Strangely padded leaves pop and ooze golden syrup under my trainers. Melting pools of gilded gloop with eyes. Crikey, I think I'm trapped in one of the more purple passages of an Iris Murdoch novel.

Dazed, I follow Albert and party into Kettlewell Village Hall. It's midday. I line up at the food platters laid out before us on a huge refectory table, and take a tuna bap. I stare at it. I know I've got to eat but the painkillers have acted like paint stripper on my stomach lining.

For God's sake, eat it. It's not a kangaroo's testicle.

One mouthful is all I can manage. Then I swallow another handful of ProPlus and have another try at coaxing water out of the drinking bladder. It's a failure. But I'm not giving up now, so there's no point worrying about any of it.

Checkpoint 13: Kettlewell (Village Hall) SD 969 723

Opens: 0200 Sunday; Closes: 2000 Sunday
Distance: 72.66 miles; Ascent: 9487 feet; Descent: 9217 feet
Manned by: Kent Group
Indoor checkpoint with hot / cold drinks & food

SIXTEEN
A Special Breed

LATE. I WAS GOING TO BE LATE. BEHIND THE wall of hawthorns where I wedged my car I could just make out a sliver of misty pasture. On my right, across the road and behind the low fence of Witley Recreation Ground, the 2008 Punchbowl Marathon had already set off with a rush of walkers, a strange parade of thermal hats, humped rucksacks, boots, trainers and Lycra, floating over the frosted grass, stretching out legs, peering at Garmins, threading through the gap in the corner towards Surrey's heaths and commons. Hurriedly I checked in and raced off to start hauling in the back markers.

The Punchbowl Marathon is a long-established event with a 30-mile route that includes the Devil's Punchbowl, Kettlebury Hill, Crooksbury Hill and parts of the North Downs Way. It's much liked by both runners and walkers, even though most years it's a mudbath. In contrast, that February Sunday was blessed with mild sun and an overnight frost that had crisped the usually soggy, slippery going. I could imagine that plunging into and out of the Punchbowl at full pelt would normally be a perilous exercise, but that day it was a joy to plummet down it alongside some 150 others swarming into the hollow, then struggle up the other side.

In the exhilarating rush I forgot the anxieties that had

begun to dog me about the Yoredale, such as uncertainty over whether I'd last the whole distance and plain fear of meeting my death through something as bathetic as being hit by a car while staggering half-asleep across the A65. I'd set myself a target for the Punchbowl that didn't seem too ambitious. My aim was not to get lost and, predicated on that, I hoped to complete the event considerably quicker than the 11 hours 17 minutes it had taken me to grope my way back to Leatherhead in the dark on the Winter Tanners.

After another couple of hours my syncopated run-walk-run brought me level with Martin Burnell and Graham Smith, editor of the *East Kent Mercury*. I was red-faced and streaked in sweat; they seemed to stroll effortlessly. We exchanged the usual pleasantries.

'Looking forward to the Hundred?' said Martin.

'I'm freaking out a bit,' I admitted.

'No need to be,' said Martin. 'You'll love it. Look on it as a holiday in the country.'

What a wimp I must sound. Vanity made me crack on. After another mile came the inevitable humiliation. I caught the sole of my Flyrocs on a protruding stone and in a flash found myself flat on the track. The damage wasn't severe – holes ripped in my tights and bloodied chin, hands and knees. Martin and Graham strode past as a pair of public-spirited dog-walkers mopped gore off me with wads of kitchen roll.

Only one other small nightmare lay in wait, that of trying to interpret the route instruction *In 280y over wide X-TK & in further 270y, at X-TK, TL (concrete blocks in TK)* with five miles to go. I found the concrete blocks eventually – they turned out to be a pair of bollards lying side by side in a shallow pit, as if they'd decided to be buried alongside each other. That apart, this was winter walking with all the rubbish bits – sopping clothes, mud that clung to the skin even after half a dozen showers – taken out. Buzzing back to Witley in the afternoon sun I could see how easy it could be to become completely taken over by this walking life.

I'd gained some insight into that when I talked to Martin earlier about his passion for Hundreds. He has spent most of his working life as a gardener, but had retrained as a plumber 'to earn some money before I retire'. It's obvious he misses his former job: 'I've got a very low tolerance to stress, which is why I loved it. I'm at one out in the open. I like the pain of physical effort, when your muscles are aching and you have to push past it.'

If you were looking for someone to play Captain Barclay in a biopic, he would be a candidate for the lead role; he emanates strength and hardiness and strides over the hills with relish. He comes over as an easy-going, friendly character, though with his mane of shaggy hair and drooping black moustache there is something scarily elemental about him. On a walk, you wouldn't be completely surprised to see him emerge from a mound of earth, a Green Man, foliage growing out of his mouth.

'At first I thought a Hundred was extreme, too much,' Martin said. 'Then I said I'd just do one, the Lakeland. I promised my wife we'd have our Bank Holiday weekend back together after that and I broke that promise straight away. I want to do at least ten before I think of giving up. You're not on a bike, you haven't got rubber and metal between you and the ground, you're feeling its texture under your feet, the springiness of the heather and the roughness of the stone path. You touch a stone wall and you feel the texture under your fingers. It's a hundred miles of pure pleasure.'

A later conversation with John Walker indicated that he seemed to see Hundreds in that positive way too, albeit from a different angle. In his case, it was the emotional connectedness that came over as important. 'If you're with someone two days and nights, it doesn't take long for your mask to fall off,' he said. 'When you're seeing your second dawn with someone, you get to know so much about them as a person. You're in this thing together. I can't think of any other way you'd get that feeling of affinity and bonding.'

A SPECIAL BREED

One fact which intrigued me particularly about John was that he lived abroad for a lot of his early Hundred career. Here was someone so committed to the event that he was prepared to return every year from as far away as Texas and India. Looking at it from the outside, wouldn't that seem rather extreme?

'I won't say you have to be crazy, but you have to be a touch unusual to want to do it,' he said. 'When you talk about it to any civilian you can see their eyes glaze over. You might as well talk to the calendar on the wall. Then again, I'm the same if anyone talks to me about cycling or something else I've got no interest in. It's, "Try and stay awake, John. Nod your head now and again."

'We are a special breed. Not necessarily a particularly successful breed when it comes to us, the normal Joe Bloggses, but anyone who has finished any Hundred has achieved something great. Something fantastic.'

To my mind, John wasn't overstating the case. Finishing is an achievement – on every Hundred, up to thirty per cent fail. But normal? Among those who have tried and succeeded are a group which, if the LDWA had any truck with that sort of word, could be called an elite – those for whom completing one Hundred, the ultimate proof of mettle and endurance, isn't enough; it's merely the first step.

This became obvious when I saw the statistics from the Hundreds database. From the first Hundred in 1973 to the 2007 Mid Wales, a total of 9,533 had been completed. What was significant about the figure was that in the event's 34-year lifetime, only 2,587 people did the completing. There were a lot of what you might call repeat offenders, of whom 618 had completed five or more, 308 had completed ten or more and 32 had completed twenty or more. Three men (Roger Cole, Martyn Greaves and Mike Gregson) had completed more than thirty.

The power of the Hundred to hold its participants in emotional thrall came home to me strongly when I spoke to David Hammond. David, who lived in a village near Carlisle and spent most of his working life as a postie, is a walker of the old school – rugged, tough, serious and fiercely independent. I can recall an agonised piece he once wrote for *Strider* about having to retire from an event he shouldn't have started because he was ill. He was deeply ashamed that he'd put a marshal to the trouble of having to come out to rescue him.

David had started ten Hundreds and finished four, and by the sound of it they didn't come easy to him. Take, for example, what he went through on the 1985 Yorkshire Dales, the one on which conditions were so harsh that nearly half the starters dropped out: 'That was atrocious. It took me 45 hours 59 minutes. It was pouring down in the Three Peaks area, very wet and windy on the night shift. I remember walking into the breakfast point, if I hadn't been used to working nights I would have given up.'

I said it sounded as if he didn't actually enjoy them very much.

'No, I don't understand this fascination of mine with it,' he mused. 'I hate it when I'm actually doing it but I miss it when I'm not. It's a mixture, really. The Hundred hits you hard. It's the unexpected. You can train as much as you want . . . you say you're going to start slowly and then you see that crowd. The adrenalin starts pumping and you just go. When you finish it, you swear blind you'll never do another. Three weeks later you're still hobbling around and you're planning for next year.

'If you drop out, you feel guilty as sin. You think you've let everybody down. Not yourself but your family, the ones who've put up with all the hassle of you doing it.' But even when he had to pack it in for a few years because he had a young daughter to support and a mortgage to feed, David couldn't break the connection. He showed me the notes he'd written about one of the Hundreds he took no part in:

Saturday I was rather apprehensive. It was the day for the Hundred and though I was not involved in any way I still watched the weather and couldn't help wondering what everyone was doing, so I wasn't there physically but I was there in spirit.

One more thing stood out from a reading of the statistics – multiple Hundreds seemed to be largely a male obsession. Female repeat offenders are a relative rarity. By mid-2007, Shirley Hume, a fifty-something lecturer in finance at Bristol University, was the only woman to have completed more than twenty.

First, the good news. 'Of the women who do start, a higher proportion of them finish,' said Shirley, a talented athlete of the kind who can notch up a sub-29-hour Hundred six weeks after a sub 3:30 London Marathon. 'Women who do Hundreds tend to be self-selecting – stronger walkers, more determined. And I think that women don't give up as easily. They're more tenacious. They have a higher endurance threshold, especially if they have had children. Their attitude is, "We've started, so we'll finish; we're here now: we've got this far." They can rationalise the kind of pain that you go through in terms of "when I stop, this'll go away", whereas men can sometimes be afraid they're going to do themselves a permanent injury.'

But the bad news from a female perspective is the old problem of making time. 'It's vitally important for a Hundred-er to be able to commit time to training – hours, days, fifties,' Shirley pointed out. 'There can be a point, for a woman, especially in her thirties and forties, when it's not possible. When the kids are small, it's the woman who has to stay at home, and it becomes the norm. If women do a couple of Hundreds then have a family, they tend not to come back. And with Hundreds, you either say, "Fine, but never again." Or you say, "Not fine, never again." Or you get hooked and go on for ever till you can't do one. If I couldn't do it one year because I was injured it would be frustrating, but I would probably do another when I was able. On the other hand if one year I didn't do one just because I broke the chain, it would be hard to do another. But men have a hangup. They can't admit they're too old, or that they don't want to walk at night any more.'

Not that male refusal to acknowledge encroaching senescence is the complete picture, according to writer and Bob Graham 24 Hour Club award winner Ronald Turnbull. (Membership of the Bob Graham 24 Hour Club is awarded to anyone completing the Bob Graham Round inside 24 hours. Turnbull is a winner of the club's 'Long Distance Achievement of the Year' award, along with the Fell Running Association's Long Distance Trophy, for bagging all the 2,000ft Scottish peaks outside the Highlands in a non-stop 390-mile run in 9 days 14 hours 25 minutes. He is also the author of, among others, a lovely book about long distance walking, *Three Peaks, Ten Tors*, which includes his account of the Exmoor Hundred.)

'Male human beings, we have a status thing,' said Ronald. 'The theory is, if you have got the status all the women will want to go to bed with you. Climbing the Matterhorn, doing a Hundred – you do it despite the fact it's completely counter-productive. Hillary – someone you'd think was a pretty well-balanced guy – on his way up to the south summit of Everest, took a detour via a part where there had been an avalanche the day before, because that way hadn't yet been done. On the Cleveland Hundred in 1993, when I'd only been doing this thing a year, there were seventeen people ahead of me by the sixty-mile mark. Over the next ten miles, along a section of former railway track, I got myself up to ninth. I knew there were five people behind me. Every time I left a checkpoint, they would be behind me. I was in pain, I had blisters, but I was running along because I didn't want these five to overtake me. It was completely irrational. Nobody would care. But guys just think like that.'

So doing Hundreds was simply another aspect of male display, along with chest-beating and driving sports cars with very long bonnets? Even the old guys thought that way?

'Even the old ones. Even the crippled-looking forty-eighthourers. People who keep going even when they're impossibly injured.'

I said I thought that might be a bit counter-productive.

'You try going round to their house and offering to have sex with them a couple of nights after.'

Cripes. Ronald did seem to have a point, though.

'It's the same as if some guy has a beautiful wife,' said Don Newman. 'It's something to boast about. When I started out, I was a computer programmer. There were forty of us in the room, and doing Hundreds made me special. You don't do it because of that, but it makes people stand up in awe.'

Don joined the Army at the age of sixteen, as a boy soldier. His ambition was to jump out of planes, which meant he had to join P Company. There was, he said, a two-week selection course. The first entailed a week in the gym, and going out running. 'I was hopeless,' he said. 'I looked around at the other people on the course, all fit and muscular, and I thought, I'm this weedy useless bloke. The second week we went to the Brecon Beacons. Walking up and down mountains, getting blisters, getting thoroughly depressed – just like Hundreds, really. What I found out was that the instructors gave you every opportunity to give up. They don't tell you you're useless, they just keep asking if you want to stop. A lot of these hundred-press-ups, sprinting heroes from the first week were saying, "Yeah, OK, I've had enough." And I was saying, "I'm fine. I'll hang on in there." That's what makes the difference between them and us. We just keep on going.'

That was no exaggeration. Don, who you'd take for a fairly average kind of guy in his late fifties, had already completed twenty-three Hundreds, with no thought of breaking the chain. 'I just have to do the Hundred every year,' he said. 'Nothing gets in the way of it. I couldn't not do a Hundred. It would come to the point of resigning if I couldn't get the weekend off at work.'

But if you think that somewhat excessive, wait for this. Don's proudest boast is that he has never given up on an event. 'The day

I fail on one, it'll be terrible,' he said. 'I don't know how I'd get over it. It means so much to me. I think I'd rather die on route.'

> *TL & in 200y TR on 2nd TK to pass in front of cottages. At end ahead down FP with fence on L, over drive and ahead around lake. Up 24 steps, TL and in 500y TL down RD for 180y &* WHEN SAFE *cross to Hall. Around RH side to Verandah and finish.* WELL DONE! **NO BOOTS IN HALL PLEASE**

Back at the finish, I eased off my trainers, mopped more blood from my knees and sat down to tea, toast and biscuits alongside other satisfyingly tired people carefully stowing certificates in kitbags and recounting how long it had taken to find the concrete blocks.

Inevitably, talk turned to preparations for the Yoredale.

'Would you say,' someone said, 'that completing your first Hundred is the most significant day in your life after your wedding day?'

The only way for me to answer that question would be to finish the thing.

YOREDALE HUNDRED 2008

14: Kettlewell (SD 969 723) to Linton (SD 998 630)
Distance: 7.12 miles; Ascent: 751 feet; Descent: 825 feet

At next junction bear right with flag pole/weather vane/seating circle on your left towards Scargill House and Conistone . . .

Getting out of Kettlewell involves one of those long dragging hauls on tarmac, now acting like a road-digger on my shins through the haze of painkillers. We have to leave the Dales Way to make a detour past Scargill House, a religious centre. It was a delightful point of interest on the recce. Now it's just an emblem of the route designer's sadism.

Ahead uphill in direction of Grassington with wall on right soon to be joined by trees on left. When walls come together go through gateway & continue up enclosed track into woodland . . .

Trees stand out in black relief against a stark sky. Nuns wait for us in a row at the top, with crisp white wimples and billowing black robes.

Leave the track and turn right (170°) in the direction of Grassington with a broken wall on your right. When wall on right turns right continue ahead & after 50yds bear right (190°) on the more level of the two paths ignoring the fainter path going uphill. Continue with rocky outcrop on left . . .

I rocket unsteadily along the wide path under Conistone Pie, simultaneously walking and drifting into snug semi-consciousness. *Rocky outcrop on left* turns out to be a big green wave poised to crash down on us. White-faced sheep float on it like little craft. On our right the grass moor slopes gently and endlessly God knows where. I position myself left of Albert and use him as a convenient bulwark to keep me from staggering down it.

Time passes. Every so often I fall asleep, only to wake a few moments later to see little bunches of walkers in front of me, all drawn by the same force towards the same distant end. And at the same time I become distantly aware that I'm tilting ever so slightly to the left, like a picture that needs straightening.

Must pull myself together. There are stiles to tackle. In fact this is Stiles Theme Park. Ladder stiles. Stepped stiles. Stiles with little picket gates that ping back and slap the backs of your legs. Max Mosley would enjoy those. And just to make things livelier, there's another self-clip point for me to find. Not to mention operate. With a grip by now as firm as a wet scarf.

Oh well. Keep going. Julian's a little ahead of us now. I've no idea where Les is but Albert's mate Dave from Cleveland is still behind us. Dave is suffering. Haystack-haired, feet dragging, gritted teeth. I find speech. 'Is he going to be all right?' I say to Albert. 'He looks terrible.'

'Oh, he always gets like that,' says Albert cheerfully.

Take left-hand path (190°). You follow this path for about 1200yds, in places picking its way through limestone . . .

Trying to hold on to consciousness like a hat in the wind, I gaze upon a plain covered in beautiful silver-white flowers, bursting out all over the tufty grass. The path before my feet is bubbling and melting. It's like walking along a fondue. We skirt around Grassington, crossing the River Wharfe beside a large stone road bridge. We climb up the endless road out of Linton, where the tarmac surface jars my shins. But I've had so much ibuprofen I feel completely detached from the pain. The Arthur Anderton Memorial Institute & Men's Reading Room is waiting for us at the brow of the hill. There's a blonde stationed by the door. She looks as if she ought to be perched on the bonnet of a car at the Motor Show. Instead she's holding out an open tub of

Vaseline. People dip their fingers in it as they emerge, then stand outside the door, hands delving down the back of their shorts.

And something else is happening to me. I've started to speak in long, silly-ass sentences. 'I say, would it be frightfully capricious of me to request a *hot* orangeade?' It's as though my brain has been taken out and replaced by a Bertie Wooster chatterbot.

It's good in here, though – a lovely, light airy place with tall windows on three sides. The tables are laid out in parallel lines like you get in a restaurant on the Route Nationale. Everywhere's spotlessly clean and the helpers are rushing about waiting on us, asking what we need. Troughing in a line like a French routier, I wonder idly what prompts these people to spend a whole weekend easing aches and pains, comforting, nourishing. I guess it's human impulse.

Checkpoint 14: Linton (Arthur Anderton Memorial Institute & Men's Reading Room) SD 998 630

Opens: 0400 Sunday; Closes: 0000 Monday
Distance: 79.98 miles; Ascent: 10238 feet; Descent: 10042 feet
Manned by: Cornwall & Devon Group
Indoor checkpoint with hot/cold drinks & food

SEVENTEEN
Delicious Fleshpots

THE MIDDLE OF MARCH, 2008. A FOGGY
Sunday, a clang as the starter opened the gates of Knole Park to
let us through and the clatter of boots and trainers as walkers and
runners set out on the 30-mile Sevenoaks Circular, organised by
Kent LDWA. The conditions were what you'd expect at that time
of year – mud, wind, drizzle and the odd clump of daffodils. It
was an easier thirty than the Punchbowl Marathon I'd done in
February and I was hoping to finish in under eight and a half
hours.

Not that day, though. About seven miles in, I hurtled down
a steep, soft field slope and slipped making a sharp left turn. One
foot was embedded in the mud, which hung on to it tenaciously.
The rest of me tipped sideways in slow motion and I felt the
tendons and ligaments stretch almost to snapping point. Then
over I went.

After swearing loudly and obscenely enough to startle a pair
of mild-looking dog-walkers, I stood up and tried to clean off. I
was so muddy that I wiped everything with more mud, and wasted
another ten minutes transferring it from my hands to the route
description and back again. Then I tried running. I failed at my
first two tries . . . got going again – these things often go away if you
run them off . . . limp, limp, wince, wince . . . My foot was already

swelling up so spectacularly I thought it might burst out of the trainer, like something in *Alien*. And then, a couple of very long, very slow miles on, at the Gover Hill checkpoint, I capitulated and handed in my tally, faintly ashamed of being a wimp.

But God, they were nice. Marshals sat me down in the most sheltered corner of the tent, wrapped a blanket round me and gave me a hot drink because I was shivering rather feebly. Half an hour later, the body bus arrived, driven by Graham Smith. A Kent Group member, he was helping out that day rather than walking. As Graham drove me back to Sevenoaks, disappointment gave way to a feeling of gratitude that was rather uncomfortable. I was indebted for my enjoyment of events to people like these, prepared to sit around for hours outside a tent beside a track on a windy, rainy hill, and more often than not I took it for granted. So this one had ended in mild slapstick and 24 hours of applying a bag of frozen peas. Even so, what I'd experienced was a standard example of the service that groups provide, unpaid, to entrants.

In fact, these affiliated groups are the backbone of the LDWA. Based in various parts of the country, they put on the events – like the Sevenoaks Circular or the Surrey Tops – that people use to build up to a Hundred, which one group will organise and others support by running a checkpoint. Without them there wouldn't be a Hundred, or it would be different, and many of the shorter events wouldn't exist.

You can see how important the groups are to the LDWA just by looking in *Strider*, each number of which publishes their walks programmes for the upcoming four or five months. There are forty-two, based with one exception – Lothian & Borders – in various parts of England and Wales. In the space of one month alone, April–May 2008, East Yorkshire offered two fifties, the Peatlands Way and the Woldsman; Cornwall & Devon was putting on the 30-mile Chagford Challenge and the 100km Wellington Boot; there was Wiltshire's 35-mile Pewsey Downsaround and Thames Valley's 40-mile The Oxon.

For most entrants, of course, the crucial benchmark of a checkpoint is the food on offer. Long distance walking uses up a spectacular number of calories. It's possible to achieve equally good results by cramming yourself with gels and energy drinks. You'd certainly end up horrendously out of pocket. The food on offer at LDWA is food for free. OK, maybe not quite; it's included in what is an almost preposterously low entry fee, roughly a quarter of the cost of an average road race. And it's great. Even shorter events like the 25-mile Stansted Stagger provide tea and biscuits when you arrive, a slap-up buffet halfway, and a hot supper at the end. As for the Hundred, it's virtually a non-stop meal.

Food is available at every checkpoint. The first is usually just an amuse-bouche in the form of biscuits and dried fruit, but after that you can stuff your face every six miles. 'I eat and drink whatever the LDWA gives me,' says my friend Fabrice, a French national based in London. 'And at checkpoints, everyone is nice. This home-cooked food atmosphere, it's fantastic. Ten minutes before I get there, I've already started thinking, Rice pudding! Tuna sandwiches in the middle of the night! It's so different from this kind of thing in France where they want to make a profit. This all comes with your entry fee, they don't want to make money out of you.'

The tradition whereby checkpoints provide home-cooked food developed over the years from the early days of Hundreds, when participants carried their own supplies and were lucky to be provided with water before the 13-mile checkpoint. Now the heroic catering is as much a feature of Hundreds as hallucinations and blisters. And, of course, the people providing it are walkers themselves; they've been through what you're going through and know what is needed. 'One of my intense preoccupations is preventing people being sick,' says Pat Ryan, a former racing cyclist who's responsible, among others, for the Stansted Stagger. 'I suffered. What a lot of people don't understand is how to eat. You must eat early. If you leave it till later on it comes straight up again. The worst thing for a walker is dry and chewy. You need cold and slippery – things like quiche, jelly. And at the hot meal stop it'll be something like soup, rolls, yogurt, fruit.'

Pat, a tall, rangy man with a neatly trimmed white beard, is treasurer of Essex & Herts, and its quartermaster. Brenda, his wife, is a plump, brisk cinnamon bun of a woman. She runs the cooking team. I really like coming back into the hall at the end of the Stagger and seeing the spread they've laid out for us on one of the scuffed folding tables, with large metal teapots dented from years of use and potatoes baking in an ancient oven behind the serving hatch. 'One year the oven stopped working, so I took all the potatoes home to cook, then brought them back in a sleeping bag,' she says. It's noticeable, too, how Brenda takes pains to credit everyone else – Sue Wingrove for her lemon cake, Jean Bowers (a very fast Hundred-er) for her flapjack, 'and John Mountain does a wonderful fruitcake'.

'You always want at least one female because they're more sensible and logical in their approach to food,' she says. 'They'll lay out better. It does make a difference – though some people are so hungry they'd probably eat the chair leg. I do tea loaf. I turn them out by the tinful and take them to Hundreds in case they need extra.'

Essex & Herts take on a checkpoint every Hundred, sometimes combining with Norfolk & Suffolk; the territory of the two groups is adjacent, and they get on well. 'The thing about checkpoints on Hundreds is that you're constrained by the building you're in,' said Pat. 'But the real crunch is the team you've got with you. We've got our A team who are competent and longstanding marshals. Gordon Facer's done seventeen Hundreds – he ran the first few. He never did any marshalling till he got married. Now he'll do anything, even clean the loos.'

I wondered what was the most uncomfortable checkpoint they'd ever had to operate from. Pat didn't take long to answer. 'The one on the Northumberland. We were in a garage behind the pub in Alwinton. It wasn't big enough, or sheltered enough. The tea urn didn't work. We had no sugar. No coffee. Brenda made four tea loaves. She could have made forty-four. People were coming in and saying, "Ah, thank God for that! We've got tea loaf!"'

An explanation is needed here. Northumbria Group, who put on the Northumberland Hundred in 2006, decided to source everything locally to put something back into the community. 'We got the Rothbury Business Club (which is basically the butcher, the baker and the candlestick maker) to quote,' says Peter Morrill, one of the organisers. 'The result was local best beef in masses of pies, and masses of bread and cakes and cheese pasties from the local bakery. And masses of leftover pies sent from checkpoint to checkpoint. And messages: Send anything but meat pies.'

I looked up the Northumberland Hundred in Keith Warman's 'Diary of a Common Man':

Checkpoint 1 at Hethpool. Meat pie and cheese pasties . . .

Checkpoint 3 in Temple Hall Hotel. Cheese pasty to augment meat pie.

Checkpoint 4 at Towford Outdoor Centre. Meat pie and pasty, for a change . . .

Checkpoint 7 at Barrowburn very busy. Ran short of food so ordered more. Apparently, it arrived in the form of van-load of meat pies . . .

Hope Farm and Checkpoint 11. Groaning tables of meat pie and pasty caused partial eclipse of the sun.

Checkpoint 12 at Wandystead Farm. Cairns of you-know-what.

78 miles . . . In early evening light, reached peaceful village of Bolton and hove into Checkpoint 13, run by Staffordshire Group, in village hall. Meat pie and pasty, thankfully brought on from previous checkpoints.

86 miles . . . I commented on how few cattle we'd seen around the route. 'That's because they're all under pastry at checkpoints,' commented Tony.

Despite the surplus of meat pies, the Northumberland was generally agreed to be a superb Hundred, with a route that was one of the most beautiful – if demanding – ever. Walkers told of running deer, black cattle, wind, sleet showers, flagstones, skylarks, swift drenching rainstorms and black, wet peat in heather, wild goats and nights lit so brightly by stars you almost didn't need a torch.

It was the most northerly Hundred to be held. The route took in the Cheviots and the Scottish borders; it went through College Valley, up steeply through forestry and open moorland, then down to Trowup Burn, before climbing to the Border Ridge where it joined the Pennine Way and entered Scotland. It was studded with wild, bucolic, romantic, eloquent names: Kirk Yetholm, Wideopen Hill, Windy Gyle, Morbattle. There was only one arable field on the entire route. One checkpoint was outside a mountain refuge hut at 1,500ft on Yearning Saddle. The final checkpoint, at 98 miles, was a shooter's hut on an estate farm – 'it had electric and kettles' – before a final 590ft ascent of Weetwood Bank from which there was no escaping because of the self-clipper on the top.

It also took some organising. On a lot of the route, there were no roads. Of the roads there were, one was a 12-mile dead end. On the Border Ridge, Search & Rescue were the only people whose vehicles were capable of reaching the checkpoints. Finding suitable places for checkpoints took a long time. 'It's a very uninhabited area,' says Peter. 'Mainly farmers' barns full of sheep shit. One was so bad we ended up setting up a tent.' He ordered Portaloos for all the barn checkpoints. 'I really didn't want entrants pissing against farmers' doorsteps. The Portaloo company was used to building sites ordering four at a time. We wanted individual ones for isolated locations. I had to take photos of where I wanted them placed for van drivers delivering on GPS.' At one point over the weekend itself, a message from Hope Farm checkpoint, run by North Yorkshire group, came through to Peter's colleague Mike Rayner. 'They said that a Portaloo had fallen over,' Mike says. 'I sent a message back: "Is there anybody in it?" Well, what are you supposed to do? It *was* very windy.'

The route planning got under way in 2004. All the planners were in full-time jobs and most had families. Peter, a tutor in the fine arts department at Newcastle University, made a list of every single household which would be passed by walkers early in the morning, estimated when they'd be coming through and when residents would see people and torches, and drove round to each one to tell them not to mistake the walkers for rustlers. 'We didn't want farmers fetching their shotguns and coming out and shooting walkers.' His efforts paid off spectacularly. Villagers applauded and offered drinks as walkers came through. 'Everyone knew about the Hundred,' he says. 'It was great. Some of the farmers came out and helped, distributing tea. And also eating some of the meat pies.'

They had two vans and two minibuses, one of which broke down on the first day so they had to find people with cars who could pick up retirees where necessary. Peter created a huge map of the whole route, with little flags showing where all the transport was: 'I felt like a Battle of Britain general, moving counters around.' There was particular difficulty reaching the 40-mile checkpoint at Barrowburn, located in a former school building converted into a camping barn. 'There were a lot of drop-outs there, after the night traverse of the Cheviots, either totally relieved that they'd come to their senses or pissed off and crying.' No doubt some were encouraged to stay by the roaring log fire. 'A lot of faster walkers who should have gone on the later start with the runners arrived too early and we couldn't let them leave because they'd have reached the next checkpoint before it opened up. So Barrowburn was heaving, full of people having second helpings.'

But one aspect of the event wasn't fun at all. Mike and Peter were on the night shift, and were trying to get some sleep during the day when Ken Falconer came in and told Peter, 'Wake up, we've lost a walker.' When Peter asked whether Search & Rescue had been contacted Ken replied that the man was dead. 'It was in a very isolated area, too. The only good thing was that the second person along was a GP on the event, who stopped and tended him, otherwise all the entrants would have had to go past the body. It was a heart attack.' This was in fact the third death on a Northumbria LDWA event, after the fatality that occurred in the first half-hour of the 1999 Durham Dales and a second in an inaccessible part of a Durham Dales 28-miler.

Did they ever stop and ask themselves whether it was worth all the effort?

'To say you spent seventy-two hours hanging around some godawful corner of Northumberland waiting for some people to turn up – you can see people can't comprehend it,' says Mike, a transport manager with Royal Mail. 'It's quite an undertaking. I wouldn't call it altruism – it's just that someone asks you and you tend to get involved. It's a sort of honour to do it. And when it's over there's a big hole left. You think, Blooming heck, what am I going to do now?'

Peter described how he felt once the event was over: 'Suddenly you'd got nothing. Three years on, you'd forgotten all the hassles. It was almost like grieving.'

We shouldn't regard event organisers as martyrs. Listening to Peter and Mike, it's clear what a buzz they got from staging a Hundred. The overriding view from Northumberland is one of pride in what they achieved against very tough odds – a remote route where communications were difficult, a death on the event and before that an appalling car crash that has left Alan Rowell, one key organiser, still in hospital and unlikely ever fully to regain consciousness.

But talk to any event organiser and the lament is unchanging. 'It's always the same people who help and we're not getting any younger.' There certainly are younger people joining the LDWA; many of them, though, are runners, and runners tend not to be group members. Tony Willey, LDWA chairman, wrote in April 2008's *Strider* about what even three years before would have been unheard of – oversubscribed events. 'One of the reasons for improved entries is the increased number of runners on events, well over a third of the entry on That's Lyth, for instance . . . This is fine and works to the benefit of all, but it needs repeating that events only happen due to the unpaid and unsung efforts of a small army of organisers and helpers. With honourable exceptions we don't see many runners in that army . . .'

And even the keenest of organisers finds a time comes when they want a break. I don't want to end on a downbeat note, but for all Brenda Ryan's enthusiasm for what she does, there are times when she and Pat seem defeated. 'What's going to happen when we're all dead?' she asks rhetorically.

'I think it'll go back to how it was before,' says Pat. 'More basic.'

You can hardly blame them for feeling tired and, perhaps, unappreciated. But we aren't, then, entitled to moan if future Hundreds take place in a different form from the ones we've come to expect. The old-timers, of course, those who think we've become too cosseted, may approve. But for the rest of us the prospect of Hundreds without home-cooked food and creature comforts hardly bears thinking about. Even the meat pies would be missed.

YOREDALE HUNDRED 2008

15: Linton (SD 998 660) to Appletreewick (SE 052 597)
Distance: 4.85 miles; Ascent: 258 feet; Descent: 426 feet

At high wall (entrance to house) bear left on enclosed path with house wall on your right for about 10yds. Turn left on enclosed path still with house wall on your right (do not cross pack-horse bridge ahead). This path leads to a wooden bridge on your left which you cross over the River Wharfe above Linton Falls. Once over the bridge turn immediately right through gap in wall & down steps in the direction of Hebden & Burnsall . . .

We're back on the Dales Way. The afternoon wears on. The path is booby-trapped with exposed tree roots and mini landslips, and punctuated by every kissing gate in Yorkshire.

Kissing gates plus maverick foliage. The gale that tried to push us back down Ingleborough passed this way too. Great branches, practically trunks, have been wrenched off the riverside trees. They're spread over the paths and grass like a drunk girl's clothes flung on the floor.

I've started to hate them. And everything else in my way. And all the things that are *around* the things in my way. I fume at the benches. I stomp along, skirting the draping branches, the undemanding endlessness chipping away at my spirits. It's like being stuck in a French train strike. You can't get away. You can't bawl at people. They just shrug if you do. There's nothing you can do except be *in* this. Where are all the stiles and climbs when you need them? Anything to get us out of this slough of tedium. On the recce it was brilliant – you didn't have to concentrate on finding your way, you could speed along enjoying the lovely sylvan setting. Now it's an opportunity to brood on how tired you are and how much everything hurts.

And how bloody annoying all these people are. I march on in a state of steadily swelling rage. God! Tourists! Why must they insist on walking towards me on this path? Some of them *two abreast*. *With dogs*. Do they expect me to stand aside for them? And make way for their sodding Alsatian? I'd kick it into the Wharfe if I had the energy. And their whooping, laughing children. Tossers.

Oh, get a grip. The next checkpoint can't be far away now. It's an Essex & Herts checkpoint. There'll be Brenda Ryan's tea loaf. And there's a white van over there. Pat's camper van with a hatch. There'll be cold drinks and date balls and cheese straws! Carry me home!

The white van dissolves. It's a hawthorn bush. Never mind. Here it is, the next field along. No, that's a hawthorn bush too. And here's another white van. And it's a hawthorn bush.

We cross a couple of plank bridges and go through a little gate. Here it is, Appletreewick. It's not a white van, anyway. It's a giant tent with canvas annexe. It looks like a corner torn off a garden centre and stuck in the middle of a field. The tent flaps are closed against the wind. The tent seems to be bouncing, as if it wants to take off.

Twenty to five. Inside, a row of slack-jawed, slightly dribbly people with lacklustre eyes sit in silence, facing the river. I join them. The river is obscured by the tent flaps, so we watch the tent flaps instead.

A plate of food appears on my lap. Even as I eat it I forget what it is. Since yesterday morning I've consumed twelve sausage rolls, five slices of quiche, three portions of baked beans (and I *hate* baked beans), six tuna baps, twenty-four cheese straws, four handfuls of Haribo sweets, eight boiled sweets, three slices of chocolate cake, nine slices of fruit loaf, one slice of carrot cake, thirty-one assorted biscuits, one baked potato, two hot dogs, five rounds of toast, three chipolatas, two fried eggs, a bowl of cornflakes, multiple ravioli, ditto apple crumble and custard, four rounds of salad sandwiches, a whole plate of carrot and celery batons and four rice puddings, one with fruit salad. Now I've reached the stage when I can barely remember how to chew, let alone differentiate one food group from another. I couldn't tell a date ball from a whole roast ox.

More painkillers, more ProPlus. I still can't get the drinking bladder to work so I wash them down with tea, which makes me feel sick again.

Albert levers up his little flock and shepherds us out. I get up and droopily go, out into the pale late afternoon light.

We trundle along again.

'What do you think of Eva?' says Albert suddenly.

Eva. Oh yeah, Eva. Albert's wife.

'She is a bold and determined woman,' I pronounce, sonorously.

Bloody hell. It's like being the last two in the pub, surrounded by empty glasses and talking bollocks after everyone else has gone home.

Checkpoint 15: Appletreewick (riverside field) SE 052 597

Opens: 0500 Sunday; Closes 0200 Monday

Distance 84.63 miles; Ascent: 10946 feet; Descent: 10468 feet

Manned by: Essex & Herts (shift 1) and Norfolk & Suffolk (shift 2)

Tented checkpoint with hot/cold drinks and some cold food. NO toilet facilities. Track access only.

EIGHTEEN
A Talent to Inspire

'SHE'S MY INSPIRATION,' SAID MARIE DOKE, the London runner. 'I want to be like her. She's never pulled out of an event, she's walked through incredible pain and discomfort. When I get to sixty-five, if I can't do as well as I did, that's no reason not to challenge myself. My attitude will be the same as hers, to do as well as you can at sixty-five. She's my idol.'

Sometimes Jill Green makes me think of Doris Day in *Annie Get Your Gun*. It's easy to imagine her coping with cheerful bravado in the Wild West, though I'm not sure whether she'd shoot intruders or invite them to come for a walk. At other times she reminds me of a bird leading the chorus at dawn. 'When I get tired I get rather morose,' said Ann Sayer. 'Not like Jill who's bubbling over all the time.'

It was a dank November day when Jill and I met in the slightly mildewy surroundings of a depopulated caravan park in Surrey. Jill's home is on the Isle of Wight but she uses the caravan as a mainland base for events. Walking seems to take up most of her life. Later in the day she was off to London for a meeting of the Centurions ('I qualified in 1992, in Leicester. I became the twenty-sixth lady, and I loved that. I've done it many times since'). At the weekend was the Gatliff Marathon, a notorious 30-mile Kent mudfest that Jill has merrily skimmed round every year since its inception. She was trying to persuade me to walk it with her; had she really not noticed I was from another, inferior species?

Jill is a marvellous walker: she has won international honours, she has done countless Hundreds and shorter events. She walks national trails for pleasure; she is a Centurion; she leads short walks for residents of an Isle of Wight hotel. There was a picture on the back cover of *Strider* of her sixtieth birthday walk – 60 miles, and all the younger blokes who went on it with her lying flat out at the end, like empties. In October 2004 she spent the weekend of her sixty-third birthday walking 105 miles non-stop to win the Tooting Bec 24-hour race. 'When I started I was sixty-two and when I finished I was sixty-three, and it was a wonderful way to spend your birthday.'

Jill doesn't dominate the skyline like Ann Sayer – she stands about five foot six, with a rosy, weatherbeaten face and neat brown curls. Only the athlete's slim, straight-backed body hints at a career that has been a whirligig of races, Hundreds and international success. Above all, as Marie said, Jill is an inspiration. Here is a woman who didn't get her chance to shine until she was nearly forty. The ability was always there, but growing up in Coulsdon, south London, it was frustrated by lack of opportunity. 'I belonged to the Girls' Life Brigade and when the other girls were buying chips I used to run round the block. I enjoyed it so much I used to run round the block again. It must have been a couple of miles. And of course I only had a gaberdine raincoat, and lace-up brown shoes, and long plaits. In those days there was nobody running round the streets, so I didn't tell my parents I was doing it because they would have said I mustn't. So really I was born before my time.'

There was another problem. Bright, engaging and articulate as she is, Jill is dyslexic, a condition not identified in the fifties; people merely dismissed you as thick. She left school at fourteen: 'Father wanted to send me to Pitman's because he thought that would sort out my spelling and writing but that would have been purgatory. So I did hairdressing, just for something that wasn't Pitman's. And it's been a good thing, because I can still earn a living from it.'

She had always liked walking as a child, but it was only after she married, had a family and moved to the Isle of Wight that it became more than a pastime. The bungalow into which she and husband Dave moved was already decorated to perfection. So – what to do? 'Let's join the Ramblers.' There she met an ancient Centurion called Harry Peel who encouraged her to take part in the 30-mile Vectis Marathon, a well-known Isle of Wight YHA event in the seventies and eighties. 'I did it for many years, and I got a team, called the Weary Wight Wanderers, to do it with me.' It was Peel who suggested to her that she could be a Centurion.

'I knew what a Centurion was – someone who walked a hundred miles within twenty-four hours,' she said. 'But when I lived in Coulsdon I used to go and watch the racewalk from London to Brighton and my impression was all men, terribly serious, doing that funny walk with the wiggly bum, on roads. Little did I know I'd one day do it myself.'

Sheer chance led her to the LDWA. Husband Dave, an aircraft engineer who worked on the mainland near Woking, met Chris Steer in the pub one Friday night. Steer told Dave that he was keen on taking part in the Vectis Marathon, an event he'd never done. 'So Dave came home and said he'd met this bloke in the pub and invited him to stay for the weekend to do the Vectis.' She agreed – 'Dave often did this sort of thing to me' – and Chris Steer came over to walk the Vectis Marathon with them.

'Chris – ever so nicely, he was a perfect gentleman – warned me not to expect to walk with him because he was fast and would probably go ahead. So I thought, Right. I'll walk as fast as I jolly well can and keep with him as long as I can.' She did better than that. 'It got to the point where Chris said, "Do you mind if you slow down? You're actually walking a bit too fast for me."'

Chris was another who told Jill she could be a good walker if she took it seriously. He invited her and Dave over to the mainland to take part in the Winter Tanners, assuring her she wouldn't get lost because they'd have a route description, and she could walk with him. 'I'd always thought the LDWA was for the elite, and didn't regard myself as a long distance walker, but I talked to other walkers and they told me about other events. I joined,' she said, 'and of course I got hooked. I liked the camaraderie of it. I found I could do it. And every time I did an event, I tried to do it faster. I know it's not competitive, but I was just trying to be better at it.'

Gradually she worked up to the Hundred. She'd been warned off the Surrey Summits because it was so hard – 100km, early in the year, over steep hills – so instead she entered the South Downs Eighty. 'Which was a run, but I was going to walk it.'

When she set off, the temperature was in the nineties. There were numerous retirements thanks to the heat, and several runners suffered the effects of over-indulging in the new salt-replacement drink that was being handed out. Jill made her way further and further up the field even though she was walking. 'During the night I passed a couple of lads and they said: "We won't laugh at little old ladies in boots again." I looked round and thought, "Bloody cheek! They mean me!" I was only forty-three.' And she came second. 'Second lady! It was such a wonderful surprise. I went home to my mum's house and in the night I was still so excited I couldn't sleep, so I went downstairs to make myself a cup of tea and of course I couldn't get back upstairs again because I was so stiff. But I thought if I can do the South Downs Eighty walking, and it's meant to be a run, I'm sure I could do those long LDWA things.'

Her first Hundred was the 1986 Downsman, which she finished in 29 hours 12 minutes. 'I was ever so pleased. Then people said, "Well, of course, the Downsman isn't a real Hundred. Too easy." That's how people talked to you in those days. So the next year I did the 1987 Snowdonia, which was a *man's* Hundred.' It was hard and steep, with a drop-out rate of 50 per cent. But Jill completed it in 37 hours.

In 1991, by which time she had participated in three more Hundreds, Jill was approached by Bob Watts, an LDWA member and racewalker who was putting together a British team to compete against France. 'He belonged to the London Vidarians.' Jill's eyes started to sparkle. 'Back in history, the Surrey Walking Club were the gentlemen, who had to be proposed and seconded. The London Vidarians was very much the club for the London working man. It was the thorn in the side of the Surrey Walking Club, and I loved that.'

The event was the first Roubaix, a 28-hour race – 'You go round and round a grubby old town near the Belgian border. Bob asked if I'd consider being in the British team. I told him I didn't do racewalking, but he said he'd noticed me when I finished LDWA Hundreds and I was still cheerful and happy and not distracted in any way, and in any case the team were one woman short.' She pointed out that she was far from young, and lived on the Isle of Wight. Watts admitted, 'Well, actually, we're scraping the barrel. Please come.'

Great Britain won it that year. They'd never told her the whole match depended on her, otherwise the pressure would have been terrible. She loved it. And then, of course, she was hooked on racewalking too.

She needed someone to teach her how. She'd met Lilian Millen on Hundreds – 'She'd racewalked for Great Britain, and we got on well and had a lot of laughs together. I knew that Boyd had taken Lilian, who had been a little round lady, and turned her into an international athlete. I thought if he could teach Lilian, he could teach me. Would he?'

He would, even though the first time Boyd saw her in action his verdict was that she walked 'like a builder's navvy'. As I listened to Jill talking about the days when she was at her peak, it was clear that racewalking has been the great love of her life. 'When you're doing it properly you're not using up any more energy. It's like pulling a rope through your body, like a cat walks, really, but you're doing it quickly. It's so different from LDWA walking, when you've got your rucksack on, and you're in the mud, and climbing over stiles.

'Sometimes when I was racewalking properly . . .' She paused. 'I was just going. You know how you're just going and nothing's hurting and it's almost like a meditation. I can feel that I've come out of my body and it's liberated me. It's beautiful. I'm just walking. And that only happens when you're walking fast and strong and it's a beautiful place and you're alone. It doesn't happen to order, but it's a wonderful feeling.'

In all, she represented Great Britain eight times on the Roubaix; one year she was first lady. She won the Soeur Selecte at the 300km Paris–Colmar – 'my digestion shut down as I got tireder and tireder and I was fed every twenty minutes with mashed potato, rice pudding with honey and jelly'; she has qualified as a Centurion in all six countries where Centurions were held (her personal best was 21 hours 15 minutes); she has taken part in 64 events of 100 miles and over (including 18 LDWA Hundreds), four of over 200 miles and 108 events of 100km or more – 'including some that were ninety-nine miles because if you do qualifying races in France the hundred miles means nothing to them – their qualifying distance is 156km.' She led a team of women to win the 84-mile Men's Cup on the Isle of Man – 'This Is The Isle Of Woman' read next day's front-page headline. She set a women's record for the 145-mile London to Birmingham canal run – 39 hours, even though she walked it.

'The blisters are a problem,' she said. 'And I lose toenails. Sometimes when you do really long things the toenails are just floating round in blisters at the top. All the time the adrenalin's going, you don't notice it, but when you finish all the pain and the trouble envelops you, and you think, I'm not the same marvellous person I was! Here I am in a crumpled heap! But it gives you such a thrill, doesn't it? Such a wonderful feeling. Because I was never good at anything. And,' she added, 'I taught myself to wee in eleven seconds so as not to waste time: I wear elastic trousers. I've been timed.'

I wondered if she ever regretted that her international career had started so late. It would have been easy to give in to temptation, surely, and speculate on what she might have achieved had it happened earlier. 'No, I'm lucky because I would have done too much and got injured and given up. I didn't start till my family was grown up and I was in my mid-thirties. I didn't have that great speed. I wasn't tempted to spoil myself. And I'm very fortunate that I have not tackled anything that I didn't believe I could finish. People have asked me to do things and I haven't done them because of that. And so far I've finished everything that I've started. I've never had to stop on any of them, and obviously I can still go on doing LDWA Hundreds for a long time.'

It was time for Jill to head off to her Centurions meeting in London. On the way to the station, I drove, she talked.

'When I'm on an event, I often ask people what they do. It's nothing to do with me, but I find it so interesting. One time one of them was Black Rod from the Houses of Parliament. But what impressed me was the other chap we were with, who couldn't read but was going to adult literacy classes. Black Rod was fascinated by him. "How do you manage? What do you do?" He said he could read the route descriptions, and then he would write a little bit about the walk and take it to his teacher. I thought, that just typifies the LDWA. That the chap who obviously came from a very privileged background could talk to this other man and respect him. I think the LDWA is wonderful because it's so levelling. It doesn't matter who you are. In mud, reading the route description, you're all equal.'

YOREDALE HUNDRED 2008

16: Appletreewick (SE 052 597) to Bolton Bridge (SE 071 530) *Distance: 6.19 miles; Ascent 567 feet; Descent: 694 feet*

You are now following a well-trodden riverside path for a mile enclosed in places, marked by posts & open in others through kissing-gates, fence gaps & stiles. You will know when you are coming to the end of the path as it crosses a 'plank' bridge over a boggy area & starts to climb above the river . . .

Eighty-four point six three miles done. Count on fingers. Sixteen left minus 0.63. Plus 0.63? Oh, sod maths. 'If we get a move on here we could go for a time,' I say to Albert.

We can do this. Yes! Fifteen-minute miles. We crank up a gear or two. Dave lurches after us, head down, manfully. He was a young man when we set out from Bainbridge this morning. Now he's limping after us like a faithful arthritic dog. I time us by my wristwatch and Albert estimates the distance covered. I forget the pain in my shins. Fields and streams and barns fly by. First mile done. This is easy. Second mile – *boomph*. I've turned into a wreck. I just can't shift this fast any more.

But on we go, making detours around branches, occasionally looking back over our shoulders for Dave, miserably traipsing behind us. I negotiate the dangerous hole in the path without falling into the river. We enter Strid Wood. The river tumbles, noisy and frothy, through a deep, narrow gorge among mossy woodland. The sound wakes me up, enough to remind me that something's happened to my shins – they feel as though someone's peeling the flesh off the bone with a nail file. And I'm dying for a pee.

'I am feeling a bit miserable now,' observes Albert.

I grit my teeth and scuttle along beside him. We leave Strid Wood and head for Bolton Priory. Cavendish Pavilion is in front of us. I dive in to the ladies' and sit, head in hands.

Maybe a sleep would help. Ten minutes' shut-eye, then I'll go like a rocket.

But I'm not sleepy. I'm droopy. I'm tilting to the left and can't seem to straighten up.

Outside, Albert is waiting in an attitude of weary resignation on the wooden bridge, leaning on the rail under a sign pointing to the Valley of Desolation.

Twisty-turny path under sunlight and shadows. Switchback. Bolton Priory a brown skeleton on the right. Dave padding glumly behind us on the made-up paths. The last of the daytrippers stare at us. There's something pitying in their gaze.

It's like dying of old age rather than hurtling to your doom in a plane crash. It's the accumulation of faults that does you in. All this – it's just a lesson in mortality, really. That's it. The Hundred has revealed to me the meaning of life. Start – being born. Going round – living your life. The disparity between aspiration and outcome. The people you fall in with. Whether you're the kind who attempts to control your destiny by planning things down to the last detail, or whether you let it all come at you and deal with it as and when, as best you can. Getting older, getting slower. Then The Finish – the great shutdown.

God, I'm depressed.

Never mind. Here's the river bank again. Here's the next checkpoint coming up. Batting away a cow, I follow Albert across the grass that morphs into a cricket field and Bolton Bridge cricket pavilion.

We are entering the world of the undead. There they are, on the wooden seats outside, as vibrant as cobwebs: Brian Harwood and

Don Newman, staring ahead with trance-like determination. Two shades watching ghost cricket.

Between minuscule sips of hot orange juice, I take in the scene. Someone's stretched out on one of the benches, snatching a sleep. Albert and I swap pills. He gets a strip of my ProPlus, I get quadruple strength super-duper painkillers, plus one of the extra water bottles he carries. I gulp thirstily, groping around the bran tub of my mind for a few facts. We did the last 6.19 miles in 2 hours 10 minutes. Not bad at this stage. Ten miles left. Let's get it over with.

Checkpoint 16: Bolton Bridge (Cricket Pavilion) SE 071 530

Opens: 0700 Sunday; Closes: 0500 Monday
Distance: 90.31 miles; Ascent: 11063 feet; Descent: 11162 feet
Manned by: Jeff Coulson & family
Limited facilities with hot/cold drinks & cold food. Adjacent to road.

NINETEEN
Where's Gerald?

THE LAST TIME I SAW GERALD BATEMAN WAS at Checkpoint 1 of the 2007 Poppyline Fifty. Feet a little splayed, a portly, bespectacled, serious figure in shorts, he was grazing at the trestle table set out on the Cromer seafront. I tallied and ran on. I didn't see him again. Usually you don't – Gerald either finishes after everyone else has gone home or marshals retire him because he's so far behind. Which is what happened on that Poppyline Fifty; he was stopped at the 31-mile checkpoint, Hanworth Memorial Hall, where he arrived 25 minutes after closing time. 'I'm just a slow walker, I'm afraid,' he says. 'I've got a bit of a reputation on that.'

Well past his seventieth birthday now, Gerald welcomes me into his Chigwell home with his usual courtly politeness. I'm invited to sit down on his left ('I'm a bit deaf in the right ear') while Vivienne, his wife, brings tea and biscuits and retreats tactfully to the kitchen. Today Gerald is limping slightly, the result of a fall on the Shotley Peninsula Fifty-Five a few days previously. He hitches up a trouser leg to reveal a blued and bloated knee with a central traffic-light red gouge. 'I don't know what I did,' he says with bemusement. 'I was in a wood in Constable country and I fell over. Pat Ryan said I'd never make it to the next checkpoint in time so I was retired.'

Gerald is a legend. Hear about his exploits and you're tempted immediately to pigeonhole him: the Eddie the Eagle of the long distance path, a heroic sporting failure in the mode of Eric the Eel, the swimmer from Equatorial Guinea who was just about starting on his final length in Sydney when the medallists were heading for the podium. You could call him Gerald the Gazelle, if you wanted to poke fun. Which I don't, or not in a horrible way.

'He was sitting down in a daze,' says Pat Ryan, who was marshalling on the Shotley. 'He wasn't with it. He had a vacant look and loads of blood running down his trousers. He was twenty minutes behind the field, so I told him he wasn't to go any further. He didn't say anything. He just looked at me, as if he was about to burst into tears.' Pat sighs. 'I've always had a soft spot for him.'

The trouble is that the equilibrium between Gerald's phenomenally slow rate of progress and the availability of marshals willing to hang around in cold corners of the countryside, waiting for him to turn up, is not always reached. You can tell that being stopped on that Poppyline Fifty still rankles. 'It was half past seven in the evening. With nineteen miles to go. I had till six in the morning. Ten and a half hours. I even drew them a graph to show the closing times didn't match. I keep complaining about their cutting down the checkpoint times. I always think of people cheering the finishers and I always miss it all.'

That's no exaggeration. He's been left further behind the field than a 500-1 Grand National shot, he's been retired more times than Frank Sinatra and was banned by one group from their Hundreds for several years. On one Poppyline Fifty, they gave him a whole marshal to himself, following him around to make sure he was all right. Bloodied but magnificently undeterred, he ploughs on, not always in the right direction, a solid, dignified figure with a neatly trimmed beard, renowned for entering a checkpoint a nanosecond before it's due to close. 'Gerald, you're going to have to go now,' are words he hears often. Marshals talk of him with a mixture of exasperation and tenderness: 'He reads one line of the route description and not the rest'; 'It's almost as if he enjoys being late'; 'We don't know where he is.'

'On one of the Hertfordshire Hobbles, he didn't appear,' says Pat Ryan. 'We couldn't lock up because his little green Beetle was still in the car park. We left some food outside, like you do for the cat.' Chris Winn, from Marches LDWA, remembers marshalling on a Three Forests Way some years back: 'A girl came in and said, "I'm last, aren't I?" and we said, "No, Gerald's still out there." Just at that moment, he came in. We reckoned he hid in a hedgerow till she came past so it wouldn't destroy his record.'

Mention that to Gerald and he laughs jovially. True or not, to him the last-gasp arrivals are something to be proud of. 'I'd say it shows it's harder for me to do it. I can't walk fast. But you don't have to walk fast, you walk to finish. I wasn't at all athletic at school. I suppose I'm not now,' he adds conscientiously, 'but I'm sure I do more exercise than most of the people who played rugby at school.'

It isn't that he never finishes anything. Let us remember that he has completed half the Hundreds he's entered, a record that bears comparison with many other walkers: the 1991 Lancastrian, the 1997 Downsman, the 1999 Durham Dales, the Millennium Hundred – 'That was horrible. Soaking. We got to Dover and it started raining. Eight in the evening. Manhole covers lifting off.' Then there was the 2004 Exmoor; he staggered in with eight minutes left on the clock. 'An Australian girl was running the hotel I was staying at. She was so intrigued by the idea of an old man walking a hundred miles that she said, "Give me a ring when you've finished and I'll come and pick you up." So I got a pint of beer and a free breakfast, and after that I was as right as rain.'

Gerald is a relic of the early days of Essex & Herts LDWA. He left his birthplace, Leeds, for London to study for a Bachelor of Divinity degree. He's a little vague about the details of the premature end of his student career, but the bright lights won out over the groves of academe and instead of becoming a priest (in which role, incidentally, you can easily visualise him) he left to become a public health inspector.

It was after he married and moved to Chigwell in the late sixties that he saw a notice in the local paper about a walk in rural Essex. Talked into doing the Three Forests Way, he put on a golf jacket, corduroys and waterproofs, borrowed his son's Cub Scouts rucksack, and turned up at Harlow Sports Centre, which was the event's HQ in the early days: 'Everybody else was in proper equipment,' he says. But off he went, slogging up towards Sawbridgeworth across ploughed fields with Essex clay accumulating on his boots, past hunt saboteurs spraying to put hounds off the scent while the huntsman's horn sounded in the distance. He hadn't brought much to eat, but a bunch of men from Middlesbrough gave him their sandwiches because they were about to retire. 'Couldn't take the Essex mud,' he says. Those he walked with included a professor, a physiotherapist from the local hospital and a group of police cadets. 'They gradually dropped out. There were a lot of retirements at the breakfast stop. I finished.'

He joined Essex & Herts and his legend started almost then and there. 'When I was first in the groups, over twenty years ago,' says Pat Ryan, 'they had a weekend away in Yorkshire to walk the night part of the Yorkshire Dales Hundred. We stayed in a rudimentary camping barn – tap, lights, sink, probably a lav. Nothing else. We slept on the floor upstairs and all of us were going down to have our breakfast except this fella curled up in his sleeping bag. No idea who he was but I thought I'd better wake him – "We're going soon and you haven't had breakfast." I went downstairs. It was freezing. Colder inside than out. White frost. This bearded figure in his vest and pants comes down. Goes outside. And he rolls around in the frost.

'I said, "Who's that?"

'"Gerald."

'I can see it now,' Pat continues. 'We set off and walked downhill from the camping barn to the river, crossed on a tiny bridge. We all continued on route. Gerald went a hundred degrees to the right. We protested he was going the wrong way but he said he was going the right way and we were wrong. We never saw him again.'

They did, of course. He virtually became the Three Forests Way's poster boy: a muddied, indestructible figure who always got there in the end. One year he did the publicity for it – they got their best ever entry. He put together a list of all the athletic and running clubs in the area and wrote a press handout: '"How would you like to enjoy a walk in the November sunshine?"' Gerald chuckles. 'Real PR. Everything's a swan, no ducks.'

He took part in every Three Forests Way, through the move to Gilwell Park scout hut and on to the early 2000s when the start moved to Blackmore. 'They dumbed it down,' he says disgustedly. 'Brought it back to October.' He finished every single one till the last. 'I was retired. I've never given up voluntarily.'

He showed me the old Three Forests Way badge, a big white W on a red background. 'I've got badges for most of the walks I do. The Poppyline Fifty, the Surrey Summits. I lost a contact lens on that, just outside Checkpoint One. I asked Ann Sayer if she'd got a mirror in her handbag. "A handbag, Gerald?" came the reply. "Can you imagine me with a handbag?"' He chuckles. 'And I was there at the checkpoint on the Blackwater Marathon when blows were exchanged after someone asked Henry Bridge how old he was.'

Ask him why he collects badges and he says simply, 'A little bit of self-esteem. Some people are a bit like squirrels. They tend to collect old things. I collect old cameras, too, and Moulton bikes. I was the sort of person who wore badges on his lapel as a schoolboy.' He used to sew the badges on a rucksack, till eventually it was completely covered. Then he was in a car accident and the vehicle went up in flames with his rucksack in the boot.

'Including my special badge from the LDWA Aysgarth AGM, a mouse nibbling a bit of Stilton cheese.'

But it's on the Hundreds that you find the *echt* Gerald performances. Take the 1990 Marchesman, based in Shropshire. 'Well before everybody had a mobile,' says Neil Fullwood, the Marches Group organiser, 'Gerald got into difficulties on the Long Mynd, on the way to the checkpoint at Clun, so he knocked on the door of the Dog and Duck and used their phone. We told him not to move from the Dog and Duck and he'd be rescued.' Almost two decades later, Neil still splutters with rage. 'He did move. It caused havoc. He could have been anywhere. We said if he hadn't turned up by nine-thirty on Monday morning we'd call the fuzz.' He arrived at twenty past nine, having gone on to reach Clun, as Gerald puts it, 'unofficially'.

Does he never wish he could go a little faster?

'I can't walk fast. You don't have to walk fast, you walk to finish. I do it for the challenge. Like climbing Everest.'

It must be somewhat akin to Everest for him. The last Hundred he completed was the 2005 Chiltern Landmarks. He'd done the first 50 miles in new trainers: 'They were too narrow. My feet were all torn. But I'd put a pair of ordinary walking shoes in my breakfast bag and I changed into them. Nobody thought I'd finish but I did.' There's a picture of him in that August's *Strider*, running into the hall wearing a big grin, hands in the air like a footballer celebrating a goal. He arrived eight minutes before the portcullis came down. The amazing thing was that he looked so good, almost jaunty bearing in mind that most walkers who finish in the final hour look completely wrecked. 'I had heard,' he says, 'I was going to be on the cover of *Strider*.'

I explained that I had already been censured by the doughty old boots and Father Timeses for a cover depicting a walker fast asleep at a checkpoint, when what they liked was photos of grinning people on top of trig points. When they got wind that

I planned to put Gerald on the cover a message was passed down that they wanted someone younger.

I'm still sorry I gave in. I think Gerald is absolutely great, though of course I've never had to sit around in a tent for hours waiting for him to show. What's more, he finished the Poppyline Fifty in 2008, thus securing his Hundred qualifier for the 2009 Wessex. 'I did 21:25,' he says.

Was he last?

'Oh yes.'

Why does he do it? Where is the pleasure in walking alone, slowly, in increasing discomfort and pain, pigheadedly going your own way when everyone else is going the other, out in the cold and rain and dark, on your own, knowing you're going to be last and that everyone will have gone home except for the resentful marshal waiting to close the hall? I still don't understand until just before I leave, when he shows me the family photos on the mantelshelf – his daughter, his son and a pretty granddaughter. 'We had three kids,' he says. 'Lost a little boy in an accident.'

It's then that I realise. Gerald is the ultimate stoic – the man who lost a child, who lost all his badges in an accident, who has suffered unimaginable pain and sadness and still carries on. But, more than that, I'm absolutely stunned by the sheer will power this man must have to keep going. It's majestic, it's almost intimidating.

We look out into the back garden, where a lean-to houses another of his collections – the four Moulton bikes. They are propped against the wall next to a 24-year-old VW Beetle, the one that's always the last vehicle left in the car park. 'It's got the original engine,' he says. 'It goes from one MOT to the other. It's refusing to be driven into the ground.'

YOREDALE HUNDRED 2008

17: Bolton Bridge (SE 071 530) to Addingham (SE 081 495) *Distance: 2.98 miles; Ascent: 235 feet; Descent: 247 feet*

We head back towards the river: Albert, Dave, Julian and me. Objects swim in and out of my consciousness – a gravel ramp, a small metal gate in a wall, a caravan site, a gravel driveway, a man, woman and dog. I recognise the dog first. It's Parsley, a friendly black mutt whom I first met on the 2003 Poppyline Fifty when I slept next to him in the hall overnight before the event. His muzzle is greying now. Well, we're all getting on a bit. And the man and woman with him are Chris and Bobbie, his people.

Another chunk of my walking life flashes before my eyes – Bobbie persuading me to walk on, all those years back, at the Shell House checkpoint on the Three Forests Way: 'You can't give up now.' If I hadn't listened to her, if I'd given up after 39 miles, I would have stopped before it really started to matter. I wouldn't have done those last five miles of utter, barmy hideousness. I would have gone home, written my article, let my wounds heal and never have gone back.

I wouldn't be here now.

I love you, Bobbie! For making me walk on! In a totally wholesome, platonic way, obviously. Wheeee!

TRAMP, TRAMP, TRAMP. *Cross parking area to notice board & ahead on path with river again on left.* There can't be more than two more miles till Addingham but I'm struggling. Really struggling. I haul my crooked body over skyscraper stiles, up tarmac mountains, in the grainy light. God, I wish this was over.

Oh, just stop bellyaching. If you want the pain to end, give up. Hail a taxi. This is a Hundred, wimp. You've got to keep on going, not snivelling and whining that your shins hurt. You haven't got any blisters. Your buttocks aren't stuck together. Everywhere you turn, there are people with even finer comedy walks than you, and they're not stopping. There's a woman so far gone her head's nearly level with her waist. And she's still carrying on. So get on with it.

Inevitably, the Addingham checkpoint is up a dozen or so steps, which at this stage of things feels comparable to the 193-step climb out of Covent Garden tube station. The place is filled with the most tragically wrecked walkers so far: piled in like clothes left out for recycling, tattered and streaked with white, salty wisps of sweat; a defiant army in their final redoubt, their shoulders slumped and their faces covered in dust. The chairs they're sitting in are livelier than they are.

I wedge myself at the end of a dark varnished table which in my fuddled state seems about forty feet long. I have a drink of hot water and more painkillers. Then Albert trowels me out, and off we trudge into the gloaming.

Checkpoint 17: Addingham (Parish Council Offices) SE 081 495

Opens: 0730 Sunday; Closes: 0600 Monday
Distance: 93.80 miles; Ascent: 11298 feet; Deswcent: 11409 feet
Manned by: Terry Griffiths & friends
Indoor checkpoint, hot/cold drinks and food

TWENTY
The Battle of Top Jelley's Hollow

IT'S THE LAST SUNDAY IN MARCH 2008 AND I'm wading through something that's half-bog and half-river, and which for all I know may be radioactive. The grass is tinted a strange, vibrant orange, as if it's been dyed by the effluvium from a hazardous chemical plant. The event is the Surrey Tops, a 50-miler organised by Surrey Group.

The route, which goes over the North Downs and the Greensand Ridge, has been designed by Keith Chesterton to test our nightwalking skills. The tops are Gibbet Hill, Kettlebury Hill, Holmbury Hill, Pitch Hill, Hascombe Hill and Hydon's Ball. With the exception of Gibbet and Kettlebury, we'll be doing them in the dark. In short, an event guaranteed to satisfy everyone's inner masochist.

The ankle I sprained on the Sevenoaks Circular two weeks ago has faded from the colour of red cabbage to a rosy pink marbled with grey. It's giving out stabs of pain when I land on it. The ProPlus and ibuprofen at the top of my rucksack are being shaken about, creating a constant *tsk-tsk* background soundtrack. It's like being stuck next to someone listening to death metal on their iPod on the tube. I splash through sloughs of runny cowshit, tripping on boulders submerged in liquid, gluey mud and at one point standing on one foot with the other in the air while retrieving my trainer from the primordial ooze that dragged it off. The next few hours provide a similar tale – continuously rained on while negotiating mud gullies with my legs wide apart so I don't fall in, leaving only my protruding head teed up for a passing boot. As I limp in a line of walkers across Abinger Common in the twilight, the wind is whistling through my running jacket, which is sopping with rain and sweat. My teeth are chattering. God, I wish I didn't have to do this any more. I wish I was curled up at home with a blanket round me and a cup of hot chocolate.

Actually, I don't have to do this any more, I realise as I shiver and hobble across the road to the 31.5-mile checkpoint, a hall set back from the Abinger Hatch pub. I have my Fifty qualification. I don't need to do another. I have two excuses: first, I'm carrying an injury; and second, my jacket clearly isn't suitable. I might get hypothermia. I might start believing I'm terribly hot and want to lie in a ditch to cool off.

For crying out loud. These people carry on when they've broken an arm. Probably when they've broken both legs. A wet jacket – not exactly life-threatening, is it? If you let yourself stop now, then who's to say you won't let yourself stop on the Hundred because your nails need cleaning or you want help taking the wrapper off your Mars bar or you don't fancy any of the sandwich fillings on offer at the 25-mile checkpoint?

But it's no good. I really don't want to do this any more.

My friend Jan, who's marshalling, is at the serving hatch where I'm collecting my stew and boiled potatoes.

'I'm quitting,' I say. 'My jacket's too thin for a nightwalk.'

At which she utters the fatal words, 'I've got a spare jacket in the car boot you can have.'

'No, no, I don't want to put you to any trouble. I can see you're very busy.'

'It's no problem,' she says inexorably.

I bolt down the stew and boiled potatoes and set off for Holmbury Hill in a new warm jacket. I'm with three men for the night, a nice sixty-something Arsenal supporter from Kent called Mike, a young guy in a Preston North End hat and a big, placid-looking man with shaggy black hair called Julian. We're making good time as we storm through night-time Surrey over sodden fields, past clumps of daffodils so bright they're almost neon-lit, lashed by rain and deafened by the yowling wind, dragging ourselves up almost vertical climbs, groping and skidding between channels and gullies treacherously strewn with glistening boulders and weeping stones into which I fall at regular intervals. Unaware of what is to come, we fling ourselves blind into dark copses, trying to avoid being given a tracheotomy by protruding branches. We have to make a special detour to visit the Toposcope on Pitch Hill, a feature that was a special favourite with our founders. We stand around for a few minutes, making our pietas in the keening gale, then slither off down again. We stomp along hunting for a house called Top Jelley's Hollow, twice passing a man clutching a route description while muttering, 'Rhododendrons, rhododendrons.' We retrace our steps, then retrace them again. We end up standing outside some kind of Ministry of Agriculture compound where around the padlocked gates are more bloody daffodils springing brightly to attention. I have no idea where I am.

There's only one thing for it. We'll have to go back to the sodding Toposcope and start all over again.

I'm almost down to the level of suicidal despair as we stumble back up the track. And then we see a head torch coming towards us. With another light bobbing three feet from the ground. Is it a long distance walking Madonna and Child? A waist-high glow-worm? No, it's Keith Warman! Who always knows the way! Thank you, thank you God. I'm on the right path. I don't have to go back to Top Jelley's Hollow.

We attach ourselves to Keith like the multitude in *The Life of*

Brian. I fall over another couple of times. Keith stalks on, rather huffy at having suddenly gained four limpets, waving his mini torch in front of him. Arsenal Mike and Preston Hat drop back. Keith, Julian and I tramp and slither up and down in the darkness. I find a small fallen bough and deploy it as a stick to keep myself upright. We follow the next bit of deranged instruction: *In 150y, reach sawn tree on R with a Cross, Insert Initials on tree in top RH corner of Route Card.*

Keep going. It's better than doing your tax returns. Or being shot in the head.

And then it's even better than that. No more tops. On the level again. Keith, Julian and I charge along like a little train, under arbours, past stone walls and through a gap in the hedge. We're back on the edge of the Witley Recreation Ground from which we started a lifetime ago this morning. Of course we don't walk across it diagonally because that's short-cutting. We go round the two sides.

It's a quarter to four. God, the bliss of unknotting sopping, gritty laces, easing your feet out of them and padding into the hall in wet socks that were dry, white and fluffy when you started out this morning. Now they're dark brown and there are holes worn in the heels.

I collapse in a dripping heap next to all the other dripping heaps. There's a man asleep with his head on the table and a girl with her socks pulled down over the back of her heels. The skin from each ankle joint to heel has been rubbed raw.

'That,' says Keith, removing two layers of socks, 'was what my friend Tim would call "sporting".' He shows me what appear to be two slabs of bleached, wrinkled tripe instead of soles. 'Look.'

'Crikey. What's that?'

'Trench foot. I got it much worse than this on the Lakeland Hundred. Folds of skin like a bloodhound's chops. And bleeding in between. Blood fissures. My feet got wet in the first twenty miles, I got to thirty and it was uncomfortable and at forty-two it was just like walking on broken glass, so I had to pull out. Took me an hour to make my mind up. I even thought of lying in the kitchen with my feet in the oven to dry them out.'

Someone else trudges in. 'Did you hear the dogs?'

'Dogs?'

He pulls back a chair and joins the comic fellowship of suffering. 'Sitting in the trees up along Pitch Hill. They were barking.'

It's the cue for everyone to start talking about their hallucinations.

'I had a car aimed at me on the Durham Dales,' said Julian. 'Probably. About one a.m. Monday, it was. I was walking on my own, a mile or two from the finish, along an enclosed footpath. It ran parallel to a minor road where you wouldn't expect to see any traffic at that time of night. But then a car comes past, headlights full on, at speed, people hanging out of the windows drinking from cans. They definitely weren't English. Texan rednecks would be close. The car does a 180 degree skidding turn. It's now directly facing me and revving up. I'm dazzled by the headlights. And I know it's aiming at me. It can't be real, I'm thinking. And it's coming towards me at great speed. I've got to be imagining it, but I still jump out of the way.

'I made it just in time, ended up standing like an idiot in a bunch of nettles. I can remember the total silence. For about three months afterwards I spent a lot of time wondering what would have happened if I hadn't got out of the way.'

Was it real?

'I'll never know but I wouldn't have chanced it.'

The outside door bangs and in comes Martin Burnell, looking grimly troglodytic, with raindrops falling from his moustache.

'It's always a mile or two from the finish when you see these things,' someone else says.

Julian nods. 'On the Lakeland, five-ish on the Monday morning, I noticed someone in a tree. They weren't moving, they were just sitting there, elbows on their knees, head resting in their hands, looking down on me. All ringlets and sort of rococo-looking. Then I saw a person in every tree, in exactly the same posture. There was nothing malign or threatening about them, my tree people. I knew I was hallucinating, I quite enjoyed the experience. They looked as if they'd just woken up from a hundred years' sleep.'

'On the White Rose in the middle of the night I went down into a muddy valley and the mud started clawing at my feet,' says Martin. 'Dripping wet foliage started crowding in on me and I had an impression that I was going down into hell. I wasn't scared or anything – quite happy, actually. I just had this feeling I was being swallowed up by the earth. I looked that bit up afterwards and it looked nothing on the map. Just contour lines.'

There's a clatter at the back of the hall. Someone sets up a stepladder and climbs to put the clock forward. Julian carries on sleepily.

'My first Hundred was the Dartmoor in 1994. I was with a walker called Conrad Power and dawn was breaking. We had to follow a dry stone wall to its corner, then get over a stile to come off the moor to the last checkpoint before the finish. In my mind's eye I could see this wall stretching to . . . if not infinity then definitely Land's End. It went on for miles and miles like one of those Escher optical illusion drawings.

'We'd been guided from the previous checkpoint by a helper who decided to walk with us, probably because I looked so totally knackered and she thought she should do the decent thing and show us the way across the moor. Thing was, as the daylight increased the feeling began to develop in my mind that she wasn't real.'

Not real?

'She appeared to be in gleaming white clothes, not a mark on them. Which is impossible, isn't it, when you're walking on Dartmoor? There were Con and me covered in ninety-five miles of mud and worse. I'd lost any concept of time passing by then, but somehow the contrast between us and her really made me think she might be all in my head. So in slow motion – I've no idea how long it took me to think of this – I worked out a cunning plan to find out once and for all. I moved in on her and gave her a quick pinch.

'She gave a sort of sharp cry. I think – I hope – she was surprised more than hurt. She had a puzzled expression on her face. Which shortly after turned to mild anxiety when I said, "Oh, sorry, I only did it to see if you were real."

'We got to the final section to the finish, which was uphill along a hedge-lined lane. There were five or six of us now, a straggling group, and one man in front of us was zigzagging along the lane in very deliberate fashion. Every time he got to the other side he'd stop and bend his knees and peer intently into the hedge. Then he'd do the same on the other side.'

'What was he looking for?' I said, accepting a marshal's offer of a second breakfast.

'God alone knows. I didn't like to ask.'

Eventually, he explained, they reached the finish, which was in a crowded school canteen. 'Then I happened to see the woman I'd pinched. I got up and moved towards her, to apologise for nipping her. She's over there, chatting, around a table, in a relaxed fashion. Until she looks up and sees me approaching. She gets up in a real hurry and edges towards the door. Always keeping a table between us.'

IT'S SIX O'CLOCK. The hall is emptying. Footsteps echo. Outside on the terrace, in the chilly spring air, I pick up my cold wet trainers and pad across the Rec in socks. Back in the car, I huddle under a duvet, letting my thoughts drift.

These hallucinations. These momentary delusions when the mind slips its handcuffs. That benign psychosis. Don Newman reckons they help you, the friendly animals, the helpful tree people, the melting sweets soaring over the beautiful hills and fields. What I think is, they're like kindly icons on your internal computer monitor. You double-click on them when things get really tough. What it proves is that we all have stuff in our heads, resources within ourselves we can call upon. You just have to believe in yourself.

Crikey. Must have been something in that toast.

I shake myself awake. I've got the beginnings of a caffeine headache from all the ProPlus I've crunched over the last 24 hours.

I start the car and drive back to London through the pearly light.

YOREDALE HUNDRED 2008

18. Addingham (SE 081 495) to Draughton Moor/Height (SE 040 511) *Distance: 2.98 miles; Ascent: 722 feet; Descent: 50 feet*

As soon as we leave the checkpoint, we enter climbing hell. Turn left up Main Street. And up . . . and up . . . Every step makes me wince. My tolerance has suddenly reached its lowest level. This short uphill promenade on the pavements of Addingham feels like a feat of marathon, heroic fortitude. I blunder along, puffy-eyed, muttering the words of the route description: *continue for 1,250 years* – ha ha, no, that should be *yards* – passing four pubs in the process. The Fleece, The Crown, The Swan and The Sailor. This must be what it's like to be a talking hare with myxomatosis on a pub crawl. Slowly I cross the road at a blind bend and pass the smart little houses. Up some more.

This lane/track/path, known locally as 'The Roman Road', maintains an almost straight line of passage for almost 4 miles to the outskirts of Skipton. In 520yds when road lane swings left continue ahead up 'No Through Road'. Reach & go through barriers to reach main road (A65). PLEASE, PLEASE TAKE EXTREME CARE CROSSING THIS ROAD. It is very busy, the traffic is travelling very fast & you will be extremely tired. Make sure you can cross safely.

I dig my nails into my palms to try and stay alert. It's the main artery between Skipton and Leeds, the verges decked with roadkill. A moment's inattention and then, *splat*. I'll be sleeping with the hedgehogs.

I look at the road from every angle. Right, left, even straight in front of me in case there's a vehicle belting through the hedge. I can't see any traffic, so I step off the pavement.

'Wait!' Albert bellows, yanking me back by the strap of my rucksack as a car whooshes by.

I cross like one of those bent figures on road signs, the ones that say CAUTION: ELDERLY PEOPLE. There are fields either side of us now. Fields and barns and dung. The road hurts. Then there's a sheep track, a pick'n'mix of rubble, stones and dung. Which also hurts. People with blood leaking through their socks and locked knees, their buttocks Siamesed by sweat, whizz past me like Sebastian Coe and Steve Ovett in their heyday. My IQ's probably down to 0.9. Tasks requiring the most basic cognitive ability are beyond me. Don't ask me to work a TV remote or expect me to explain what shoes are for. All I can do is shuffle forward, occasionally wincing. The finish comes no nearer. I – just – want – to – stop – walking.

But we're nearly at the end of the climb now. There's a shaggy-maned, broad, solid figure at the top. Framed in the last of the sinking sun, it looks like some sort of magnificent horse-god. It's Julian, waiting for us. I shuffle up the sheep track to the gate.

Draughton Moor checkpoint is a tent and a van at the roadside. I stand there, thinking, That took an hour and ten minutes – yes, an hour and ten minutes – to do less than three miles. I've been under the impression I've been 'walking' when actually I've just been shifting from one foot to the other without going forward.

People give up, even at this stage. I've always thought they must be off their heads to have come so far and then given up. Now I begin to understand.

Four and a half miles more. It's only walking.

Checkpoint 18: Draughton Moor Height SE 040 511

Opens: 0600 Sunday; Closes: 0700 Monday
Distance: 96.78 miles; Ascent: 12020 feet; Descent: 11459 feet
Manned by Andy Ward & friends (shift 1) and Cumbria Group (shift 2)
Tented checkpoint, hot/cold drinks and cold food. Adjacent to road.

TWENTY-ONE
This Walking Life:
April–July 2008

Sat–Mon May 24–26: Yoredale 100

100ml in 48hr. Start Aireville School, Gargrave Rd, Skipton GR SD977519 via Gargrave, Malham, Settle, Ingleton, Ingleborough, Horton-in-Ribblesdale, Hawes, Stalling Busk, Stake Moss, Buckden, Addingham and Draughton Moor and back to Skipton. 12,000ft ascent. Start: 09.00, also 10.00, 11.00 and noon for faster walkers, joggers and runners. Maps OL2 and OL30, or LR 98, 103 & 104. (Two small sections not on OL 2 & 30 will be made available to entrants.) Entries close May 1, limit 530. Organised by West Yorkshire LDWA . . .

Strider,

The Journal of the Long Distance Walkers Association
April 2008

AMONG THE OBITUARIES IN APRIL'S STRIDER was one for Tony Youngs, who joined the LDWA in 1973 and was a member of Surrey Group from its early days. He completed five of the early Hundreds and devised the Founders Challenge, whose route visited five points associated with Alan Blatchford and Chris Steer: Tanners Hatch youth hostel, Blatchford Down, Steer's Field, the Pitch Hill Toposcope and the old Peaslake post office.

'William Blake as a Walker', an article by Tony Hewitt, told of Blake's 40-mile rambles over the hills of Dulwich and Norwood through Croydon to Walton on Thames.

Among the routes featured in 'News of Long Distance Paths & Challenge Walks' were the 89-mile Kintyre Way in Scotland, the 50-mile Oxford Green Belt Way in Oxfordshire and a new 60-mile Jubilee Greenway which was being developed to circle inner London in time for the Queen's sixtieth Jubilee and the 2012 Olympics.

In 'The Anatomy of a Badge', Rod Heywood, founder of The Irregulars and designer of more than 500, described the evolution of a walk badge.

Hilary Scott, of East Lancashire Group, wrote of the joys of 'Gate Spotting', inspired by the 230 gates encountered on the 130-mile Thirlmere Way.

Reports of 'Past Events' included Peter Russell's 'View from Checkpoint 3 on the Winter Tanners': 'The regular women looked better than ever this year and their favourite biscuit was the low-cal choc digestive whereas for men who were more worn out it was the fig roll.'

Few social walks featured on the late spring Bank Holiday weekend as most of the groups would be in Yorkshire, helping out on the Hundred. For Marches LDWA, Chris Dawes wrote that 'we look forward to staffing the checkpoint at Horton', and included an update on the group's plans for their next Hundred, the Housman. The Group Social Walks programme also included last-minute appeals for checkpoint help and car shares. Merseystride Group's Hundred Weekend schedule included checking-in at the Skipton start, followed by a social walk on the Sunday. Paul Hatcher, completing his final year as national group secretary, signed off, reminding members that he would be at the

Yoredale Hundred, helping out with Cumbria LDWA on the last checkpoint, Draughton Moor.

There were three big walks in 'Events Diary' during April. Some Hundred-ers would be heading to Yorkshire for The Peatlands Way and The Woldsman, both fifties. Others would go to the West Country for Cornwall & Devon's 100km Wellington Boot.

I had entered for the Wellington Boot but opted instead to go up to Skipton to recce with Avril. We did 15 miles a day over five days. Ken Falconer emailed us his notes from the marshals' walk, which included a somewhat minatory description of the final descent: 'The last part from Addingham looks easy and navigationally it is. However, after crossing the minor road the track is very rutted and after the rain it was boggy and slippery. The steep muddy descent to the road by Jenny Gill is particularly awkward – I slipped several times and others remarked that the combination of wet and trainers made it lethal.'

In fact it was the part of the route I was dreading most: bad enough on a dry day, horrible in darkness when crocked, boss-eyed and psychotic with lack of sleep. All I had to do, though, was go back to that night on the Surrey Tops. I had to remember the kaleidoscope of emotions I went through as I struggled up and down those appalling hills in the rain and mud and darkness. The apprehension and exhilaration, the loneliness and panic, relief, euphoria, mastery, despair and vexation. But above all, it was the resolve.

You like cycling. You enjoy going out for a little jog. This was different. Pitch Hill wasn't K2, of course. The Surrey Tops wasn't the Olympic 10,000 metres. It was simply a long, long walk which kept you out there a long, long time. But I was a small, middle-aged mother of three. I didn't have the athleticism and suppleness and balance to run sub-three hour marathons. I never had. Otherwise I would have been counting my Olympic medals and hanging out for my damehood, not writing books and hack journalism for a living. Plus I loved the enchantment: daffodils bright yellow in the midnight ground, a line of head torches beading the black hillside, a hard cold circle of water a thousand feet below. And it was the real deal. You didn't get cowshit in cyberspace.

Fussy, neurotic, stressed-out people who grind away in gyms, calculating to the second each sanitised plod on the Stairmaster, listening to crap music on the PA system, in a puddle of someone else's sweat, wearing twatty little shorts . . . whose life consists of staring into a computer screen, communicating with imaginary friends . . . who would you say was mad?

At the time Jan lent me her jacket I was fairly ambivalent, as it meant I'd have to spend a night scrabbling around twenty miles of Surrey wilderness in the dark, so I probably didn't look very grateful. But looking back I knew it was the best thing that could have happened. I knew after that I could rely on all those unfashionable virtues – resolve, steeliness, bloody-mindedness, stoicism – that I had never been aware I had.

More to the point, I knew I was going to need them.

YOREDALE HUNDRED 2008

19: Draughton Moor/Height (SE 040 511) to Skipton (SD 977 519) *Distance: 4.30 miles; Ascent: 246 feet; Descent: 815 feet*

Leave checkpoint & continue along track with wall on left. After 260yds go through gate. After another 120yds go through another gate. In a further 340yds go through a further gate. The wall is still on your left but on your right you now have the felled Back Plantation for 800yds . . .

I can't see where I'm going because (1) I'm skewed to the left like a motorcyclist taking a bend and (2) I'm too weak to raise my head. I'm trundling along with my nose practically in the rubble and rough grass. Julian takes my rucksack and hooks it over his shoulder.

Ahhh, isn't that great of him.

Actually, he probably just hopes it'll make me get a bloody move on.

After 390yds the track enters a wooded area & the wall on the left goes off above it. On leaving woodland, path narrows to go through an area of gorse but it is easy to follow for 210yds. Here you have a small piece of wall/fence with a stile in it. Continue forward for a couple of yards to find a small well defined path on the right.

We keep going, Albert, Julian, Dave and me, along this hideous track in a line of utterly slaughtered walkers with feeble, watery legs, in the weird, low light of evening just before it becomes night. Skipton is a shadowy fuzz beneath the moor top, from which the only escape is a narrow gash between some yellow gorse bushes that I had trouble identifying on the recce when I was fresh. Then suddenly the amber lights of the A65 appear at the edge of the black moor, which makes it look strange. And absolutely beautiful. Relief and excitement fill me. I'm going to finish. There's no more despair. No more this-will-never-end. I am going to finish. Here's the yellow gorse now, bursting in front of me like an exploding planet. Walkers are starting to descend through the nick in the bushes. I'm there.

I pause in perplexity at the edge of the narrow path down. Seconds tick by as for some mad reason I'm overcome by courtesy and wait for a young couple to go first. And then I can't stop. I let a whole load more file past me. They're in much better condition than me. I'll wait till they've all gone past so I don't hold them up.

'What are you buggering about at?' Albert barks masterfully. 'We can't stand here all night.'

I ease my contorted body through the narrow nick in the gorse. Grey stones form shallow steps leading past sundry patches of twilit vegetation.

We're off Draughton Moor at last.

Take care on this rutted/rough track as it descends to eventually become a tarmac road on entering the outskirts of Skipton.

Roots arch above the parched track, forming interstices of dusty air, trailing crooked woody fingers. The floor is littered with rocks and leaves and little stones. Paths peter out. People are hacking at branches and stumbling and cursing. Darkness falls abruptly, as if someone has switched off the lights.

I make it down by feeling my way along a stone wall from which thistles and brambles sprout in sleeve-grabbing clefts. Wave after wave of us pour off the chaotic path as it rearranges itself, becoming a short downward stretch of track. Then tarmac and order.

I force my head up so I can see the homecoming lights. A man's giant head is suspended in astonishing disproportion over the rooftops of Skipton, a great square blond face with a cleft chin and thoughtful, benevolent gaze.

As I step gingerly on to the unforgiving tarmac, John Sparshatt, former Scene of Crime Officer with Leeds Constabulary, is waiting to apprehend me. Sideways, wonky, head lolling drunkenly, I'm frogmarched like the town wench by Sparshatt and a Kentish Brobdingnagian called Nick Dockree, on the crook of whose elbow I have settled like a ladybird. My legs are barely touching the ground as they steer me past town walls and railings, over pavements and crossings.

I blink and my right contact lens falls out. I find it resting on my eyelashes and, holding it between finger and thumb, carry on being dragged over the swing bridge and into the park, past the signs pointing to the finish, past young guys drinking in the park. 'She's had one too many!' cries John.

'We've just walked a hundred miles!' hollers Albert.

'Is that further than Bradford?' one of the lads calls after us.

I've started to notice what's going on again. Here's John Westcott, outside the doors. He's taking the air; he looks as if he's standing vigil. Here's the entrance into the Aireville School hall. I crash into a door jamb, vaguely registering applause as I steady myself at the top of the steps. My shoulders are slumped, my head is skewed to one side. I look like a cross between Anubis and Mrs Overall, with Andy Murray hair. I am also struggling to control a full scale blub. It's been so hard and I've made it back. I haven't been found wanting.

THIRTY-EIGHT HOURS 33 MINUTES. I sit on a stair, trying to gather my wits. It's coming up to 11.45. I've hit my target, to get in before midnight on Sunday. Ken Falconer is kneeling beside me, being very helpful and patient, though I have a faint impression of being an interesting specimen of fauna to be regarded with detached scientific interest, curiosity and mild amusement as I fumble in my bag for my mobile.

'Would you like me to get the number for you?' Ken offers, adding tactfully, 'I do find after a Hundred people can get the number wrong.'

'No! No! I'm fine! I'll do it!'

Obviously I get the number wrong, so Ken punches it out for me. Everyone at home is in bed when I get through.

'What would you like to do now?' says Ken.

I'd like a shower. And a sleep. Only . . .

I can see what's going through Ken's mind. Fancy you not bringing a sleeping bag!

I can see it going round the hall. She hasn't brought any wash things!

My mind has been so focused on the Hundred that I haven't thought beyond anything but finishing. Ken lends me a sleeping bag and a towel and I'm taken away by another kind person, wearing a sweatshirt with Beds, Bucks & Northants LDWA on the front. She sets the shower up for me. The plughole is blocked. Water, leaves and gunk swill all over the floor and race for the gap under the door. Stark naked except for my fleece, I gather my things and dry and change in the corridor in front of a man snoring on a gym mat.

In the women's morgue, it's chilly. A girl is sleeping with her pants over her head for warmth. I make my sweatshirt into a pillow and try to sleep. It's impossible. Not just the chorus of snores from the adjacent men's morgue, or the fire alarm going off at 3.20, or someone announcing from the corridor: 'There's a naked man asleep in the ladies' shower,' but the fact that my legs are still walking.

Finish – Aireville School, Skipton SD 977 519

Opens: 0900 Sunday; Closes: 0900 Monday
Distance: 101.08 miles; Ascent/Descent: 12270 feet
Manned by: West Yorkshire Group
Indoor with every facility aching bodies and painful feet could want

CONGRATULATIONS & WELL DONE

TWENTY-TWO
This Walking Life: August–December 2008

Sun Dec 28: 8th Stansted Stagger

25ml in 10hr from URC Hall Stansted (GR TL513249).
Start: walkers from 8.00; runners from 09.00. Entry: in
advance only £4 (non-LDWA £5); late entries up to 24 Dec
by phone & email + £1; no entries after 24 Dec or OTD. Incl
cert, 1 cp midway giving drinks, cakes & sandwiches. Mug
required. Drinks and snack meal at finish. Limit 200. Small
hall, therefore staggered start would help all. Organised by
and chqs to Essex & Herts LDWA . . .

Strider,

The Journal of the Long Distance Walkers Association
August 2008

IT'S A MILD WINTER'S DAY IN RURAL ESSEX
and I'm running down Chapel Hill past Keith Warman.

Ahead bearing R with Rd going parallel with station car park.

There's the car park. I cross and storm up the hill. God, I'm
fit. I've shaken the Hundred out of my body at last. If I keep this
up I'll be back in six hours.

When metalled Rd ends keep ahead on TK.

Um. Is this a metalled Rd? Not yet. I run a bit further, past suburban houses. Pavement stretches as far as the eyes can see. So I turn back to the car park and set off on the metalled road that runs on its other side, but this doesn't end in a track either. After ten minutes I turn back again and spot a marshal, who directs me to the turning I should have taken at the foot of the road. Here's the station car park. The other was just a car park, duh. Bugger it, twenty minutes gone and I haven't even started yet. I pass Keith Warman for the second time and run on, past the windmill, across the footbridge over the Stort. The arable fields roll around me like giant rumpled blankets and the ground is crisp and dry underfoot. I pass Gerald Bateman, deliberating which path to take. I catch Brian Harwood and walk some of the way with him while he tells me about the events he's done in the past month.

I'm a bit tired now. I need a sugar hit, and my right hip hurts after all those stiles. I am not getting any younger. These days, I don't have to remind myself of that; my body does it for me. But I'm still running, slowing to a walk, foraging intermittently, running again. I love the feeling I get on these short events, of being a small wild animal moving insignificantly around my terrain.

In the village hall at Arkesden, 13 miles in, I eat flapjack with a mug of tea. Someone has left a copy of August's *Strider* on a chair. I flip through it, turning the Hundred over in my mind. Of the 489 starters on the Yoredale Hundred who left Skipton on Saturday morning, 367 completed the route. First home was Ian Hill, who arrived back at Aireville Park at 9:20 on Sunday morning while I was still heading for my private cartoon showing at Buckden. Marie Doke was the first woman to finish, in 26:08; she would have been faster except that for the last ten miles she was running with a stress fracture of her foot. 'This year I felt so strong. I thought it was my year. Then in the last ten miles I thought, My foot's a bit sore. A few of the really good chaps who had started later started coming past me. The minute I got on to the flat at Skipton, I had to run on my heel. But I knew that even if I had to limp, I'd finish.' Marie might have been a runner, but she *carried on*. She was a real long distance walker.

Sixteen walkers received their Ten Hundreds badge, including Merv Nutburn, who finished in 34:05, and my friend Avril, who brought Ian McLeod back with her in 46:02. Four women, Ann Atkinson, Ann Bath, Eileen Foxton and Celia Hargrave, completed their twentieth Hundred, and Keith Hewitt completed his thirtieth. Roger Cole completed his thirty-fifth, in a time of 35:46. In his Notes, he wrote 'Very nice. Perfect. No problems.'

The last back was John Walker, as bent as an angle bracket: John Sparshatt stopped the clock at 47:59 so he could get his badge and certificate. 'I was taking Betty round again,' he said later. 'We got lost trying to find Bolton Bridge and when we got there Betty was near dead. Didn't know what planet she was on. Val Bridges, who was one of the marshals, said to me, "John, she ain't going to make it. You've got to go on. Leave her here and if the sweeper comes, he can take her on."

'I said, "No, if she can't make it I'll stay with her." Because she wouldn't have been there if it hadn't been for me encouraging her to do it. I couldn't just leave her. But then ironically she finished before me because I fell apart!'

The main difficulty, according to *Strider*, was 'the high blustery wind, making the ascents of Ingleborough and along the Pennine Way particularly energy-sapping. Even in the dales there was very little respite from the buffeting. Another major problem was the very hard and often stony ground resulting in many sore and blistered feet.'

Comments from walkers were all positive: 'High points: Cornwall & Devon's Rhubarb and Custard and the lady at Buckden with sun cream'; 'These events are like giving birth, so painful at the time but you forget the pain and remember the pleasure!'; 'A successful and memorable weekend.' Also included was a hysterically perky post I had left on the LDWA website forum about the kindness of the checkpointers, and the pride I felt at having finished.

As ever, as far as *Strider* was concerned, the Hundred wasn't the only game in town. For walkers more interested in doing the trails, 'News of Long Distance Paths & Challenge Walks' featured the new 105-mile Hadrian's Coastal Way in Cumbria, the Three Downs Link, a 102-mile route connecting the South Downs Way and the Ridgeway, and the 100-mile Ayrshire Coastal Path.

Tony Willey reported on the 2008 AGM at Frodsham in March, where after a Saturday spent walking, 'The hotel dance floor was filled to overflowing for the country dancing until well after midnight.'

Tony Rowley's byline appeared under an obituary of Mac MacArthur, who founded Bristol & West LDWA's Malvern Midsummer Marathon and who after eighteen issues of the LDWA Newsletter came up with the name *Strider*. 'This perfect name for our journal remains a lasting memorial.'

Keith Chesterton's article 'Is Your Number Special?' told of a recent Surrey Group social walk on which LDWA membership numbers came up for discussion. Keith pointed out that his own number, 81, is the only one, apart from 1, whose square root was the same as the sum of the digits in the number itself. 'There are a lot of other interesting numbers . . . These speculations are the ideal way to pass the time while on long stretches of road, such as on a Centurion's walk.'

'Forthcoming Hundreds' included news of the 2010 Heart of Scotland Hundred, the first ever to take place completely in Scotland, with 'a route for fast times and a high completion rate' and 'only a wee bit heather-bashing'. The route ('the inspirational brainchild of Chris Dawes') of the 2011 Housman Hundred is to pass through part of the Welsh Marches 'immortalised by A.E. Housman in his timeless masterpiece, *A Shropshire Lad*'.

My byline appeared under 'The Curious Case of the

Disappearing Nuns', illustrated by Isobel Falconer, Ken's wife.

Among reports in 'Past Events' were those by Neil Fullwood on the South Shropshire Circular organised by Marches LDWA, Alan Castle on Quakers, Monks & a Lighthouse, organised by Morecambe Bay & Bowland LDWA, and Adrian Robson on East Yorkshire LDWA's 50-mile The Woldsman.

The Group Social Walks programme included Kent's South Downs Thirty, led by Mike Pursey, Merseystride's Around The Horn (50km for 50 years), led by Paul Aird, and South Lancashire's 24-mile Six Stations Stomp, led by Jim Rigby. In November, I had been one of twenty-one walkers setting out on a mild autumnal Saturday morning on The Irregulars' Dovedale Figure of Eight: '20 miles. Badge and cert £3'. The walk was being led by Arthur Read. I walked with Peter Wood, who had helped put together the Yoredale Hundred route description, and a nice woman called Jackie, a sexual health doctor from Derby: 'The stories I could tell.' On the following Sunday, I was one of ten on Graham Smith's 14-mile walk for Kent Group, A Bit of a White Cliffs Challenge.

I flip over to *Strider*'s 'Calendar of Events', which stretches into October 2009. I could plan almost a whole year's walking – the Winter Tanners in January, the Punchbowl Marathon in February, the Sevenoaks Circular in March, and for a pre-Hundred Fifty in April, the Peatlands Way or the Woldsman.

Back on route again after Arkesden, I pass the time reliving more memories of the Yoredale. Some are blurred, others clearer than yesterday's: the miraculous way my back was as straight as a stick of celery again after a couple of hours in the morgue; talking garbage in the middle of the night with Tony Rowley; a head-on-the-table half-hour with my forehead nudging a plate of half-eaten toast; Keith Warman staring at me with dazed incomprehension when I greeted his return just after eight o'clock – 'Who is this woman?'; Betty Lewis, the oldest woman finisher, floating in like an immaculate falling leaf; waking up from a sleep at a motorway service area on the way back to London to see Martin Burnell walking past my car, looking exactly the same as he always looks, brawny, hairy and healthy.

It took ages to detach myself. For weeks afterwards, I was aware of a rolling sensation going on in my head that I think must have been a subconscious ingested rhythm, as if my motor cortex wasn't entirely convinced the Hundred was over. Part of me was still back there emotionally, too. I knew I had been very lucky to fall in with Albert and Julian. Both could have finished faster if they hadn't stayed to drag me along with them. That brought home to me more than anything the spirit of the Hundred, that people are prepared to put the interests of others before their own. What I remember still, and always will, is the kindness of strangers: the man with the lovely, warm smile at Buckden, the woman in the Beds, Bucks & Northants sweatshirt who helped me shower and take a rest at Skipton. I'd been helped through the darkness, fed with generosity, sent out mended, had my burden carried. I don't think you could find a nicer lot of people anywhere than in the LDWA. It's true what Garfield Southall says – that someone has the power to leave such a mark on you is profound.

Which is to say that I got the point. It's being in it that matters. Once we set off in that great exuberant stream from the start, we are no longer individuals. Bound up in each other, we are a phenomenon of nature, like migratory birds, answering to some internal instinctive compulsion to carry on going till we arrive wherever it is we have to get to. In being part of it, we are creating it. We are the Hundred.

For me, it meant the connectedness, the emotional unfolding over a long period of physical effort when the normal ways of living in the world were irrelevant. In that strange period between dawn and dusk on the second day, layers of social, work and family behaviour peeled away and you were left with the core of who you were. I'd done it the way I did because I was the person I was. I'd tried terribly hard, been unnecessarily competitive, ignored advice, found a few nice men, ended up looking rather silly and undignified. But I'd done it. I had *carried on*. The moment I stumbled across the threshold of the finishing hall wasn't the moment all the failures were wiped away – that had been when I finished the Surrey Tops. It was validation that I'd received at Skipton. I was a real long distance walker at last. I didn't have a definition of a Hundred. I had a definition of myself.

And it is very hard to let go. More than six months later, I'm still deliberating whether or not to do another. The Yoredale was a perfect experience. There is no unfinished business to return to. I didn't give up. I did what was by my standards a decent time. Maybe I should leave it at that, because otherwise I'll probably become a lifer. I'll do Hundred after Hundred till one day, tottering white-haired into a ditch, I can do no more. Already, after eighteen months' immersion in long distance walking, the carapace of civilised behaviour has been worn away. I have become more feral. I have let my hair grow long; even now, as I bounce along the fields behind Ugley Green, I can feel it sprouting wildly. I remember being slumped on a stair in the finishing hall at Skipton, ineffectually patting the scruffy tangles, wiping dust and tears and snot off my cheeks as vanity reasserted itself. Another few years and perhaps I won't care. I'll become like that hideously barmy woman with straggly hair who went along bleating on the 2003 Poppyline Fifty. Or a doughty old boot in shapeless hat and elastic-waisted trousers, ticking off the National Committee at the AGM. Not long now, I reflect, as I take the last half-mile at a run, reeling in the figures in front of me.

It's my best time yet for the Stagger. Negative splits – the second half faster than the first. Back in the hall of the United Reformed Church, I sit down guarding my certificate and eating a slice of tea loaf. The tables are set out in rows, like a school dinner. There's already a crescendo of chomping and chatter, and the rattle of cutlery on plates. Opposite me, Keith tucks into jacket potato, baked beans, grated cheese. At the next table are

OUT ON YOUR FEET

more friends: Merv, Brian, Bobbie the sweet, round-faced girl, Chris her partner and Parsley the dog. Rod Heywood, founder of The Irregulars and badge enthusiast, is down from Yorkshire for the event. I chat to Brenda Ryan, who hands me my own personal tea loaf, wrapped in foil, then join a discussion about whether Yorkshire mud is worse than the Essex variety. Cocooned, I put off the moment when I have to leave the warmth and comfort of this small, friendly world and set off back to London in the raucous motorway traffic.

An hour passes. By the time I stand up to go, calling, 'See you at the Winter Tanners,' all the walkers are back except one. Closing the door behind me, I catch up with a tall, shadowy figure on the way down the drive. It's Pat Ryan, heading off into the dark to see where Gerald has got to.